PRESENTED TO:

_____

FROM:

_____

DATE:

_____

# JESUS,
## OUR PERFECT HOPE

365 DEVOTIONS

# CHARLES F.
# STANLEY

THOMAS NELSON
*Since 1798*

Published in Nashville, Tennessee, by Thomas Nelson. Thomas Nelson is a registered trademark of HarperCollins Christian Publishing, Inc.

Thomas Nelson titles may be purchased in bulk for educational, business, fund-raising, or sales promotional use. For information, please e-mail SpecialMarkets@ThomasNelson.com.

All Scripture quotations, unless otherwise noted, are taken from the New American Standard Bible®. Copyright © 1960, 1962, 1963, 1968, 1971, 1972, 1973, 1975, 1977, 1995 by The Lockman Foundation. Used by permission. (www.lockman.org)

Scripture quotations marked AMP are taken from the Amplified® Bible, Copyright © 1954, 1958, 1962, 1964, 1965, 1987 by The Lockman Foundation. Used by permission. (www. Lockman.org)

Scripture quotations marked GNT are taken from the Good News Translation in Today's English Version—Second Edition. Copyright 1992 by American Bible Society. Used by permission.

Scripture quotations marked HCSB are taken from the Holman Christian Standard Bible®, copyright © 1999, 2000, 2002, 2003, 2009 by Holman Bible Publishers. Used by permission. HCSB® is a federally registered trademark of Holman Bible Publishers.

Scripture quotations marked KJV are taken from The King James Version. Public domain.

Scripture quotations marked NKJV are taken from the New King James Version®. Copyright © 1982 by Thomas Nelson. Used by permission. All rights reserved.

Scripture quotations marked NLT are taken from the Holy Bible, New Living Translation, copyright © 1996, 2004, 2007, 2013, 2015 by Tyndale House Foundation. Used by permission of Tyndale House Publishers, Inc., Carol Stream, Illinois 60188. All rights reserved.

Scripture quotations marked NIV are taken from the Holy Bible, New International Version®, NIV®. Copyright © 1973, 1978, 1984, 2011 by Biblica, Inc.® Used by permission of Zondervan. All rights reserved worldwide. www.zondervan.com. The "NIV" and "New International Version" are trademarks registered in the United States Patent and Trademark Office by Biblica, Inc.®

Scripture quotations marked TLB are taken from The Living Bible copyright © 1971. Used by permission of Tyndale House Publishers Inc., Carol Stream, Illinois 60188. All rights reserved.

ISBN–13: 978-0-7180-9886-5
ISBN–13: 978-1-4041-0852-3 (Custom)

*Printed in China*

20 21 22 23 24 / WAI / 10 9 8 7

# JANUARY

Sing to the LORD a new song, for He has done wonderful things, His right hand and His holy arm have gained the victory for Him.

PSALM 98:1

# SOMETHING NEW

*"Behold, I will do something new . . . will you not be aware
of it? I will even make a roadway in the wilderness."*

ISAIAH 43:19

Perhaps you've grown hopeful about something new—whether it's a new year, the start of a relationship, an exciting opportunity, or something else. Maybe you feel optimistic that you can shake free from your past mistakes and tiresome burdens. But then your heart sinks when you realize that the issues that plagued you December 31 will continue on into January 1 and beyond.

No doubt, that was the way the people of Israel felt as they awaited the Messiah year after year. What they didn't realize was that even when they couldn't see the incredible plan the Lord was setting in motion, He was working to fulfill His promises to them in an incredible way they could never have imagined (John 1:12–13).

The same is true for you. God is making a way for you even when you don't see it. So don't be discouraged because everything looks the same from one day to the next, your burdens remain, and new opportunities don't seem to work out. Trust that at the right time, He will make you aware of all He's done on your behalf.

*Lord, thank You for working in the unseen and in unimagined
ways to set me free of the things that bind me. Amen.*

> My hope is in Jesus because He
> is making a new way for me.

# FIXED ON JESUS

*Let us keep our eyes fixed on Jesus, on whom*
*our faith depends from beginning to end.*

HEBREWS 12:2 GNT

When you read the news headlines or think about the daily struggles you and your loved ones face, it is easy to lose heart. The challenges can certainly seem too overwhelming to overcome.

But that is why Scripture calls you to have a different focus—not looking at the circumstances before you, but having a gaze fixed on Jesus. Why? Because He is greater than whatever is happening to you. Your relationship with Christ opens the door to every blessing the Father has promised in His Word and provides all the resources you will ever need. Jesus is the reason you can have an unshakable, eternal hope that everything is going to be okay, regardless of the situation.

So no matter what you're facing today, don't think of it in terms of your strength or knowledge. Instead, consider what Jesus—the all-powerful, all-wise Savior who defeated sin and death on your behalf—can do. Certainly, He is the anchor that will always hold you steady, no matter how severe the storm may be.

*Jesus, when I get distracted or overwrought by circumstances,*
*always remind me to look to You. Amen.*

> My hope is in Jesus because He
> is greater than anything I face.

# HIS LOVE

*We have come to know and have believed*
*the love which God has for us.*

1 JOHN 4:16

Read today's verse again. We *know* and *believe* God's love. Do you realize the incredible love the Father has for you? Many times, our perception of love may be marred because of our past experiences—we may think of it as conditional, having unsustainable requirements, being easily lost, or even a tool of manipulation.

Yet, John painted a different picture: "God showed how much he loved us by sending his one and only Son into the world so that we might have eternal life through him" (1 John 4:9 NLT). His is not unattainable or pain-causing love. Rather, the cross is the ultimate expression of God's care—it is unconditional, generous, healing, and always seeking the best for you.

Friend, you don't have to be afraid of God's attitude toward you even when you face difficult circumstances. What's crucial is that you *know* and *believe* that He loves you in increasing measure. Because when you do, you realize that everything that touches your life must first pass through His loving purposes for you, and that even the challenges are sent for your good (Romans 8:28–39).

*Jesus, help me to embrace Your perfect love*
*and love You more in return. Amen.*

My hope is in Jesus because
He loves me unconditionally.

# THE WORD OF PRAYER

*In the beginning was the Word, and the Word
was with God, and the Word was God.*

JOHN 1:1

We know that in the beginning, the Lord spoke the world into creation. "God said, 'Let there be light'; and there was light" (Genesis 1:3). His agent of creation was His Word, and John 1:14–18 tells us that His Word has a name: *Jesus.*

In Hebrews 7:25, we read that Jesus "lives to make intercession" for us. Think about that. The One who carried out creation is the One who prays for you. But consider what that means—what happens when He speaks out His desire to help you.

The same voice that called the universe into existence is moving people, engineering situations, and orchestrating circumstances so as to carry out His wonderful will for your life. He declares the details, the limits, the solutions of your experiences—all to teach you, to prepare you, and to draw you closer to Him.

Jesus uses His unfathomable wisdom and creative power in order to help you. So when you grow disheartened, remember who your Advocate is. He was there before the beginning, He *is* God, and He always speaks for your good. Praise Jesus' holy name.

*Jesus, with a word, You make all things possible
for me. I trust You and praise You. Amen.*

> My hope is in Jesus because
> His voice moves the universe.

## JANUARY 5

# HE SEES YOU

*"How do you know me?" Nathanael asked. Jesus answered,*
*"I saw you while you were still under the fig tree."*
JOHN 1:48 NIV

Jesus sees you—the real you. If you've ever felt that people don't truly understand who you are or what's in your heart, then know for certain there's One who does.

This may be surprising to you. It certainly was to Nathanael. John 1:47 reports Jesus saw Nathanael and said, "Behold, an Israelite indeed, in whom there is no deceit!" This was astounding to Nathanael because Jesus saw him under the fig tree. We are never told what Nathanael was doing there, but apparently, he was having a holy moment—one only observed by heaven. We know this because of Nathanael's response: "You are the Son of God!" (v. 49). Nathanael recognized that Jesus saw his inmost being—his heart laid bare.

Jesus sees your inmost being as well. Regardless of how others treat you, you never have to feel unloved, unrecognized, or even invisible because your Savior *sees* you—your past, present, and future. Jesus knows your hopes, thoughts, fears, struggles, and wounds. And He loves you deeply. So trust that you matter to Him and that He leads you in the best way forward.

*Jesus, thank You for seeing, loving, and providing for me. Amen.*

> My hope is in Jesus because He knows
> me fully and loves me completely.

# TRUTH IN PROFOUND PLACES

*Behold, You desire truth in the innermost being, and in the hidden part You will make me know wisdom.*

PSALM 51:6

Sometimes our most enduring childhood memories are formed when we feel lonely and fearful. For example, my first memory is from when I was two years old. I had an earache, my mother was at work, and I felt miserably alone with no one to comfort me.

Such experiences make an impact on our young hearts—at times creating wounds that have a profound influence on unanticipated areas of our lives. Whether we realize it or not, they ingrain certain survival instincts within us. And often, our pervasive feelings of anxiety, loneliness, unworthiness, and anger, as well as our needs for self-reliance and control, can be traced back to those early ordeals. But these are the wounds we must overcome if we are to experience the fullness of the life Jesus has made available to us.

So today, pay attention to the early memories you have. Seek God to make sense of them for you. Ask Him how they impact the trials you're facing today and why you're responding to them as you are. Then trust Him to heal those areas of your life in the way only He can.

*Jesus, You know my blind spots. Expose these areas of my life so I can trust You fully. Amen.*

My hope is in Jesus because He sets me free with His truth.

# THE FAITHFUL WITNESS

*Jesus Christ, the faithful witness. . . . Him who loves*
*us and released us from our sins by His blood.*

REVELATION 1:5

If you ever want an idea of what God is really like, all you have to do is look at Jesus. Jesus is the exact representation of the Father's unconditional love, mercy, and presence (Hebrews 1:3). He is "GOD WITH US" (Matthew 1:23).

Before the incarnation, people could only catch a glimpse of the Lord through the Law, the testimony of the prophets, and His intervention in Israel's national situation. Sadly, they tended to view Him as legalistic, distant, and full of wrath.

But Jesus said, "He who has seen Me has seen the Father" (John 14:9). So when we read about Jesus forgiving sins, healing the sick, and comforting those who suffer, we see an incredible picture of who God *really* is.

Jesus gave His life so you could be liberated from everything that enslaves you. That's who your loving God is. So trust Him with whatever is troubling you. Certainly, He provides everything necessary so you can live the abundant life He created you to enjoy (Romans 8:32).

*Jesus, thank You for making such a sacrifice*
*to show me who You really are. Amen.*

My hope is in Jesus because
He is God, and He loves me.

# INVESTING IN FOREVER

*"Whoever wishes to save his life will lose it; but whoever loses his life for My sake will find it."*
MATTHEW 16:25

Do you know why it's important how you live your earthly life? It matters because you set the stage for eternity with it. This life may only last a few decades. But eternity is everlasting—infinite. And right now, you are creating your résumé for how you will exist forevermore—for how you will serve and the privileges and responsibilities you're given in the unending kingdom of God (2 Timothy 2:12).

This is what Jesus meant when He spoke about storing up your treasures in heaven (Matthew 6:19–21). This life is only a breath in comparison to what is to come, so it only makes sense for us to invest in those things that will last. Not worrying about titles here, but exalting the ever-reigning King of kings and Lord of lords. Not agonizing about who you rule on earth, but focusing on who you serve and witness to here so that more souls may enjoy heaven.

So live for Jesus! Certainly, that's an investment you'll be glad you made forevermore.

*Jesus, sometimes my vision is too earth-bound. Help me always to invest my energy and passion in Your eternal kingdom. Amen.*

> My hope is in Jesus because He leads me to bear fruit that lasts in eternity.

# DREAMING

*"Listen to this dream which I have had."*

GENESIS 37:6

Joseph had a dream—a vision of his life that came from almighty God. Who wouldn't be excited about that, especially when such a dream promised great blessing and authority? Yet the mistake that Joseph made was thinking that the dream was an immediate reality rather than something the Lord would work in and through his life over the years.

It is an honest mistake that many of us make. We may believe that the path of God's plan will be easy and full of blessing. However, when we look at Joseph, David, and even Jesus, we see that the fulfillment of the Father's plan takes commitment, faith, and patience. Yes, the path of God's will *is* glorious—eternally so! But if you are struggling today because what the Lord has shown you has not yet come to pass, fret not (Psalm 37:3–9). This time of pressure and waiting are part of the process of making you into the vessel worthy of carrying out all He has planned for you to accomplish (Ephesians 2:10).

*Lord, the waiting and the challenges are so difficult, but I will trust in You because You always fulfill all Your promises. Amen.*

My hope is in Jesus because He is making the dreams He has given me into reality.

# STOP SHIFTING BLAME

*When I refused to confess my sin, my body
wasted away, and I groaned all day long.*
PSALM 32:3 NLT

It is human nature to deflect responsibility for the things we do wrong. We see it as early as the garden of Eden, when Adam said, "The woman whom You gave to be with me, she gave me from the tree, and I ate" (Genesis 3:12).

However, blaming someone else for our sins—though perhaps making us feel better temporarily—does nothing but damage our relationship with God and increase our woundedness. Our heavenly Father is calling out, "Stop doing this—it's destroying you." And we're hiding behind excuses: "They hurt me, so I'm justified in hurting myself." Do you see the problem?

God is calling you away from sin so you can experience the fullness of the life for which He created you. Not to shame you or make you feel worthless, but so you can enjoy His abundant purpose and peace. So stop hiding behind others and focus on Jesus. Agree with what He says. He is pointing out your sins to liberate you from them. Cease looking for people to blame and start walking in His freedom.

*Jesus, it's difficult to stop sinning. Please help
me to confess, repent, and be free. Amen.*

My hope is in Jesus because He
addresses issues in my life for my good.

# IN A MOMENT

*Weeping may last for the night, but a shout*
*of joy comes in the morning.*
PSALM 30:5

In just a moment, everything can change.

Joseph spent many seemingly interminable days in an Egyptian prison, during which it certainly must have appeared that the great dreams God had given him would never come to pass (Genesis 39–41). But then, in the twinkling of an eye, Joseph's circumstances were transformed *radically*.

Genesis 41:14 reports, "Pharaoh sent for Joseph *at once*, and he was *quickly* brought from the prison" (NLT, emphasis added). A few verses later we read that Pharaoh proclaimed, "You will be in charge of my court, and all my people will take orders from you. Only I . . . will have a rank higher than yours" (v. 40 NLT). Joseph went from prisoner to ruling the palace—just like that.

However your circumstances may appear, the one thing that's certain is that *they will eventually change*. So appreciate and cling to what's good while you have it and don't despair over the burdens and disappointments. God's help *will come*. And just like that, He will transform your situation in ways you could never imagine.

*Jesus, help me to hold on until Your help comes.*
*My life is in Your hands. Amen.*

> My hope is in Jesus because He can change
> everything in the twinkling of an eye.

# DECIDE TO BELIEVE

*"Did I not say to you that if you believe,
you will see the glory of God?"*
JOHN 11:40

There may be times when your struggles are so overwhelming that you'll pray, "Lord, I just can't do this anymore—not one more day, hour, second." It may be the emotional pain that has you devastated. Or perhaps the toll on your body is too much to handle. Or maybe you've just gone too long without a glimpse that God will make a way for you. If that's where you are today, I can honestly say I know how you feel.

However, I can also confirm that Jesus consistently used those times to stretch my faith—just as He is doing with yours now. And no matter how impossible the situation, He *always* came through for me. He will for you too. But if you want to make it through the next day, hour, or minute, *you've got to get your focus on what He can do.* You must *decide in your heart you will trust Him.* Because when you do, He will comfort you with a peace that transcends understanding.

*Jesus, help me see You and love You more so I can trust You
more deeply—even when things are at their worst. Amen.*

My hope is in Jesus because
He always comes through for me.

# THE MORE IMPORTANT WAR

*He who is slow to anger is better than the mighty, and*
*he who rules his spirit, than he who captures a city.*

PROVERBS 16:32

There are people who will irritate and even infuriate you every time you see them. When you lay eyes on them, the anger rises up and you find yourself tempted to tell them what you really think of their character and behavior—even if your opinion is based on second-hand information.

In the world today, it may seem normal to air your grievances as long and as loudly as your heart desires. You may tell yourself you're standing for what's right and prevailing in an important battle. But the truth is, when you spout off uncontrollably, you're really losing—hurting yourself, others, and even Jesus' work through you.

Friend, it is always better to act like Christ in every situation: remaining patient, being loving, understanding the hurts of others, forgiving freely, and praying for those who persecute you. In that way, you're always sure to win the more important war for the greater kingdom—the one that really counts.

*Jesus, purge this anger from me and replace it with compassion. Help me to forgive, love, and be the peacemaker You call me to be. Amen.*

My hope is in Jesus because He
leads me to the victories that count.

# DON'T FORGET

*I shall remember the deeds of the LORD. . . . You
are the God who works wonders; You have made
known Your strength among the peoples.*
PSALM 77:11, 14

Unless you are a brand-new believer, you have most likely had experiences in your life that have taught you that God is always there for you. You've bowed before Him in prayer when you were heartbroken and felt His comfort. You've turned to Him in time of need and seen His provision. You've laid the messes of your life on the altar before Him and been surprised at the good He has brought from them.

Today's struggle may be greater than all the previous ones and may tear at your heart more deeply, but the result will undoubtedly be the same. God *will* come through for you when you submit yourself to Him. The problem is that it is too easy to forget how loving and kind He really is when circumstances block your view. So today, take time to remember all the ways He has helped you and praise Him for that. Certainly, whatever is troubling you now will not seem so overwhelming.

*Jesus, thank You for always helping me. Bring to mind all the
ways You have blessed my life so I can praise You. Amen.*

My hope is in Jesus because
He has never let me down.

# BE IN AWE

*I saw the Lord sitting on a throne, lofty and exalted.*
ISAIAH 6:1

Have you embraced the wonder and majesty of the living God? In your heart, is He the Great I AM? Do you recognize that the all-powerful Lord of creation is near to you and aware of your every need? Does a sense of worship characterize your relationship with Him?

Scripture instructs that we should "fear the LORD" (Deuteronomy 6:24; 10:12, 20; Joshua 24:14, etc.). But don't mistake that to mean God wants you to be so afraid of Him that you avoid approaching Him. Rather, His desire is that you stand in awe of His wondrous power and ability so you'll be confident of His loving help in time of need (Hebrews 4:16).

With this in mind, imagine God lifted up, exalted, with all of creation as His footstool. Picture Him easily coordinating the workings of the universe with His unfathomable wisdom and might. Then remember that His desire is for you to know Him and be known by Him. Worship, love, and honor Him, recognizing that of every creature that exists, He has singled you out as His own to love, and He will never leave you or forsake you.

*Lord, I don't deserve You, but how grateful I am for Your loving-kindness. To You be all honor and glory forever. Amen.*

> My hope is in Jesus because He is sovereign over all creation.

# OVERCOME

*In all these things we overwhelmingly*
*conquer through Him who loved us.*
ROMANS 8:37

There are experiences in life that are extremely difficult to get over. Whether it's the loss of a loved one, the end of a career, failing health, or other circumstances—the impact can be devastating. We can be left feeling that our identity, worth, and security have been undermined and even destroyed. Those difficulties can also rock our understanding of God to the core. We may try to move on, but really, it takes everything we have just to exist; our progress is strangled by the hurts of the past.

Is this you? Are you unable to move forward because of something that's happened to you? Certainly, there are losses that take time to heal. But you know when you're stuck—when you feel you'll never get over something.

Don't just exist—there's *more* for you! Release your injury to the Great Physician. Forgive whomever God reveals is a source of bitterness—even if it's Him; even if it's yourself. Not only will He help you get over your experience, but He will give you meaning in it. So allow Jesus to lead you to victory by submitting even your greatest hurts to Him.

*Lord, You know how painful this experience is. But I trust*
*You to bring healing and significance from it. Amen.*

My hope is in Jesus because
He helps me overcome.

# TRUSTWORTHY GUIDANCE

*Study this Book of Instruction continually. . . . Be
sure to obey everything written in it. Only then
will you prosper and succeed in all you do.*

JOSHUA 1:8 NLT

*Guidance.* It's one of those important things we all long for. We
want to take the best path for our lives—the one that leads to success. However, it seems many people ignore or reject the one source
for godly direction that never fails. They mistakenly believe that
God's Word is intended to deny us pleasure or keep us oppressed.
However, nothing could be further from the truth.

The Lord has given us Scripture for our good. He made us—He
understands our limitations, drives, and faults. He recognizes what
will give us the greatest sense of freedom, fulfillment, purpose, and
hope. He also desires to teach us the best way to give and receive
love so we can function in a healthy manner. In other words, He
has given us His Word so that we can experience the fullness of the
life He's given us.

So, don't ignore God's Word. Embrace Scripture and allow
Him to teach and guide you through it. In it is the path of success
for which you long.

*Jesus, increase my love for Your Word and guide me through
it—for Yours is the only success I truly long for. Amen.*

My hope is in Jesus because
He is the living Word of God.

# MOTIVATED TO CLEANSE

*He poured water into the basin,*
*and began to wash the disciples' feet.*

JOHN 13:5

It's one of the most beautiful pictures in the Word of God: the Savior of the world takes on the task of the lowliest servant of a household and bathes His disciples' feet. He does so to foreshadow the greater cleansing He will accomplish on the cross, washing us free from our sins.

Yet notice what motivated His loving act: "Jesus knew that the Father had given him authority over everything and that he had come from God and would return to God. So he got up from the table . . . and poured water into a basin" (John 13:3–5 NLT). Knowing all power was His, understanding that He would soon return to His heavenly throne, recognizing that He could do absolutely anything—*He chose to cleanse them.*

That is the Savior you serve. With every resource at His disposal, He sets out to free you of whatever may hinder you from experiencing His love. So don't be afraid of what He is doing in your life, no matter how confusing it may seem. Trust and obey Him because He truly has your best interests at heart.

*Jesus, thank You for not rejecting me because of the impurity*
*in my life, but instead choosing to free me from it. Amen.*

> My hope is in Jesus because
> He does what's best for me.

# ASPIRE TO SERVICE

*"Since I, your Lord and Teacher, have washed
your feet, you ought to wash each other's feet."*
JOHN 13:14 NLT

We often think about the pinnacle of success as being a great leader or achieving astounding feats. Yet, what we read yesterday was that with all power and authority at His disposal, Jesus chose to wash the disciples' feet in a beautiful act of service. And the wonderful thing is that He did that in order to help us.

When Jesus models what He wants us to do, it is something that any of us can accomplish: *we can serve others.*

The world may not put a premium on what you do and may even look down on you for it. But when you are lovingly serving others in Jesus' name, you are pleasing the only One who counts— and that is God Himself. So don't fret when you're asked to complete a task that appears "below you." Instead, think of Jesus, serve faithfully, and count on the fact that when you "humble [yourself] in the presence of the Lord . . . He will exalt you" (James 4:10).

*Lord Jesus, being humble is difficult, but I will
follow Your example and serve with love. Amen.*

My hope is in Jesus because He's the
One who gives worth to my service.

# GOD HELPS THOSE . . .

*My son, be wise, and make my heart glad,*
*that I may answer him who reproaches me.*
PROVERBS 27:11 NKJV

At times, whether we realize it or not, we live out the proverb "God helps those who help themselves." Of course, that saying isn't found anywhere in the Bible. But it speaks to the fact that we think we need to fight our own battles. Yet God is clear: He is the One who wins every skirmish for us; we must simply submit to His combat plans.

Today's verse is evidence of that. When you walk wisely, it clears the path for God to answer your enemies—those who stand against His purposes for your life. He takes their opposition as an affront *to Himself.*

So what does it mean to be wise? Proverbs 15:33 reminds us: "The fear of the LORD is the instruction for wisdom." Acting in reverence to God is the key to winning every conflict you face because that is when He takes up arms and fights for you.

So regardless of the battles before you, refuse to fight them on your own. Instead, keep walking in His wisdom, which clears the way for Him to give you the victory.

*Jesus, You are my Commander-in-Chief, and I*
*know You can win this battle for me. Amen.*

My hope is in Jesus because
He is always victorious.

# UNCONDITIONAL

*God demonstrates His own love toward us, in that
while we were yet sinners, Christ died for us.*

ROMANS 5:8

It's an ache you cannot escape. If you've never truly embraced God's unconditional love, then chances are you always feel as though you're falling short. The subtle message constantly plays in your mind as you face unmet needs, unfulfilled expectations, disappointments, and challenges: "The reason this is happening to me is that I haven't adequately earned God's love. I'm not good enough."

Understand your Savior's provision. While you were as utterly undeserving as you could possibly be, Jesus died to give you the greatest gift you could ever receive—salvation. He gave it freely—with absolutely no contribution on your part. And He did it because He loves you. And yet, there may still be areas where you're engaging in religious disciplines in order to earn God's approval. Each heart creates its own standards. But the telltale sign is always the feeling that you're not measuring up.

Understand your struggle doesn't honor the Lord; it actually belittles what Christ did on the cross. So ask Jesus to reveal where you've not yet fully accepted His unconditional love, and rest in His perfect provision of salvation.

*Jesus, help me to embrace Your unconditional love in the
areas I am still trying to earn Your acceptance. Amen.*

My hope is in Jesus because I can never lose Him.

# THE NEW YOU

*You are no longer a slave, but a son;*
*and if a son, then an heir through God.*

GALATIANS 4:7

You may have some negative thoughts about yourself that were ingrained in you during childhood. You know what they are. It's possible they entered your mind this morning as you prepared for your day: *I can't handle this. I'm a failure. I'm worthless. No one wants me. I feel so alone.*

But understand that those thought patterns were formed in you before your salvation, which is when you became a permanent child of the King of kings and Lord of lords. You are as different now as a slave and a true son: From sold cheaply to treasured as priceless (Luke 12:7). From menial in purpose to eternal in significance (Philippians 1:6). From having nothing to possessing everything (2 Corinthians 6:10). From having no say to having the most powerful Advocate (Hebrews 4:14–16).

So act like it! Cast down those slavish thoughts and embrace who you are now: a child of the living God who is adequate, capable, loved, and worthwhile in Christ.

*Jesus, thank You for making me a new creation—a*
*beloved child with both worth and purpose. Amen.*

> My hope is in Jesus because He makes me
> more than I could ever dream of becoming.

# THE GLORIOUS REST

*Return to your rest, O my soul, for the*
*LORD has dealt bountifully with you.*

PSALM 116:7

Do you feel tired? Most people I talk to do. And it's not just a physical fatigue that people feel—it goes much deeper. It's a mental and spiritual weariness that comes from so many years of struggling, carrying burdens, and doing the right thing.

The reality of facing seven years of devastating famine probably made Pharaoh feel very drained. And yet, after hearing the plan God spoke through Joseph, Pharaoh did something interesting. He renamed Joseph *Zaphenath-paneah* (Genesis 41:45), which can be translated as "the treasury of glorious rest," or "the one who furnishes the nourishment of life." He saw the wisdom God had spoken through Joseph as a cause for peace and repose.

We would do well to learn from this. What we have in our relationship with Jesus is an unfathomable treasure of glorious rest and life—we can always find tranquility and refreshment in His leadership, provision, and care. So if you're feeling tired today, return to the Prince of Peace, who will never fail you (John 14:27). Seek Jesus to give rest to your soul (Matthew 11:29).

*Jesus, I need Your rest. Help me to cast my cares*
*upon You, knowing You lead me faithfully. Amen.*

My hope is in Jesus because He is
my source of ultimate, glorious rest.

# REVEALING GOD

*"No one truly knows the Father except the Son and
those to whom the Son chooses to reveal him."*

MATTHEW 11:27 NLT

Do you ever feel so distant from God that you wonder if you'll ever really know Him or His will for your life? Then take heart. The word for *reveal* in today's verse is *apokalupto*. The prefix *apo-*means "separation." The word *kalupsis* means "to hide or veil." In other words, *apokalupto* means "to separate the veil."

Think of that in terms of what Jesus did at the crucifixion. Mark 15:37–38 tells us, "Jesus uttered a loud cry, and breathed His last. And the veil of the temple was torn in two from top to bottom." Remember: the veil separated everyone from the Holy of Holies, where God's presence was said to dwell. Only the high priest was allowed to approach Him there one time a year. But when the veil was torn from top to bottom, it signified that Jesus had succeeded in removing *all* that separated us from the Father.

So if you know Jesus as your Savior, but there's something dividing you from the Lord or something you need to know about Him—do not fear. Instead, pray and trust Jesus to separate the veil for you in His time and way.

*Jesus, thank You for revealing the Father to me! Amen.*

> My hope is in Jesus because
> He reveals all I need to know.

# SAFE ARRIVAL

*He caused the storm to be still. . . .*
*He guided them to their desired haven.*
PSALM 107:29–30

As Jesus and the disciples made their way to the other side of the Sea of Galilee, a tremendous storm arose. Certainly, in His perfect knowledge, Christ could have avoided making the crossing until the tempest had subsided. Likewise, in His unlimited power, He could have prevented the squall from even occurring. But He didn't. Instead, He called them to set sail and then fell asleep in the stern of the boat.

You know the story. Out of fear the disciples awakened Jesus, and He calmed the winds and the waves (Mark 4:35–41). The very next verse reveals, "Then they came to the other side of the sea" (Mark 5:1 NKJV). They all arrived safely, just as Jesus said they would. He had a plan, and He fulfilled it, but He also allowed a storm to test their faith.

That's the way God often works. He'll call you to trust that He will accomplish His plan for you. But He'll also permit trials that test whether you'll believe your eyesight more than His promises. Friend, be wise. Trust God in the tempests. With Him, you always arrive on time.

*Jesus, I accept that this storm is a test for my faith.*
*I will continue to believe in You. Amen.*

My hope is in Jesus because He calms the storms.

# SO NEAR

*What great nation is there that has God so near to it, as the LORD our God is to us, for whatever reason we may call upon Him?*
DEUTERONOMY 4:7 NKJV

When you feel helpless, remember how the children of Israel wandered in the wilderness for forty years. All they had were the garments they'd worn as slaves—a grim reminder of who they used to be. Without earthly allies, armaments, land to call their own, or anywhere to plant crops, the years must have seemed endless as they traveled. Perhaps, like them, you wonder where your provision and security will come from, since there's no help in sight. Yet God *never* let them down.

The Lord supplied their water and food. Their shoes and clothes didn't wear out. He led them with a pillar of cloud by day and of fire by night. When they were surrounded by enemies, He delivered them. They had no way to achieve anything for themselves, but they had everything they needed because God was with them.

The same is true for you. Ultimately, there is no true defense, provision, or hope apart from the Lord. But as you trust and obey Him completely, you will see that no matter what your situation looks like, He is your unfailing help every step of the way.

*Jesus, I don't know how I'll get through this, but I trust You. Amen.*

My hope is in Jesus because He is
my unfailing Provider and Defender.

# ALWAYS BE LISTENING

*"When He, the Spirit of truth, comes,*
*He will guide you into all the truth."*
JOHN 16:13

The Spirit of the living God is always calling to you—always draw-ing you into the Father's presence. God works within your needs. When you feel lonely or helpless, He is revealing the necessity for you to enter into intimate communion with your Savior. When He brings a verse or an issue to mind, He is asking you to deal with something that is hindering you. Even in your temptations, He is showing you that you require liberation from bondage in a certain area and that He has provided a way out through faith in His wis-dom and obedience to His Word.

The trouble is that learning to listen to Him is both a learning process and a discipline. He teaches you how to hear Him and then gives you opportunities to put what you've learned into practice. So listen with a wise ear to how God is calling you. Assume that everything is an opportunity to connect with Him—because it is. And trust that when you listen and respond to Him, you've made the choice to experience life at its very best.

*Holy Spirit, help me to realize when You are speaking*
*and how to respond in obedience to You. Amen.*

My hope is in Jesus because He
leads me to truth and freedom.

# ALLOWING THE STORMS

*"O my afflicted people, tempest-tossed and troubled,*
*I will rebuild you on a foundation."*

ISAIAH 54:11 TLB

Though Jesus could stop the storm, oftentimes He doesn't. Isn't that the issue that makes us all struggle? If He is God and He is good—*and He is*—then why would He allow all the difficult things we have to face? Why does life have to be such a struggle?

With the disciples, we understand Jesus was building their faith. He led them into squall after squall—not to *dishearten* them, but to make their hearts *stronger*. He did so because He knew what was ahead for them—that they would suffer for His name. And He needed to tear down all of their own strongholds of self-reliance so they could be established on the much more enduring foundation of His power and wisdom.

Don't imagine His reason for you is so different. God has kingdom purposes He will fulfill through you as well, and He is equipping you with everything you need for success. That means enduring some storms. But be not afraid—He *will* get you through them. And He is building eternal qualities in you that you'll be glad you have.

*Father, thank You that You have worthy purposes in mind*
*for allowing this tempest. I will trust You. Amen.*

My hope is in Jesus because He
even brings good from the storms.

# WAIT FOR HIS GUIDANCE

*I will instruct you and teach you in the way which you*
*should go; I will counsel you with My eye upon you.*

PSALM 32:8

Perhaps you don't know what to do today. There is a problem that consumes your mind, but you cannot see a clear way forward. If you don't know what to do, the only thing you *can* do is seek God and wait to see what He will reveal to you. That's what having patience means. It doesn't mean you sit and do nothing; but, rather, you persevere by actively anticipating that the Lord will respond on your behalf (Isaiah 64:4).

However, to wait in an effective manner, you should answer some important questions in your own heart: Do you believe that God is indeed all-powerful, all-wise, and ultimately good and loving toward you? Do you trust that when you ask the Lord for wisdom, He reveals it to you willingly (James 1:5)? And do you have confidence that even if you cannot see the benefit in a trial, that your loving heavenly Father will eventually bring good from it (Romans 8:28)?

If so, then what do you have to fear? Rest in the fact that God will show you what to do when the time is right.

*Lord Jesus, I will trust You to show me the way I should go. Amen.*

> My hope is in Jesus because He
> always provides perfect guidance.

# CONFESS AND BE FREE

*If we confess our sins, He is faithful and righteous to forgive
us our sins and to cleanse us from all unrighteousness.*

1 JOHN 1:9

You *will* make mistakes. You will act outside of God's will—and even against it—and immediately know in your heart you've failed. But understand that the Lord doesn't reveal your sins in order to shame you or make you feel miserable—though those may be natural by-products of what you've done. Rather, He does it so you can be free.

If you've ever had a loved one who is an alcoholic or drug addict, you understand the concept. You would do anything to see your loved one liberated of the habit that is both controlling and destroying him or her. The same is true for Jesus: His desire is to free you of the devastating hold that sin has on your life. That's why He's always there welcoming you with open arms when you return to Him.

So when you fail, remember that God wants you back. Then, confess that He is right about what you've done and trust Him to teach you how to turn away from it forever.

*Jesus, I know the sins You are pinpointing in my heart.
I agree with You and want freedom from them. Teach
me how to walk in a way that honors You. Amen.*

My hope is in Jesus because
He always works to set me free.

# FULLY KNOWN

*Now I know in part, but then I will know*
*fully just as I also have been fully known.*
1 CORINTHIANS 13:12

Sometimes the longing to be loved, respected, and appreciated can be overwhelming. This is because you were created for *intimacy*—for such a close relationship that you can bear your soul and still feel worthy, accepted, and protected.

Of course, we may try to ignore that need for intimacy if we've ever been hurt. We can also try to meet it with other things that will never satisfy—such as possessions, prominence, or addictions. But those will never truly replace the communion we yearn for or the comfort and significance it brings to our lives.

Jesus understands this, which is why He shared in your humanity (Hebrews 2:17). He is the only One who can genuinely satisfy your soul or supply what you need. And He did—Christ provided everything necessary so you could interact with Him in a profoundly meaningful way that would fulfill your deepest longings. He desires to encourage, edify, and empower you to the core.

So open your heart to your Savior and discover the sincere contentment, the purposeful existence, and the future hope you were created for. Because certainly, He is the Source for your every need.

*Jesus, You're the only One who really understands me. Draw*
*me into a profoundly intimate relationship with You. Amen.*

My hope is in Jesus because He knows me fully.

# FEBRUARY

In all these things we overwhelmingly conquer through Him who loved us. For I am convinced that neither death, nor life, nor angels, nor principalities, nor things present, nor things to come, nor powers, nor height, nor depth, nor any other created thing, will be able to separate us from the love of God, which is in Christ Jesus our Lord.

ROMANS 8:37–39

# His Workmanship

*We are His workmanship, created in Christ Jesus for good works,*
*which God prepared beforehand so that we would walk in them.*

EPHESIANS 2:10

You are God's *workmanship*. That word in Greek means "a person of notable excellence." The Lord calls you this because *He made you.* You are His prized creation.

Of course, you may not like yourself. You may have a thousand complaints about your looks, failings, background, weaknesses, and inadequacies. But know for certain: God loves you and did a great job putting you together (Psalm 139:14). He delights in your personality, appearance, and talents because He planned for you to have them. And He made you that way and in your circumstances *for a reason* (Acts 17:26–27). True, there are issues in your life He is working on—such as sin, unforgiveness, destructive habits, and damaging coping mechanisms. But who you are—your inmost being and personhood—those He sees as His masterpiece.

This is important to understand because at times you might think of your physical and internal makeup as a punishment. But the Lord did not make any mistakes with you. So embrace who He created you to be and live the life He planned for you to enjoy.

*Jesus, thank You for how You put me together. Help me*
*to reach all the potential You see in me. Amen.*

My hope is in Jesus
because He made me.

# ALWAYS

*"Come to Me, all who are weary and
heavy-laden, and I will give you rest."*
MATTHEW 11:28

If you are wondering if God wants to meet with you—if it's okay even after all you've done wrong or the times you've already approached Him about a matter—know for certain *He does*. The Savior *always* welcomes you into His presence, regardless of how you're feeling or what mistakes you've made. *Always*.

Unfortunately, the emotions of embarrassment, fear, and failure can keep you from realizing this, which is one of the reasons the evil one will tempt you to sin. The devil knows that if he can get you to rebel against the Lord, you'll feel so guilty about it that you'll avoid His presence altogether. The more the enemy can get you to focus on your shame and inadequacy, the easier it is for him to keep you from the One who takes it away.

God wants you. *Always*. Don't avoid Him for *any* reason. Instead, go to Him—often! Pray to Him, turn from your sin, and accept His grace. His loving arms faithfully await you—*always*.

*Jesus, thank You for always welcoming me into Your
presence and forgiving my sins. I am so grateful
for Your grace and loving-kindness. Amen.*

> My hope is in Jesus because He
> takes away my pain and shame.

# EVICT THE IDOLS

*"You shall have no other gods before Me."*

EXODUS 20:3

It is that one issue, person, or object that you know is more important to you than God because it constantly causes you to doubt Him and even tempts you to give up on Him. It could be a job, possessions, reputation, a relationship, or many other things. But you wonder why He doesn't answer your prayers. *If He were good*, you reason, *He wouldn't make me go on hurting this way.*

Be careful. You have no idea what the Lord is accomplishing by making you wait. And He is God—He deserves your utmost respect and total trust. So if there's something in your life that's causing you to question God, then you need to examine if you've placed it above Him in your life—if it's become an idol to you.

An idol is anything that you value more than the One who saved you. It competes for your devotion to Him and causes you to doubt, avoid, and even forget Him. But understand, God won't stand for competition and will target anything that could potentially hurt your relationship with Him.

So consider: Has anything besides Jesus come to represent your identity, worth, comfort, or security? If so, then confess and repent. Turn back to the only One who can really satisfy your soul.

*Jesus, there is nothing I desire above You. Remove the idols from my life and help me draw closer to You. Amen.*

> My hope is in Jesus because
> He is the only true God.

# GOD SPEAKS

*God, after He spoke long ago to the fathers in the*
*prophets in many portions and in many ways, in*
*these last days has spoken to us in His Son.*
HEBREWS 1:1–2

Throughout history, God has communicated with humanity in the ways we could understand Him. He taught Adam and Eve as He walked with them in the cool of the day. He addressed Moses through the burning bush and Joseph through dreams. Elijah heard His whisper, while it took a large fish to get through to Jonah.

In these last days, we've seen how God communicates through Jesus, who used daily life circumstances to teach important lessons. And now, His Holy Spirit indwells us to lead us to all truth (John 16:13). But why does the Lord use so many methods? Could it be that the God who knit us together in our mothers' wombs understands the best way to communicate with us? Of course!

Friend, that's why you need never be afraid of missing God's will if you're in an intimate relationship with Him. The One who created you can overcome any inability you have to hear Him. You can trust the Father to speak and even to move heaven and earth to show you His will. So be listening.

*Father, thank You for always communicating*
*in the way I can best hear You! Amen.*

 My hope is in Jesus because He
is the greatest Communicator.

# THE PROFIT OF FAITH

*The word they heard did not profit them, because it
was not united by faith in those who heard.*

HEBREWS 4:2

As we saw yesterday, the God who created you can overcome any inability you have to hear Him. What He will not accept is your *refusal* to listen. This means that you must receive whatever the Lord tells you by *faith*.

Today's verse from Hebrews refers to the Israelites' unbelief as they stood on the border of the Promised Land (Numbers 13–14). Even though God had miraculously delivered them from Egyptian bondage and sustained them in their travels, they did not believe that He'd give them their own land because of the enemies they saw there. In other words, how they saw their obstacles was greater than how they viewed God.

But understand, whenever the Lord makes you a promise, the only way to take hold of it is by faith. You will have to trust that God is in control regardless of how big the challenges appear. So don't refuse Him. Instead, unite His promise with faith and believe that He is able to accomplish all He reveals to you.

*Jesus, I want to accept all You tell me by faith—regardless of how
my circumstances appear. Help me always to trust in You. Amen.*

My hope is in Jesus because He is
greater than every challenge I face.

# WHAT TO DO?

*"I have called them but they did not answer."*
JEREMIAH 35:17

I have often said God will move heaven and earth to show you His will. And the last couple of days, we've been talking about the fact that the One who created you can overcome any inability you have to hear Him. What He won't accept is your *refusal* to listen.

But maybe you are truly struggling today. Maybe you're thinking, *I have been listening, but I don't think He's talking to me.*

I've found that when people say that, it's possible that God has indeed spoken, but either they don't like His answer or they're having trouble believing Him. It could also be that He hasn't told you the next step because you have not yet obeyed the last thing He instructed you to do.

So what do you do? Ask the Lord to search your heart and root out any fear or unbelief. Then go back to the last time you were sure of God's instruction and do it—step out in faith even if you don't understand it. And be confident that the Father not only *wants* you to do His will but is eager to *reveal* it to you.

*God, I really need to hear You—please open my heart to*
*Your truth so I can follow You in obedience. Amen.*

> My hope is in Jesus because
> He's never let me down.

# THOUGHT WAR

*We are taking every thought captive to the obedience of Christ.*

2 CORINTHIANS 10:5

As you pray, do you ever have stray thoughts that seem to invade your time with God? What do you do with them? Most people try to push them out of their minds so that they may get back to their conversation with God. But that doesn't always work, does it?

Today's verse suggests a different tactic—taking the thoughts you have as bound prisoners to the Savior. Realize that at times, God will expose what's really on your mind and heart in order to bring your unseen bondage to the surface.

Is it an old memory that comes up? Perhaps the Lord is revealing a stronghold formed early in your youth. Is it an immoral rumination? He may be uncovering some sin that you need to actively turn away from. Is it a person or issue that dominates your deliberations? He may be showing you that you've set up an idol in your heart that must be taken down.

Take your thoughts to the Savior as if they were enemy combatants. Your wise Commander-in-Chief will show you what to do with them and will help you win over every spiritual battle you experience.

*Jesus, thank You for revealing the bondage within me.*
*Help me to be sensitive to Your promptings. Amen.*

My hope is in Jesus because He is
my victorious Commander-in-Chief.

# THE TRANSFORMATIONAL WORD

*Holy and clean, washed by the cleansing of God's word.*
EPHESIANS 5:26 NLT

The fact that you are a believer in Jesus means you understand that sometimes you get things wrong. You realize that you don't always look at situations in the right way or have the best perspective. You've acknowledged it is good and right to turn to God to help you, teach you, and guide you.

Thankfully, as you read God's Word regularly, the Holy Spirit works through it to change the thought patterns of your mind. He teaches you to respond to life as Jesus would. Likewise, He builds in you the attitudes and beliefs that set you free from bondage and glorify God, which in turn affect your behavior.

God's Word changes you. Not only do you know the Lord Almighty through it, but He also uses it to transform you into the person He created you to be. So don't just read the Bible as part of some holy checklist you think is necessary for pleasing the Lord. Rather, embrace the fact that the power of God flows through His Word to change your life for the better.

*Jesus, I know there is power in Your Word. Help me to know You better through it. Thank You for working through it to transform my life. Amen.*

My hope is in Jesus because He makes my life better in eternal ways.

# ENOUGH

*By grace you have been saved through faith;*
*and that not of yourselves, it is the gift of God;*
*not as a result of works, so that no one may boast.*
EPHESIANS 2:8–9

How much prayer is enough to please God? How many hours of Bible reading does He require of you? How many good works do you need to do?

The reality is, you can *never* do enough. Just when you think that you've met all the requirements, feelings of guilt, inferiority, and rejection arise. This is because Christ has done everything necessary—paying the sin debt that can never be satisfied by earthly disciplines. Jesus forgave you *fully* when you accepted Him as Savior, and there's nothing more you need to do. And if you're trying to pay God back for saving you, then you haven't really accepted His gift of grace.

So then, why read the Bible, pray, and serve? Out of love and devotion—to know God better and embrace His wonderful will for your life. Our motivation should be solely because we love God, not because we think we have to impress or appease Him. Then we can obey Him out of gratefulness, love, and joy and experience life at its very best.

*Thank You for saving me, Jesus! Help me*
*to walk in gratefulness to You. Amen.*

My hope is in Jesus because
He paid the price for me.

# PROFOUND HEALING

*Jesus said to them, "It is not those who are healthy who need a physician, but those who are sick; I did not come to call the righteous, but sinners."*

MARK 2:17

Are there things about yourself that you don't like or are ashamed of? Sometimes your mistakes and past experiences can be so painful that you just want to block it all out. You wish you could forget your failings, and you certainly don't want anyone else to know what you've done—especially not God.

But understand, the Savior already knows everything about you and is not surprised by your issues, fears, or sins. And His response is to pursue you and heal you fully—it's the very reason He came to save you.

This is also why Jesus invites you into a profound, intimate, and transformative relationship with Himself. He wants you to experience His presence in the inmost depths of your soul, where true freedom and healing take place. So don't be afraid to be honest and transparent with Jesus about your fears, failings, and painful feelings. Because He will certainly lead you down the path to genuine transformation, recovery, and hope.

*Jesus, my sins and my past are so difficult to bear. Thank You for healing me and helping me to walk in Your freedom. Amen.*

My hope is in Jesus because He heals the deepest part of my soul.

# TRUSTING HIS VISION

*It is the glory of God to conceal a matter.*

PROVERBS 25:2

At times, one of the hardest things about God is that we do not see nor do we comprehend what He is doing—especially when trouble strikes. Of course, it's human to want to reason everything out and understand what's happening to us—and even more so to try to plan our way out of trouble.

But realize that at times, God hides details from you on purpose. Why? In order for your faith to grow—in order for you to learn to rely fully on Christ. He calls you to trust Him—to realize that He sees the circumstances of your life from beginning to end from His all-knowing and eternally wise perspective. And He wants that to be enough for you. This is why at times you will be forced to submit the confusing dilemma before your eyes to God and simply rest in His guidance and leadership (Hebrews 11:8).

So when trouble strikes, don't be disheartened if your limited, earthly understanding fails you. Rather, be encouraged by focusing on the fact that the Father has your life in His wise, all-powerful hand and is working all things out for your good.

*Jesus, I thank You for seeing my situation clearly—especially when I can't. Grow my faith and help me to trust You. Amen.*

> My hope is in Jesus because He leads
> me with His perfect love and vision.

# THE FRUIT OF LOVE

*The fruit of the Spirit is love, joy, peace, patience,
kindness, goodness, faithfulness, gentleness, self-control.*
GALATIANS 5:22–23

Have you ever considered that the order in which Paul lists the fruit of the Spirit implies that the first fruit is love and that all of the other qualities associated flow from the presence of His love in you?

*Joy* is delighting in God's love and the wonders of His creation. *Peace* is resting on His promises and trusting they will be fulfilled because you know your Beloved wouldn't let you down. *Patience* is waiting for the Lord because you trust that in His love, He always gives you His best. *Kindness* is reacting lovingly to those around you. *Goodness* is choosing to do what is right out of love for God. *Faithfulness* is remaining true to the Lord out of gratefulness for the love He's shown you. *Gentleness* is lovingly empathizing with people in need or pain. And *self-control* is actively resisting temptation out of love for Him.

As you open yourself to the fullness of God's love, these character qualities are going to flow from your life. So receive the Savior's love with a sincere, open, and humble heart.

*Lord Jesus, I want to know and love You more. Reveal
Yourself to me, my Savior, and allow Your fruit to
grow in me and flow through me. Amen.*

My hope is in Jesus because the fruit
He produces in me is wonderful.

# ACCEPTED AND LOVED

*"He who has My commandments and keeps them is the one who loves Me; and he who loves Me will be loved by My Father."*

JOHN 14:21

Perhaps you realize that Jesus accepts you because of His sacrifice on the cross. But you're not really certain He likes or loves you. You know your faults and the mistakes you make. Could God possibly love you despite all of that?

Unfortunately, this uncertainty can impede your relationship with Him. You may constantly imagine His displeasure, which can actually drive you to more sin, discouragement, and feelings of alienation. You may fear that you'll do the one thing that could lose His favor and blessings forever. Friend, that's no way to live.

Your heavenly Father is just that—a *Father*. He is not like our imperfect human dads, but One who is unfathomably wise and unconditionally loving. He knows you are growing in the faith—that you'll have questions and make mistakes. But He asks you to obey Him because He wants to teach you how to be free. It is for your own good—not to earn His love. He knows your potential and longs to see you embrace the abundant life for which He created you.

*Thank You for being my loving Father. Teach me to walk in Your ways. Amen.*

> My hope is in Jesus because He is a kind and faithful Teacher.

# LOVE RECEIVED AND GIVEN

*We know love by this, that He laid down His life for us;*
*and we ought to lay down our lives for the brethren.*

1 JOHN 3:16

The full understanding of God's love for you doesn't happen in a day. It is an ongoing process. The more you seek His love, the further He expands your capacity to receive it, and the more profoundly you will comprehend your true identity in Jesus. You belong to Him as you've never belonged to anyone else. You are worthwhile to Him, and He sees all your wonderful traits and potential. And when you get to the end of all of your self-efforts at striving for perfection, you'll discover that your gracious heavenly Father has been loving you unconditionally all your life. Nothing is more liberating than that discovery.

There is no end to God's love, and there ultimately will be no end to your ability to experience it. You need never feel love-starved again. His desire is to heal you, free you from bondage, and teach you. Because that is when you begin to truly reflect His image and not only love Him but also love others freely and unconditionally in His name (John 13:34–35).

*Jesus, expand my capacity to both receive and give Your*
*love. Thank You for loving me so profoundly. Amen.*

My hope is in Jesus because of
His unconditional and healing love.

# GREAT SERVICE

*"You shall say . . . 'I AM has sent me to you.'"*
EXODUS 3:14

Have you ever felt God calling you to serve Him in some capacity? Likely, if the call was really from Him, the task felt beyond your abilities. Perhaps you even thought, *There's no way I can do that.*

If so, you're in good company. That was Moses' response when the Lord called him to address Pharaoh and demand that the enslaved Israelites be permitted to leave Egypt. But this just goes to show that God doesn't call us to tasks that are easy; rather, He commissions us to assignments that will only succeed if we rely on *His* wisdom and power. In that way, He glorifies Himself through us.

If we could accomplish those tasks on our own, there would be no reason for anyone to trust God more. And that is the ultimate goal—that others would believe in Jesus because of our service to Him. So He calls us—not to be superstars but to be humble servants who trust Him completely.

So if the Father has called you to accomplish something that seems too great for your strength and ability, then rejoice! That means He sees you as someone He can work through to reveal Himself to others.

*Jesus, I will obey however You call, trusting*
*You to glorify Yourself through me. Amen.*

My hope is in Jesus because He empowers my service to Him.

# UTTERLY TRUSTWORTHY

*We have fixed our hope on the living God,*
*who is the Savior of all men.*

1 TIMOTHY 4:10

You can trust Jesus today for whatever confounds you. Why? Because throughout history, He has proved Himself to be absolutely trustworthy. Not one of His promises has failed (Joshua 21:45).

He is the Son of the living God—God Himself! There is nothing He cannot accomplish. He was present at the foundation of the world, when He faithfully planned for everything you would ever need. Yes, even that thing you lack today, He knows how He will provide for you in His perfect way and time (Philippians 4:19).

He is the Way, the Truth, and the Life (John 14:6). You can be confident that as you follow Him, He will never lead you astray because He's the only One who knows the end from the beginning and is able to see all His good plans fulfilled (Isaiah 46:10–11).

Finally, and most important, Jesus loves you unconditionally—even laying down His life to save you. If He was willing to give His life, how will He not also give you everything you truly need (Romans 8:32)?

No matter what you're facing, you can trust Jesus today. Think about who He is and believe in Him.

*Jesus, I know I can trust You today. Help me to*
*rely on You regardless of what happens. Amen.*

My hope is in Jesus because
He is utterly trustworthy.

# BEING MOLDED

*"Behold, like the clay in the potter's hand, so are you in My hand."*
JEREMIAH 18:6

There's something inherently painful in realizing that God is working on us. That there's something about us that doesn't quite please Him or fit His purpose. It hurts to think we fall short.

But as our Great Potter, God sees the process differently. He works on us because He sees potential in us and has something important in mind for our lives. It is actually a great honor because He is continuously molding us into the image of His Son—giving us an appearance that is unmistakably His, with increasing faith, capacity for His power, wisdom, and endurance.

In other words, the Father applies His discipline to our lives not out of anger or frustration, but out of His unconditional love and a wonderful vision of our place in His kingdom. It isn't something we should fear; rather, we should embrace it as making us more worthwhile, valuable, and effective.

So don't grow frustrated as God molds you. Instead, ask Him to show you what He is forming in you, accept His leadership, and grow stronger in Him.

*Jesus, I trust You not only to mold me into something useful*
*for Your service but to form Your image in me. Amen.*

My hope is in Jesus because everything
He does is out of love for me.

# FOR YOUR GOOD

*"Obey My voice, and I will be your God, and you will
be My people; and you will walk in all the way which
I command you, that it may be well with you."*

JEREMIAH 7:23

Don't ignore God. When He brings His truth to mind, convicts you of some behavior, or shows you something in His Word—don't disregard what He's saying. Rather, obey Him immediately. He is communicating with you for your good.

When we ignore the Lord, we are the ones who suffer because we miss an opportunity for blessing. This is because God is our wise and loving Father, and He wants us to be completely free from anything that could hinder or ensnare us. Of course, we might think that He is a cruel taskmaster because of the things He asks us to give up. But nothing could be further from the truth.

The Lord is a loving God who cares for you, hears your cries, carries your burdens, heals your wounds, and understands your fears. And He realizes that when you obey Him, trust His love, and experience His liberty—the bondage of sin will fall away. So listen to Him, give Him your heart, and do whatever He asks of you. Because certainly, you will be blessed.

*Lord, help me to obey You always. I know
You only speak for my good. Amen.*

My hope is in Jesus because
He is my Help and Deliverer.

# AN ACTIVE MINISTER

*"Where I am, there My servant will be also; if*
*anyone serves Me, the Father will honor him."*
JOHN 12:26

Do you realize God has called you to active ministry and has important assignments for you to fulfill in this world (Ephesians 2:10)? That does not necessarily mean that He intends for you to be a full-time pastor, missionary, or evangelist—though He may. However, Jesus was clear that He desires for you to share the gospel with others (Mark 16:15) and to use your gifts for building up the kingdom (Matthew 5:16). You have a very special role in the kingdom of God, and it is better for everyone when you participate.

Now, this is not as difficult as you may think it is. All it really means is that you ask the Lord daily to guide your steps and show you how to serve Him. He will enable you to minister to others in the way He created you to—through your unique mix of personality, talents, and gifts. And when you do, you will feel not only the extraordinary joy and satisfaction of fulfilling your purpose in life but also God's pleasure. And that is something you don't want to miss.

*Lord, I want to fulfill Your purposes for me and feel*
*Your pleasure. Show me how to serve You. Amen.*

My hope is in Jesus because He
gives me an eternal purpose.

# WALKING IN VICTORY

*Because the Sovereign LORD helps me . . . I have
set my face like a stone, determined to do his will.
And I know that I will not be put to shame.*

ISAIAH 50:7 NLT

As you discover the purpose for which God created you, you'll find joy and a sense of fulfillment that goes straight to your core. Even better, you'll learn that your success doesn't depend on you, but on the Holy Spirit who leads and empowers you. Certainly, it's wonderful to walk in God's will.

But be warned—this doesn't mean life will always be easy. On the contrary, the Father will use challenges to keep you humble because it's as you cling to Him that He pours His power into you (2 Corinthians 12:7–10). Likewise, your ultimate calling is to be like Jesus, which requires additional refining of your character and faith. Finally, God works to keep you understanding toward others so you can comfort them with the same consolation He's given you (2 Corinthians 1:3–4).

So life may get tough. But the key to walking in victory is abiding in Christ and choosing to believe He's actively helping you even when things are at their worst. Because He is. So keep trusting God and walking in His will—because that's truly life at its very best.

*Jesus, teach me to abide in You, do Your will, and
trust You regardless of my circumstances. Amen.*

My hope is in Jesus because
He leads me to victory.

# YOUR FRIEND

*"I have called you friends, for all things that I have
heard from My Father I have made known to you."*

JOHN 15:15

Do you realize that Jesus considers you His friend? It is good and right to have reverence for Him as God. But it's also imperative that you realize that as your Sovereign, Jesus longs to share His heart, mission, and kingdom with you through an intimate relationship.

Just ponder the wonder and beauty of that. The King of kings is willing to tell you His plans and minister to your wounds; He even delights when you enjoy His presence. Best of all, your relationship with Him can never be destroyed because He's promised to never let go of you (John 10:28).

So the next time you're tempted to think that Jesus doesn't care if you hurt or are lonely, consider all it cost Him to come to earth and be your Friend. Contemplate the privilege of having the almighty Creator of all that exists seek you out for fellowship. Then read the Bible—His love letter to you—and recall all He has done on your behalf. Certainly, He is the very best Friend any of us could ever hope to have and is worthy of our praise.

*Jesus—You are my Friend! What a beautiful and humbling thought!
Lead me ever deeper into this intimate relationship with You. Amen.*

> My hope is in Jesus because He's
> the best Friend I could ever have.

# GO TO LISTEN

*Guard your steps as you go to the house of God and draw*
*near to listen rather than to offer the sacrifice of fools.*

ECCLESIASTES 5:1

There will be some burdens that will cause you to go to the throne of grace over and over again. You know the ones—they are the problems that keep you up at night and are first on your mind when you wake in the morning. You want the Father's guidance as you persevere through these challenges, and that's great. But are you going before Him just to talk, or are you actually stopping to listen to Him?

Friend, God has the wisdom you need today. Don't doubt that. He already understands all there is to know about your troubles. Yes, go and share your heart with Him, but remember—He is God and you are not. Show Him the respect He deserves by being quiet and allowing Him to speak to you.

Get on your knees before Him in prayer, open His Word, give Him ample time to speak to you, and agree with what He says. Keep seeking Him and don't lose heart. Certainly, the Lord will guide you, give you the wisdom you need, and lead you to overcome all you're facing.

*Jesus, You know the questions on my heart. Thank You for*
*answering my every need and guiding me always. Amen.*

My hope is in Jesus because He shares
His unfathomable wisdom with me.

# NOT CONDEMNED

*There is now no condemnation for those who are in Christ Jesus.*
ROMANS 8:1

Are you feeling burdened by your own failings—by your sins, the mistakes you've made, the way you've treated people, and even the ugly attitude you may be feeling at this very moment? Then reread today's verse and take heart: *you are not condemned.*

Yes, God sees all the painful things in you, and He has allowed them to surface so you can be set free of them. That is what His grace is all about. He is not content simply forgiving you of sin; He wants you to be completely liberated from its destructive influence on your life.

Jesus is not looking at you as a stern, unloving Judge who is just waiting for you to mess up. Once you accept Him as your Savior, the only judgment you will face is the one where He rewards your faithful service.

So do not fear, He will never turn away from you. You may be troubled by your own failings, but God loves you and is working to set you free. So accept what He says fully, repent, and embrace the grace He offers you freely.

*Jesus, thank You for forgiving me so fully and*
*setting me free of all the sins in me. I repent, Lord.*
*Teach me to honor You with my life. Amen.*

My hope is in Jesus
because He sets me free.

# NOTHING

*I am convinced that neither death, nor life, nor angels, nor principalities, nor things present, nor things to come, nor powers, nor height, nor depth, nor any other created thing, will be able to separate us from the love of God, which is in Christ Jesus our Lord.*

ROMANS 8:38–39

Do you realize the power and beauty of the passage above? Every one of the things mentioned is beyond your control. Can you stop your own death or create life for yourself? In a very limited fashion, maybe—but certainly not as God can. Can you affect the paths or purposes of the angels, principalities, or powers? No, most of the time you don't even perceive their activity—not without the Lord revealing it to you. What about things to come? I think you'll agree how difficult it is to influence a future you cannot even foresee.

The point is that you cannot control any of these things, but the Lord God Almighty, the Sovereign of all that exists, can and does. And He has assured you that nothing—not even things completely out of your control—can separate you from His love. His power and wisdom keep you absolutely secure.

*Thank You, Jesus! So much is out of my control, and I'm so grateful to know that You care for me so deeply and completely! Amen.*

My hope is in Jesus because
His love is perfect and permanent.

# STIFLED PRAYER

*The Holy One of Israel, says: "Only in returning to me and resting in me will you be saved. In quietness and confidence is your strength. But you would have none of it."*

ISAIAH 30:15 NLT

Do you ever feel that your prayers aren't going anywhere? That somehow they no longer have the influence they used to?

God's message to the nation of Judah through Isaiah can give us some insight. As enemies threatened to invade, the Lord told the Judahites what to do: *Repent and trust. Stop depending on outside sources for security. Turn to Me and be secure.* Yet as we see from today's verse, they would have none of it.

Is this you? Are you asking God for guidance, help, and protection, but then insisting on having it your own way? Do you refuse to give up the destructive habits that undermine your relationship with Him? That very well may be the source of your stifled prayers.

The Savior wants you to be His—*only* His. Don't refuse Him by clinging to that which keeps you enslaved. Rather, when you pray, listen to and obey Him. Humble yourself before the Lord, return to Him with all your heart, and make Him your only source of confidence and strength. In trusting Him lies the answer to your prayers that will bring rest to your soul.

*Jesus, I will return and rest in You. You only are my confidence, security, and strength. Amen.*

My hope is in Jesus
because He is my Defender.

# SOW WHAT'S WORTHY

*Whatever a man sows, this he will also reap.*

GALATIANS 6:7

What are you sowing into your life? What are you planting into your mind, spirit, and heart? You are having a quiet time, which is an excellent first step. But are you truly allowing God's truth to take root in you? Are you responding to the opportunities and challenges He allows with faith and obedience?

This is important for you to take seriously because the principle of sowing and reaping directly impacts your future—shaping even what you become in eternity (2 Timothy 2:12). You are reaping *what* you sow—you are growing either in intimacy with the Father or in rebellion against Him. You are reaping *more than* you sow—even the smallest decisions impact the generations after you, whether you realize it or not. Finally, you are reaping *later* than you sow—the choices you make continue to have either increasing consequences or accumulating blessings in eternity (Philippians 1:6).

Therefore, make sure that you're always sowing what's good and worthy each and every day—sow faith and obedience to God. Because in due time you will reap an extraordinary harvest if you don't lose heart (Galatians 6:9).

*Jesus, help me to sow only those things that bring You honor,
so that the harvest of my life will glorify You. Amen.*

My hope is in Jesus because what He
produces through my life continues in eternity.

# AFTER HIS LIKENESS

*Be imitators of God, as beloved children.*

EPHESIANS 5:1

The Father cares for you so much that He made you *in His own image*. To be His child. To be His representative in this world. Think about how profound that is. It means He created you with the ability to experience Him in a deep, intimate relationship. Likewise, He made it possible to pour His life into you and work through you in ways that will impact eternity. His desire is that when people see you, they are reminded of Him and give Him the glory.

So no matter how you feel about yourself, embrace the truth: You bear the image of the living God. You have the capacity to know Him, walk with Him, and carry out His wonderful plans—with His power, wisdom, and leadership. He loves you, enables you, and works out His will through you. Pondering being created in His image not only will bless your life, but can absolutely transform the world in a manner you never imagined possible. So walk in His ways. Obey God and do your best to represent your Father well.

*Lord, thank You for creating me in Your image and calling me Your own. Teach me Your ways and how to reflect Your likeness faithfully. Amen.*

My hope is in Jesus because He formed me with His perfect love and wise purposes.

# SUCCESS THROUGH THE SPIRIT

*We have received . . . the Spirit who is from God, so that*
*we may know the things freely given to us by God.*

1 CORINTHIANS 2:12

Proverbs 16:3 promises, "Commit your actions to the LORD, and your plans will succeed" (NLT). This may seem difficult to believe if the tasks you face today are especially challenging. You want God to guide and empower you, but how can you be certain He will?

You can be confident because when you accepted Jesus as your Savior, He sent His Spirit to indwell you (Ephesians 1:13–14). The Holy Spirit of the all-knowing, all-powerful, sovereign God lives within you to carry out all His purposes through you. Though the challenges you face today may be tough to you, they are nothing to Him. And He invites you to seek Him, entrust your future to Him, and obey Him—so He can demonstrate His awesome power and wisdom to you. Things may not turn out as you expect, but they will ultimately work together for your good (Romans 8:28).

So don't deny your loving Savior; rather, claim the promise of Proverbs 16:3 and surrender your day to Him. He will guide you, give you strength, and prompt you in the way you should go.

*Jesus, thank You for leading me to triumph! Make me sensitive*
*to Your Spirit and help me obey You in all things. Amen.*

> My hope is in Jesus because
> He always leads me to victory.

# TRUST HIS "NO"

*"If you . . . know how to give good gifts to your children,*
*how much more will your Father who is in heaven*
*give what is good to those who ask Him!"*

MATTHEW 7:11

Has God ever said no to one of your requests? Have you ever asked the Father for something that He refused to give you? It's certainly painful. However, the Lord is committed to leading you in the best way possible. He loves you profoundly and has intricately woven every fiber of your being (Psalm 139). It makes sense, then, that He knows exactly what you need—and what you don't.

"But this is all I really want," you might say. "Why doesn't God change my desires if He's not going to give it to me?"

Only the Lord can answer that. However, there is one thing I know for certain, and that is your heavenly Father is kind and gracious. "No good thing does He withhold from those who walk uprightly" (Psalm 84:11). So when He says "no" or "wait," it is for a worthy reason.

Your heavenly Father is careful on your behalf. So rest in the assurance that He answers your requests in absolute wisdom, in His perfect time, and with regard to your ultimate welfare.

*Jesus, I trust Your "no." Help me to accept Your leadership*
*and wisdom in every area of my life. Amen.*

> My hope is in Jesus because
> He knows what I really need.

# MARCH

I waited patiently for the LORD; and He inclined to me and heard my cry. He brought me up out of the pit of destruction, out of the miry clay, and He set my feet upon a rock making my footsteps firm. He put a new song in my mouth, a song of praise to our God; many will see and fear and will trust in the LORD.

PSALM 40:1–3

# HE UNDERSTANDS

*He had to be made like His brethren in all things,*
*so that He might become a merciful and faithful*
*high priest in things pertaining to God.*

HEBREWS 2:17

Are there days when it seems as if no one understands or respects the unique pressures you face? It's possible that with your particular family dynamics, burdens, and challenges, few really could. However, there is One who knows and appreciates how you feel. That, of course, is Jesus, who sees your situation from such a profound perspective that it's difficult for the human mind to grasp.

Because Jesus is fully God, He has heard the hidden cries of your soul and can influence the dynamics of your circumstances from His omniscient and omnipotent viewpoint. Yet, He is also fully man, so He also realizes how defeated you can get when you're exhausted or emotionally spent, how fearful the unknown can be, and how it feels when someone you love betrays or rejects you. So He ministers to your heart as well.

Always remember that Jesus understands you very well—even better than you comprehend yourself. As fully God and fully man, He can help you overcome any challenge you face. Therefore, trust Him and rest in His perfect care.

*Jesus, thank You for understanding and loving me. No*
*matter what happens, I know You'll help me through. Amen.*

My hope is in Jesus because
He understands me.

# A Different Nature

*If anyone is in Christ, he is a new creature; the old*
*things passed away; behold, new things have come.*
2 Corinthians 5:17

Are you trying hard to be a "good Christian" and feeling exhausted? Then be comforted by the fact that you cannot make yourself into a new creation—no one can. We often view the time when we become a believer in Christ as one of making the transition from sinner to a moral person.

But the truth is that you become a Christian when Jesus forgives you of your sins and makes you spiritually alive—forming you into a *different* creature. You are new in form, nature, and substance. That's not just an ethical or behavioral transformation; rather, it means you have an added capacity to communicate with and be empowered by the Lord God. He shows you that certain attitudes and behaviors no longer fit who you are and leads you to become all He created you to be through the leadership of His Holy Spirit, who now indwells you.

So how can you cooperate with God as He transforms you? Every morning say, "Lord, I'm Yours. I trust You to teach me to think and act as Jesus would." Then obey whatever He shows you.

*Jesus, thank You for transforming me into a new*
*creation. Teach me to walk in Your ways. Amen.*

My hope is in Jesus because He
does what I can't—He makes me new.

# THE LIVING WORD

*The grass withers, the flower fades,*
*but the word of our God stands forever.*
ISAIAH 40:8

Have you considered the fact that the Word of God is not like any other book? In fact, in Hebrews 4:12, we learn, "The word of God is living and active and sharper than any two-edged sword, and piercing as far as the division of soul and spirit, of both joints and marrow, and able to judge the thoughts and intentions of the heart."

Think about the fact that Scripture is *living*—it is a dynamic force with vitality and transformative power because of the Holy Spirit's work through it. And as we see from today's verse—it lasts *forever*. It is *eternal*. This means that God's Word is not just black-and-white words on the page, like other works of literature; rather, it is the Lord's own messenger of resurrection life through which He works on you and grows you spiritually.

Friend, this is great news! Because in God's Word you have living guidance, living counsel, living comfort, living hope, and living confidence. No matter what you're going through, Scripture speaks to you. It is always relevant, true, and right. So get in God's Word and embrace the life He has for you.

*Jesus, speak to me and transform me through Your wondrous*
*Word! Thank You for the gift of Scripture! Amen.*

My hope is in Jesus because He
breathes resurrection life into me.

# ACTIVE DIRECTION

*Your word is a lamp to my feet and a light to my path.*

PSALM 119:105

As we saw yesterday, Hebrews 4:12 teaches that "the word of God is living and active." Today, let's consider what it means that Scripture is *active*.

Think about Psalm 119:105. We often approach God's Word as if it were *passive*—like a flashlight *we* hold to illuminate the steps ahead. There's nothing wrong with that, of course. However, that's not the picture God gives us of it being a lamp that reveals our path.

Nehemiah 9:12 explains that when the Israelites wandered in the wilderness: "You led them . . . with a pillar of fire by night to light for them the way in which they were to go." In other words, the Lord's leadership was *active*. No Israelite held the pillar of fire or pointed it in a certain direction. Rather, through it, God led them on the path of His will—taking turns they wouldn't have considered on their own.

The same is true for Scripture. If you always approach it thinking, *How can I solve my problems?* you'll find answers. However, you won't experience all it offers you. Instead, open the Word saying, "Lord, lead me to do Your will." Certainly, He will guide you in ways that defy imagination and bring joy to your heart.

*Jesus, lead me to do Your will through Your Word! Amen.*

My hope is in Jesus because
He actively leads me.

# HIS LOVE

*I pray that you, being rooted and established in love, may . . .*
*grasp how wide and long and high and deep is the love of*
*Christ, and to know this love that surpasses knowledge—*
*that you may be filled to . . . all the fullness of God.*

EPHESIANS 3:17–19 NIV

It's a key to faith that we sometimes take for granted: Jesus loved us so much that He died on the cross (John 3:16). He acted out of *love*—that was His motive.

Yes, it's a *sacrificial* love. He left His throne in heaven for more than three decades and then humbled Himself to death on a cross. He was willing to give up everything for you. Likewise, it's a *saving* love. He takes away your sins and restores your relationship with the Father—providing what you couldn't give on your own.

But what can impact your faith today is that it's also a *rooting*, *establishing*, and *filling* love. The love of Christ grounds you, steadies you, builds you, and satisfies you in a manner that's intensely personal and unique to your being. He lovingly reaches into the deepest places of your inadequacy, fear, hurt, and despair and fills all that's lacking to overflowing. That's why you can trust Him in *every* situation and always walk in faith.

*Jesus, Your love is amazing! Help me to love and*
*trust You with all that is within me. Amen.*

My hope is in Jesus because
I can trust His love.

# IN THE DETAILS

*"I know the plans that I have for you . . . plans for welfare*
*and not for calamity to give you a future and a hope."*
JEREMIAH 29:11

It's clear from Scripture that the Father has a plan for your life. After all, God's not a reactor—He's a planner. You can see it in the way He made Jesus your Savior—how He worked through Israel, the sacrificial system, and even Christ's lineage to fulfill thousands of prophesies and provide everything necessary. He coordinated your redemption with extraordinary forethought and detail.

When it comes to His will for your life, the same is true. This thought should be comforting to you today. Your life is not random. Your gifts, personality, talents, and background are not a mistake (Acts 17:26–27). And as you seek an intimate relationship with the Savior, He can eliminate your doubts and fears. He can fill you with a sense of certainty, confidence, and purpose as you follow Him.

So how do the details you are facing today fit into His plan? How do the struggles, frustrations, obstacles, and challenges further you on the path of His will? It won't always make sense. But one thing is certain: God loves it when you to go to Him to find out (Jeremiah 29:12–13).

*Jesus, I trust Your will for my life. Lead me, my Savior! Amen.*

> My hope is in Jesus because
> I can trust His detailed plan.

# CHOOSING HIS WILL

*Do not be unwise, but understand what the will of the Lord is.*

EPHESIANS 5:17 NKJV

Yesterday, we discussed how God has a plan for your life and that He's working in the details you face. But maybe you're not convinced you want to walk in His will. Perhaps it's daunting because of the behavior you'll need to give up, what you'll be required to sacrifice, and how different His way is from the life you're living now. After all, you read about what Abraham, Moses, and the disciples had to endure, and you wonder if it's really worth following the Lord.

But understand, you were formed in your mother's womb to carry out God's will. Anything short of that and you will always lose out—feeling as if there could have been more to your life and greater things you could have accomplished. This is because God's purpose for your life is honorable and eternal. Only He knows your maximum potential and can develop it in you. Only He can satisfy you to the depths of your soul. And He accomplishes it all as you walk in His purposes.

Doing His will is indeed worthwhile—eternally so. So choose Him and don't miss out.

*Jesus, Your plan is best. Calm my fears, increase my faith, and help me to always walk in Your will. Amen.*

My hope is in Jesus because
He knows me better than I do.

# STEP-BY-STEP

*[May] our Lord Jesus . . . equip you with all you need for*
*doing his will. May he produce in you, through the power*
*of Jesus Christ, every good thing that is pleasing to him.*

HEBREWS 13:20–21 NLT

You have everything you need. Right here, right now—you have all that's necessary for doing God's will and pleasing Him. This doesn't imply you'll please everyone around you. Rather, it means He has equipped you to obey and honor *Him*. That includes knowing all of His will that's necessary *at this moment*.

"But," you may say, "I've been seeking His will and He's not shown me what to do." It may be that you're asking to see His whole plan, while He's only showing you one step at a time. If you recall, even Abraham "went out, not knowing where he was going" (Hebrews 11:8). Yet God successfully led him to the Promised Land.

One thing is certain: if God hasn't revealed His plan to you yet, it's because you don't need to know it yet. Obey Him in whatever He's already shown you and trust Him to guide you every inch of the way. You have what you need—the power, giftedness, wisdom, and strength—for what is before you today. Let Him take care of tomorrow.

*Jesus, I trust You to lead me every step of the*
*way. Help me to have faith. Amen.*

> My hope is in Jesus because
> He is faithful to lead me.

# SHINE THE LIGHT

*God, who said, "Light shall shine out of darkness," is the One*
*who has shone in our hearts to give the Light of the knowledge*
*of the glory of God in the face of Christ. But we have this*
*treasure in earthen vessels, so that the surpassing greatness*
*of the power will be of God and not from ourselves.*

2 CORINTHIANS 4:6–7

God's ultimate desire is to reproduce His supernatural, resurrection life in and through you—for His power, wisdom, and strength to flow through you in extraordinary ways. For you to be a light in this world that directs others to Him (Matthew 5:16).

But in order for that to happen, the Lord must reveal Himself to you and bring you into a profoundly intimate relationship with Himself. He must remove your dependency on yourself, others, and artificial crutches so that others see it is God—and only God—who is doing the extraordinary work through you. And He must grow your love and devotion to Him.

That is *why* you're facing *what* you're facing today. That is God's goal. With that in mind, spend time with Him in prayer, release whatever it is He reveals to you, and experience the extraordinary life for which He created you.

*Jesus, I want You to shine Your life through me—*
*a bright light that draws others to You. Amen.*

My hope is in Jesus because He
gives my life power and purpose.

# ALL OF ME

*Search me, O God, and know my heart; try me and know
my anxious thoughts; and see if there be any hurtful
way in me, and lead me in the everlasting way.*

PSALM 139:23–24

Does Jesus have access to your whole heart? Does He have a say in everything you think, express, and do? As your Savior, He wants to. He realizes there are places within you that are still bound to sin, and you will tend to shut Him out of them—keeping Him away from your well-established walls of protection and coping mechanisms. But those are the very areas where you need Him most because they are the ones that cause you to struggle and despair. Even today, they may be causing you to feel weak and hopeless.

The answer to the pain you feel is going even deeper in your relationship with God, saying, "Jesus, here is my heart. I am willing to unwrap myself before You—my soul, my spirit, and everything I am. I don't want to hold anything back." This is true intimacy with Him. And it is the victorious path to freedom and healing for you.

*Jesus, I want You to have all of me—every part, including the
ones that are painful. Search me, see if there be any hurtful
way in me, and lead me in the everlasting way. Amen.*

My hope is in Jesus because
His goal is my freedom.

# HE IS

*Without faith it is impossible to please Him, for he
who comes to God must believe that He is and that
He is a rewarder of those who seek Him.*

HEBREWS 11:6

Today, there will be opportunities for you to put today's verse, Hebrews 11:6, into practice in ways that will shape the character of your life. This is because without faith—without trust in God that results in obedience—it's not possible to honor the Lord.

First, you "must believe that He is"—or that He exists. You may believe in God with your mind, but do you demonstrate it with your life? For example, if He asks you to give up everything today, do you trust that He'll provide what you need tomorrow?

Second, you must believe that "He is a rewarder of those who seek Him"—that His character is trustworthy and He always works for your benefit.

Friend, it isn't when everything is going well that it's difficult to have faith. Rather, it's when your world falls apart that you'll be tempted to doubt that God is in control and that He'll work everything for your good. But regardless of what's happening today, set your heart to have faith. God has never let you down and never will. His way will always be best.

*Jesus, I believe You exist and that You always
work for my good. Help my unbelief. Amen.*

My hope is in Jesus because
He is and He is good.

## MARCH 12

# SOWING FAITH

*Whoever sows to please their flesh, from the flesh
will reap destruction; whoever sows to please the
Spirit, from the Spirit will reap eternal life.*

GALATIANS 6:8 NIV

Every day, you'll have choices you must make—ones that come back to what we discussed yesterday in Hebrews 11:6: *Do you truly believe that God exists, and do you have confidence that He is a rewarder of those who seek Him?* Those decisions are seeds that are planted in your life, and with each one, you're either nurturing your relationship with Jesus or undermining it.

Please understand, today's verse doesn't mean that you are *earning* eternal life through obedience. Rather, it recognizes that "this is eternal life, that they may know You, the only true God" (John 17:3). In other words, the more you make decisions that honor the Lord, the more He reveals Himself to you and allows His life to flow through you. You're either choosing God or choosing yourself to be in control. Either Jesus sits on the throne or you do.

Plant faith in your life—with every decision, declare that He is God. Because then you're sowing to the Spirit and you know that the harvest of your life will be good and worthwhile.

*Jesus, help me to make decisions that honor You and
always sow eternal life according to the Spirit. Amen.*

My hope is in Jesus because He
sows and reaps eternal life in me.

# BELIEVE HIM

*He believed in the LORD.*

GENESIS 15:6

Has God spoken to you about some profound desire of your heart? Did you believe Him? Real faith—the faith that honors the Lord—is not just belief in a certain promise fulfilled or blessing given. Instead, it's trust in your Savior's unfailing wisdom, power, and character, regardless of how things look. You trust that He means what He says and will accomplish what He promises (Isaiah 14:24).

Of course, like Abraham, you may have waited a long time to see your hopes fulfilled—and like him, each day you wait may make its fulfillment seem more impossible. However, what's truly important to decide is this: Do you trust your heavenly Father? Do you have confidence He has your best interests in mind?

Like Abraham, you don't have to keep pleading for God to do what He's promised—He never fails to do as He says. In fact, the more you think about what you want, rather than on the Lord Himself, the more frustrated you'll become. Instead, focus on your Savior's perfect character and unfailing ability. Because then you'll be looking in the right direction when He keeps His word.

*Jesus, I believe You always keep Your promises to me—no matter how impossible my situation looks. Strengthen my faith, beloved Savior. Amen.*

> My hope is in Jesus because
> He is the fulfilled Word.

# FOCUS ON GOD

*The LORD longs to be gracious to you; therefore he will rise up
to show you compassion. . . . Blessed are all who wait for him!*
ISAIAH 30:18 NIV

No matter what you're waiting for today, ultimately, you're better prepared for it if you focus on God during the delay.

Why? Because when you continually think about what you lack, it always ends up producing despair in your heart. It tempts you to obsess over your own limitations and to meet your needs in your way rather than the Lord's—which is the very definition of sin (Jeremiah 2:13). It's a disheartening cycle that never ends: you fixate on what you don't have, which puts you in danger of sin, which makes you feel even more depressed and hopeless, which causes you to idolize your desire even more because of the hope that it'll deliver you from your despondency. What a mess!

But when you focus on God, you realize the incredible strength, wisdom, and power that are orchestrating all things on your behalf. You have confidence because the Lord knows and provides what is absolutely best for you. And because He is unaffected by the obstacles that limit and intimidate you, your reasons to fear can utterly disappear.

Be wise; focus on God!

*Jesus, You are the ultimate desire of my heart.*
*Help me always to focus on You. Amen.*

> My hope is in Jesus because
> He truly satisfies my soul.

# SOVEREIGN OR NOT?

*The LORD has established His throne in the*
*heavens, and His sovereignty rules over all.*

PSALM 103:19

You will not make wise decisions unless you wholeheartedly believe this one basic, theological fact—the truth that *God is absolutely sovereign.* That He is indeed God and that He rules over all things, at all times, in all circumstances. Why is this important? Because it will make all the difference as to whether you obey Him or not.

For example, take David (1 Samuel 17). When he was a young man, the champion of the Philistines, Goliath, challenged the bravest of Israel's soldiers to a duel. Sadly, Israel's warriors were all terrified of the mighty Goliath. That is, all except David—who understood that the battle wasn't about human strength, but about the divine power of God. David was able to triumph over Goliath because he was confident that the Lord was sovereign—and that He didn't like His name being taken in vain.

Likewise, God may direct you in ways that seem absolutely impossible or that you don't understand. Ask yourself: is He the omnipotent, omniscient God or isn't He? Answer that question and you'll have the confidence to do as He asks.

*Lord, You are God! You deserve both my respect*
*and trust. Help me always to obey You. Amen.*

> My hope is in Jesus because He
> is the sovereign King of kings.

# DIVINELY REASONABLE

*There is no [human] wisdom or understanding or
counsel [that can prevail] against the LORD.*
PROVERBS 21:30 AMP

At times, God will direct you to do things that don't seem logical.
But He doesn't require you to understand His will; He only asks
that you obey it, even if it seems unreasonable.

For example, throughout Israel's history, the Lord called His
people to depend on Him rather than make military alliances.
From the human standpoint, this made no sense—especially since
Israel's army was so weak. But God saw each and every battle as
an opportunity to reveal Himself to the world. And whenever He
supernaturally delivered Israel, their enemies would fear Him.

Likewise, the Lord may lead you to do something that—
humanly speaking—is counterintuitive. What you have to decide is:
*whose understanding do I trust more: mine or God's?* Remember that
common sense may not be enough to judge your situation, and you
probably don't have all the facts—at least, not like He does. So don't
lean on your own understanding. Trust the Lord's wisdom, which
never fails, and do as He asks.

*Lord Jesus, I don't understand Your wisdom and
Your ways—but I acknowledge that Yours are far
greater than mine. I will trust and obey. Amen.*

My hope is in Jesus because His
wisdom is unfathomably great.

# GOD ALONE

*My soul waits in silence for God only;*
*from Him is my salvation.*

PSALM 62:1

Have you wondered why God has allowed the challenges of your life—especially the ones that seem to undermine everything you depend on? When we encounter serious difficulties—and often, many at once—we may be tempted to feel hopeless. We find ourselves longing to have the Lord's help and wisdom to face the obstacles ahead.

You may not realize it, but this is God drawing you to Himself. He brings you to the point of realizing that all earthly resources and security have failed you. After that, there's only one place to go, and that's to God Himself. This is a positive thing!

David faced this repeatedly as he waited to become king of Israel, and it was why God called him "a man after His own heart" (1 Samuel 13:14). David realized there was only one Source to help him in every instance—only One worthy of his complete devotion and trust. God is bringing you to that understanding as well.

So as David said in Psalm 62:8, "Trust in Him at all times, O people; pour out your heart before Him; God is a refuge for us."

*Jesus, I know You are my refuge, strength, and salvation.*
*In all these trials, You are my hope and I rest in You. Amen.*

> My hope is in Jesus because
> only He can save me.

# PURPOSE

*I cry out to God Most High, to God*
*who will fulfill his purpose for me.*
PSALM 57:2 NLT

God has a good plan for your life. Do you believe that? Or do you automatically think of the failings and limitations that would disqualify you from serving Him? Don't devalue yourself because of something in your past. The Father wants to reach others through you, and He's given you gifts and talents to that end. He loves to make the most of every life He touches.

For example, I recently heard about a group of death row inmates who had accepted Christ as their Savior. They made it their goal to reach other prisoners with the gospel and have absolutely revolutionized their jail with their love for the Lord. God has made them a bright light in a very difficult mission field.

God can work through you as well. He has important plans for you to fulfill, and He's with you every step of the way. Don't worry—He's already considered all the things that are causing you to hesitate. Before He called you, He knew how to overcome every challenge you would ever encounter. So don't deny Him. Let Him make your life more than you ever dreamed possible.

*Jesus, I am willing. Work through me—make*
*my life into whatever You wish. Amen.*

> My hope is in Jesus because
> He sees the potential in me.

# BE A BLESSING

*Blessed be the . . . God of all comfort, who comforts
us in all our affliction so that we will be able to
comfort those who are in any affliction.*

2 CORINTHIANS 1:3–4

Do you realize that God formed you to be a blessing to others?
He absolutely did. In fact, even the things you've been through in
life can be a source of great encouragement to believers who are
struggling. They can see they're not alone in their trials when they
witness how God successfully got you through yours. That in itself
is incredibly comforting.

The issue isn't *if you can* be a blessing; it's *if you will* tell others
how faithful God has been to you. You don't have to be a theolo-
gian; all you need is to start right where you are in your own quiet
time. What are you struggling with, and how is the Lord teaching
you through it? Because when you comfort others from your own
struggles, it's very personal and powerful. God will speak through
you in ways you can't imagine.

So open your eyes to opportunities, your heart to others, and
your mouth to all Jesus has done. You'll be astounded at how the
Lord works through your faithfulness.

*Jesus, I want to be a blessing to others. Give me the
words that exalt You and comfort them. Amen.*

My hope is in Jesus because
He turns my trials to triumphs!

# THE WAY TO GO

*"I am the LORD your God, who . . . leads
you in the way you should go."*
ISAIAH 48:17

Are you confused today because you don't know what to do? Are you confounded because God isn't showing you what direction to take, though you've been asking Him? Don't despair—He hasn't forgotten you, and He isn't ignoring you.

The Lord *will* show you how to proceed. In fact, He is actively working in your situation and guiding you even as you read this, though you may not realize it. You see, God *wants* you to honor Him, and He understands that you don't always know how to do so. Therefore, He takes responsibility for teaching you how to walk in His ways, instructing you as a patient and loving Father would— one step at a time, building your faith, character, and obedience.

What this means is that it would be completely out of character and contrary to His purposes for Him to hide how He wants you to go forward. So stop fretting and continue listening. God will move heaven and earth to show you His will and help you walk in it. He will certainly give you the wisdom to advance with Him one step at a time.

*Jesus, I trust You to show me what to do today
and every day—step-by-step. Amen.*

> My hope is in Jesus because He
> faithfully shows me how to proceed.

# NEVER

*Lord, for what do I wait? My hope is in You.*
PSALM 39:7

Are the *nevers* of life plaguing you today? "This will *never* get better. I'll *never* receive the love and respect I long for. I'll *never* have what I really want." It can be difficult if you've waited a long time to see God work in some situation that's especially important to you. But this is the challenge of faith. It's the ability to keep trusting in Him when the days pass without answers to your pleas at the throne of grace.

But today, know one thing for certain: the only "never" that really matters is that God will *never* let you down (Deuteronomy 31:6, 8). So whatever it is you've been praying for—no matter how long you've had to wait—trust that the Father is leading you and know for absolute certain that He has your best interests at heart. Human reason may tell you to give up on Him, but don't. Instead, keep clinging to the Savior. And remember: the One who came through for Abraham, David, and Joseph after their long periods of waiting is working on your behalf too. Just as He kept His promises to them, He will do so for you as well.

*Jesus, I will never give up on You. You are my help and my hope—in You I trust always. Amen.*

> My hope is in Jesus because
> He never lets me down.

# PRINCIPLE OR PREFERENCE

*"Everyone who hears these words of Mine and acts on them, may be compared to a wise man who built his house on the rock."*

MATTHEW 7:24

Today you have a choice: You can live by your *preferences*—choices based on your likes and dislikes and whatever seems best at the moment. Or you can live by God's Word—His fixed *principles* of conduct and character.

In today's verse, Jesus explains that if you want to be strong enough to withstand the storms of life, you must base your beliefs on something that cannot be moved—that nothing in eternity can overturn. You stand unmovable on the outside because internally, your life is resolutely established on infallible truth. And, of course, the firmest foundation you could ever build your life on is God—His unshakable character, wisdom, and purposes.

But how do you do so? You believe the Lord and obey however He directs you. You allow Jesus to shape how you respond to whatever happens. He loves you and never fails you. So you can know for certain that when you live by the principles of Scripture, you're setting the foundation to stand strong no matter what occurs.

*Jesus, sometimes obeying You is so difficult because it is so counter to what I am used to. But I will trust that You know best. Amen.*

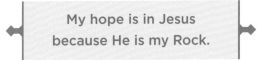

My hope is in Jesus
because He is my Rock.

# CONFESS JOY

*"I have told you these things so that you will be filled with my joy."*
JOHN 15:11 NLT

Today, know with certainty that God loves you, He's in control of all that concerns you, and He is at work in your life in a powerful way. In fact, proclaim it out loud: "God is active on my behalf, and I will trust Him!"

It's always important for us to confess this because when we look at our troubles apart from His intervention, we can grow disheartened—realizing that we don't have the ability to overcome them on our own.

But when we fix our eyes on Jesus, who defeated sin and death, rose from the grave, and rules all creation—we see that our problems are as nothing to Him! Nothing touches our lives without His permission, and He ensures that all will work together for our good. In fact, He uses our difficulties to prepare us for the great plans He has for us. Can anything give our hearts more hope and assurance than that?

Our God is sufficient for every circumstance we face, and He's leading us to become more than conquerors. Truly, He is the unshakable Source of all our joy and is fully worthy of our praise!

*Jesus, You are the unassailable Source of all my hope and joy! Thank You for leading me victoriously! Amen.*

My hope is in Jesus because
He gives me true joy.

# A Crossroad of Faith

*When we obey him, every path he guides us on is
fragrant with his loving-kindness and his truth.*

PSALM 25:10 TLB

What can you do when you get close to receiving what your heart longs for, but then the door gets shut? The job you wanted is given to another. The relationship you were so excited about ends. The cure that was supposed to help instead causes more issues. It can leave a soul depressed and questioning.

When this happens, realize that you've come to an important crossroad in your faith—a crucial decision that will shape your life. You can grow either bitter or better. You can either get angry and walk away from God—or accept His will and acknowledge that He knows best for you.

Friend, don't give up on the One who saved you—not for anything. If Christ has shut this door, it's for a good reason (Romans 8:28). He gave His life for you and always strives to give you the absolute best (Romans 8:32). So let go and trust Him. You may not understand His reasons at the moment, but eventually you will. And no doubt, you'll be grateful for the wisdom and love He's shown on your behalf.

*Jesus, I don't understand, but I will trust You, knowing
You always lead me in the best way. Amen.*

My hope is in Jesus because He
leads me in loving-kindness and truth.

# GREATER THAN YOUR SIN

*God had mercy on me so that Christ Jesus could use
me as a prime example of his great patience with even
the worst sinners. Then others will realize that they,
too, can believe in him and receive eternal life.*

1 TIMOTHY 1:16 NLT

Never talk down what God can do in you. How do you do so? When you say things such as: "I don't think God can forgive me." Or, "I'm too flawed for Him to use." Or, "I'm a lost cause—Jesus can't fix someone as broken as I am." You may think you sound humble, but you're actually doubting God's power and wisdom.

Paul addressed this when he wrote today's verse. As a man who had once persecuted the church, he felt himself to be the worst of all sinners—the person least deserving of God's grace. Yet Paul said that Jesus had mercy on him, so that even at our lowest, we can know for certain Christ wants to forgive and help us. What a beautiful message!

You may feel conviction because God wants to set you free of bondage, but never take that to mean you are too lost for Him to heal. Instead, praise Him for loving you even when you feel most unlovable.

*Jesus, You make me worthy when I feel worthless. Thank
You that Your grace overcomes all my failings. Amen.*

> My hope is in Jesus because
> His grace is greater than my sin.

# CLOSE TO GOD

*Woe is me, for I am ruined! Because I am a man of
unclean lips, and I live among a people of unclean lips;
for my eyes have seen the King, the LORD of hosts.*

ISAIAH 6:5

At times, you will grow closer to God—ridding your heart of idols, renewing your commitment to Him, and shedding all that encumbers your relationship with Him. Then suddenly, out of seemingly nowhere, you will be absolutely convicted of your sinfulness to the point of utter brokenness.

It will be surprising because you'll *feel* further from God even though you've been more dedicated to Him. But take today's verse as encouragement. It was when Isaiah got *close* to the Lord that he truly understood his sinfulness. He was not being rejected by God. On the contrary, the Lord was readying Isaiah to draw *even nearer*!

The same is true for you. The closer you get to God, the more aware of your sins you'll be so He can free you from them. The discomfort is not forever and afterward "produces a repentance without regret" (2 Corinthians 7:10) that will lead you to a deeper and more fulfilling experience of His love and all Jesus has provided for you in salvation.

*Jesus, this pain as I draw near You is difficult, but I trust
You to set me free and draw me even closer. Amen.*

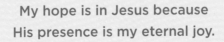

My hope is in Jesus because
His presence is my eternal joy.

# COMPELLED TO TELL

*I heard the voice of the Lord, saying, "Whom shall I
send?" . . . Then I said, "Here am I. Send me!"*
ISAIAH 6:8

Yesterday, we saw how Isaiah understood his sinfulness when he
got *close* to the Lord because God was readying Isaiah to draw *even
nearer*. Today, we see the result. Isaiah was so grateful for the mercy
he'd received, he was willing to do whatever God asked.

Forgiveness has that effect. In fact, David said the same thing:
"Restore to me the joy of your salvation. . . . Then I will teach trans-
gressors your ways, so that sinners will turn back to you" (Psalm
51:12–13 NIV). When you're liberated from bondage, guilt, and
shame, it's natural to want to help others find the same. Out of
gratefulness and compassion, you tell them how to be free so they
can enjoy all God has given. This is the very heart of the commission Jesus gave us (Matthew 28:19–20).

If the desire to tell others about Christ doesn't flow from you
out of thankfulness to Him and mercy for others, then examine
your heart. Make sure you've received the fullness of His freedom
and forgiveness. Because when the joy of His salvation is in you, it
can't help but overflow.

*Jesus, sometimes I don't feel compelled to share. Fill me with
the desire to exalt You and to minister to others. Amen.*

My hope is in Jesus because
He sets people free!

# ALWAYS PRAY

*"GOD IS OPPOSED TO THE PROUD, BUT GIVES GRACE TO THE
HUMBLE." Submit therefore to God. Resist the devil and he will
flee from you. Draw near to God and He will draw near to you.*

JAMES 4:6–8

The one thing Satan doesn't want you to do is pray. So if you feel
distant from God—as if He doesn't want to hear from you or you
should handle your troubles on your own—you know where it's
coming from. You're experiencing spiritual warfare.

The enemy knows that if he can keep you off your knees and
away from the Lord, then he has accomplished his mission. He has
cut you off from the Source of your power, worth, identity, guidance, and purpose. That's a victory for him. You see, after you
know Jesus as Savior, the enemy cannot separate you from Christ
ever again. All he can do is undermine your effectiveness for God's
kingdom by telling you that the Lord doesn't want you (a lie) or that
you don't need Him (also known as *pride*).

Don't fall for the devil's trap. No matter how you feel, humble
yourself before God. Tell Him you need Him and will obey. Then
praise Him for the spiritual victory He'll lead you to.

*Jesus, I submit myself to You in prayer. Lead
me to triumph over the enemy. Amen.*

My hope is in Jesus because
He leads me to spiritual victory.

# WAIT FOR HIM

*Wait for the LORD; be strong and let your heart
take courage; yes, wait for the LORD.*

PSALM 27:14

Time is one of God's most effective tools for teaching you to rely on Him. This has been true throughout history—seen often in the lives of great saints such as David, who wrote the psalm above.

David was a teenager when the prophet Samuel anointed him to succeed Saul as king of Israel. Although this was a great honor, it was only the beginning of a long and difficult wait—one filled with devastating losses and uncertainties. At one point, David was forced to flee from Israel altogether, making the fulfillment of his dreams seem impossible. But David trusted the Lord to do as He said, and because he did, David eventually took the throne. And through it all, the Lord molded David's character—fitting him to be a godly king of Israel.

You can be certain the same is true for you. In your waiting, the Father is preparing you for His awesome purposes. So today, no matter the disappointments, delays, or seeming impossibilities, take the advice from a man who knows: Wait for the Lord; be strong and be encouraged. Yes, wait for the Lord.

*Jesus, I will wait for You. Prepare me
to do Your will, my Savior. Amen.*

My hope is in Jesus because
He always keeps His promises.

# BEHIND THE SCENES

*"Thus it shall be done to the man whom the king desires to honor."*
ESTHER 6:11

You don't know what God is doing behind the scenes or how He is orchestrating important details on your behalf.

Take Mordecai for example. He was hated by an evil man named Haman, who was second in command to King Ahasuerus of Persia. Haman was determined to execute Mordecai and even built gallows for that purpose. However, the night before Haman planned to ask the king if he could kill Mordecai, Ahasuerus couldn't sleep. He asked to be brought his kingdom's chronicles, and, while reading, discovered that five years earlier, Mordecai had saved his life by exposing an assassination plot. What a moment for the king to realize Mordecai's service to him! Not only was Haman's plan foiled, but Mordecai was honored instead!

This is the perfect illustration of how God works on your behalf—in the unseen His all-powerful hand engineers what you need. So don't lose heart no matter how impossible your situation seems. Instead, focus on God, respect His leadership, and trust Him to provide for you in His perfect wisdom and time.

*Jesus, I know You can change my impossible situation in the twinkling of an eye. I will trust You and wait. Amen.*

My hope is in Jesus because
He is working in the unseen.

# DEPENDABLE LOVE

*God is love.*

1 JOHN 4:8

Are you reticent to trust God because of how others have let you down? If so, then understand that the Savior's love for you is not like most human love—moody, unpredictable, self-serving, and dependent upon your response. Rather, God's love for you is based on His holy character—which is sacrificial, unchanging, completely trustworthy, and committed to providing the very best for you.

Today's verse explains that love is His very nature. What this means is that He cannot cease to care for you, because to do so He would have to stop being Himself. Likewise, your Savior won't love you more when you're obedient or less when you're sinful, because His affection is based on *His* steadfast disposition—not on *your* worthiness.

This is why you can always count on Jesus to help you. He is loving, good, and faithful (2 Timothy 2:13). You never have to worry about Him saying one thing and doing another, or acting in a way toward you that is harmful or cruel. Instead, you can rely on the loving assurances He's given you in His Word every day of your life.

*Jesus, thank You for loving me profoundly,*
*unconditionally, and faithfully. Help me to live in a*
*manner worthy of Your love for me. Amen.*

My hope is in Jesus because I
can count on His unfailing love.

# APRIL

Blessed be the God and Father of our Lord Jesus Christ, who according to His great mercy has caused us to be born again to a living hope through the resurrection of Jesus Christ from the dead.

1 PETER 1:3

# WHAT'S IN YOUR HEART?

*Every man's way is right in his own eyes,*
*but the LORD weighs the hearts.*

PROVERBS 21:2

Take a moment and consider what thoughts and emotions are flowing from you. Are you fearful, angry, or miserable? Do unkind or even profane words, complaints, doubts, or curses rise up in your heart? Are there unclean, impure machinations?

You will learn a lot when you listen to yourself. The arguments and feelings that surface reveal who you really are and what's going on in you. Certainly, you may believe you're doing well—that you're honoring the Lord and living a holy life. But there's no evidence that can condemn you like that which comes from your own heart (Proverbs 30:12; Matthew 15:18–19).

Friend, whatever God surfaces—don't deny it. He is revealing it to you for a reason. Ask Him to reveal the source of your thoughts and emotions and what you need to do in response to what He shows you. Then obey Him fully. Remember: His goal is to liberate you from your bondage to sin and heal the wounds within you (Romans 7:24–25). So don't be afraid. Rather, trust that your Savior continues on His mission to conform you to His image and fit you for everlasting life.

*Lord, I repent. Help me to break free from this*
*bondage and live a life worthy of You. Amen.*

My hope is in Jesus because
He truly heals my heart.

# Your Defender

*The Lord said . . . "I will deliver you."*
Judges 7:7

Are you facing a battle where you can't help yourself—you just don't have the resources or strength to fight what's coming against you? God wants you to realize how completely you can depend on Him. He is not just the Savior of your soul, but your Defender and Deliverer in every moment of your life, and you are always safe relying upon Him.

This was certainly the case for Gideon. The Lord called Gideon to stand against the immense invading armies of the Midianites. However, being from the smallest tribe, Gideon felt ill-equipped to face them. So God lovingly assured him: "I will be with you" (Judges 6:16). Ultimately, He delivered Israel in a miraculous manner that Gideon could never have foreseen or engineered on his own.

The same is true for your battles today. It could be that not only is the challenge too big for you, but you've been cut off from the resources you're accustomed to relying upon. You're more limited, weak, and powerless now than ever. Stand by. Your omnipotent God is orchestrating your deliverance in a manner you could never have imagined so you can see the mighty workings of His power on your behalf. Count on it.

*Jesus, this battle belongs to You. I will trust Your deliverance. Thank You for helping me. Amen.*

My hope is in Jesus because
He is my Defender.

# His Mighty Hand

*"I give eternal life to them, and they will never perish;
and no one will snatch them out of My hand."*

John 10:28

What's the first thing you usually think about when you face a trial? Is it how you feel about it or what you could lose? Do you realize the difference it could make if your first thought was about God? If you asked, "Lord, what are You up to? What do You want me to learn from this?"

Friend, nothing touches your life without Him first allowing it. Think of the assurance Jesus gave you in today's verse. You rest in the palm of His hand. Yes, this speaks to your eternal security when He's your Savior. But it also speaks to your life as a whole—you are safely protected within His mighty hand. So anything that comes to you must first make it past Him. And since nothing in all creation can move even God's finger, anything He permits must ultimately be for His greater purposes (Romans 8:28–29).

So when you experience circumstances that you don't understand, watch for what the Lord is trying to teach you about Himself. And trust His mighty hand to guide and guard you regardless of what happens.

*Jesus, thank You for holding my life in Your hand. I
know that I can survive anything with You. Amen.*

My hope is in Jesus
because His grip is eternal.

# GOOD FRUIT

*"Bear fruit in keeping with repentance."*
MATTHEW 3:8

We all long to be happy people—comfortably situated in fulfilling lives. And there are thousands of products that promise to help us achieve that. However, the emphasis on most self-help items is on what *we're* supposed to do, own, or think. Although they make inspiring claims, and even make us happy short-term, they never produce the genuine, long-lasting peace and contentment we truly desire.

This is because these aren't feelings you can generate on your own or through earthly means—they are solely the work of the Holy Spirit within you. Love, joy, peace, patience, kindness, goodness, faithfulness, gentleness, and self-control are all His fruit—manifestations of His renewing work in your life (Galatians 5:22–23). This is what is born in you when you repent—when you agree with God and walk in His ways.

From the moment you accepted Jesus as your Savior, the Holy Spirit has been working to transform you into Christ's likeness and free you from the bondage to sin. That's how you become the joyful, peaceful, loving person you desire to become—you yield to His activity. So don't fight Him. Obey how He prompts you and enjoy the harvest He brings forth from your life.

*Jesus, bear good fruit in me! I yield to Your*
*wonderful transforming work. Amen.*

My hope is in Jesus because
His fruit is always good.

# No Compromise

*"Let your heart hold fast my words; keep
my commandments and live."*

PROVERBS 4:4

There will be times when it seems that the best course of action will be to compromise your core beliefs. Perhaps you're tempted to bend your standards of integrity for a business deal or seek counsel from an ungodly source to achieve success in a certain area. But this is never a good idea. Satan's deadliest attacks are usually very subtle.

Take King Solomon, for example. The Lord warned Solomon against alliances with Egypt; but because Egypt had the best horses, Solomon ignored God's command. It was a small area of compromise—what could it hurt? But eventually, Solomon agreed to a treaty with Egypt that involved marrying Pharaoh's daughter. That opened the door to him taking more pagan wives.

The result was terrible. "When Solomon was old, his wives turned his heart away after other gods; and his heart was not wholly devoted to the LORD" (1 Kings 11:4). Consequently, the nation of Israel became weaker until it was ultimately torn asunder.

Even the smallest compromises can lead to devastating consequences. Don't fall for the trap. Listen to God, hold tight to His commands, and trust Him to provide better for you.

*Jesus, Your ways are best. I will obey all You've taught me. Amen.*

My hope is in Jesus because
His instruction is trustworthy.

# WHO HE IS

*"He who has seen Me has seen the Father."*

JOHN 14:9

When you think about God, what are the first emotions you feel? Are they love, peace, and hope—or fear, uncertainty, and disappointment?

This is important because how you *see* the Lord will shape how you feel about Him, how you interact with Him, and how you live your life. Of course, the best way to form an accurate view of the Father is to read about Jesus in the Gospels. After all, Christ is "the exact representation of His nature" (Hebrews 1:3). When you read about Jesus, you're seeing the very character of God at work.

Witness Jesus as He healed those who were sick or as He held the children and blessed them. Think about how He had time for and compassion on all who came to Him. Then consider the Savior on the cross. He sacrificed Himself so that you could know the Father intimately—love was His motivation.

When you get a clear picture of Jesus, you'll realize there's really no reason to be uncertain, fearful, disappointed, or angry at God. On the contrary, there's no one as loving, faithful, kind, or merciful as He is. Rather, you'll find ample reason to respect Him and give Him your full devotion.

*Jesus, reveal the Father to me so I can love*
*Him more and serve Him better. Amen.*

My hope is in Jesus because
He is my loving Savior.

# THE POWER OF YOUR LIFE

*Our gospel did not come to you in word only,*
*but also in power and in the Holy Spirit.*

1 THESSALONIANS 1:5

Are you weary? Do you feel as if your service for God has become a burden? There's good news for you today: *you were never meant to live the Christian life in your own strength.* The true Christian life is not so much that you live *for* Jesus—which is what most religions require. Rather, it's Jesus living *through* you; empowering you to do the work only He can do.

Think about the disciples. They were uneducated, simple men, who had no resources on their own. They were completely incapable of taking the good news of salvation to the whole world on their own. But then, no one would ever say that the gospel spread and endured because of those disciples. Rather, it was the power of God that fueled it from start to finish.

Remember: the Father never asks you to do anything for Him in your own strength because then you'd get the glory. No, He's chosen you for the tasks before you so He can shine His power through you—so that when the work's accomplished, people won't look to you; they'll look to Him and believe.

*Jesus, work through me in the way only You can—*
*and may many believe in You! Amen.*

My hope is in Jesus because
He's the power of my life.

# TAPPING INTO THE POWER

*"My grace is sufficient for you, for My strength
is made perfect in weakness."*

2 CORINTHIANS 12:9 NKJV

Have you ever noticed that Jesus' Great Commission begins and ends with His power and presence? Christ told the disciples, "All authority has been given to Me in heaven and on earth. . . . and lo, I am with you always, even to the end of the age" (Matthew 28:18–20). As we said yesterday, it was only by relying on Jesus that those believers could take the good news to the world.

The same is true for us—anything we do for the Father must begin and end with His power and presence. But how does one tap into it? It may surprise you to discover that brokenness is key. Why? Because first we must come to the end of our own ability and strength. Only then do we stop fighting Him and discover that God's power in us can move mountains. We stop relying on our-selves and instead depend on the Lord, who can do anything.

So if you're feeling weak and ineffective today—rejoice! You're in the perfect position for God to pour His power into you and work in miraculous ways through you.

*Jesus, I praise You that when I am weak, You are strong!
Work through me in a powerful way. Amen.*

> My hope is in Jesus because He
> turns my brokenness to triumph.

# THANKFUL FOR WEAKNESS

*I have received such wonderful revelations from God. So to keep*
*me from becoming proud, I was given a thorn in my flesh.*
2 CORINTHIANS 12:7 NLT

Have you ever thanked God for the burdens and trials that keep
you reliant upon Him? He put those limitations in your life for the
purpose of liberating you from your dependence on yourself, keeping you close to the Father, and allowing you to know Him better.
And, as we saw yesterday, they also help you experience His power.

Paul understood this, which is why he wrote today's verse. He
had received such incredible revelations that God worked through his
infirmities to make sure he wouldn't become conceited or exalt himself. Paul recognized the Father's good purpose, and he praised the
Lord for keeping him reliant upon Him and humble toward others.

This is true for you as well, and it's why you should praise Jesus
for your inadequacies. It's in your weaknesses that you relate to
others better (2 Corinthians 1:3–4) and that Christ is magnified.
That's where the real ministry and miracles of God take place. So
don't hide or despise your flaws and limitations. Instead, thank
Jesus for them and glorify Him.

> *Jesus, thank You for the weaknesses that keep me*
> *close to You and allow others to experience Your*
> *power. May You always be exalted! Amen.*

My hope is in Jesus because
He's strong when I'm weak.

# UNSEEN BATTLES

*Be strong in the Lord and in the strength of His might.*

EPHESIANS 6:10

God is always looking out for you. He is always preparing you for the future and safeguarding you from forces you're not even aware of. In fact, that's the essence of today's verse. Jesus invites you to be strong in Him—putting on His might as you would protective clothing because there's a battle for you raging where you cannot see it. There is an enemy who will oppose the godly lifestyle Christ has called you to and will do everything in his power to keep you from serving Jesus.

It's important that you be aware of this battle because, at times, the discontentment or anxiety will rise up within you and may completely overwhelm you. You may be more tempted than ever to give up on God. But don't. This is the time to pray more, love Him more, seek Him more. And most especially—to obey Him more.

His commands and His ways may not make sense, but with everything He instructs, He is guarding against something that is beyond your vision. So understand that sense of unrest in your spirit—you're under spiritual attack. Fight to win by reaffirming your faith in Jesus and doing as He says.

*Jesus, everything seems like defeat right now, but I trust You. Lead me to victory, my Savior. Amen.*

My hope is in Jesus because
He defends me in the unseen.

# STAY IN THE WORD

*The word of the LORD is tried; He is a shield*
*to all who take refuge in Him.*

PSALM 18:30

God loves you so much that He wants you to have His very best—both in this life and in the one to come. However, you cannot experience either outside of knowing Him. This is why it's so important to spend time studying His Word.

By investing time in Scripture, you gain the wisdom you need for every challenge, trial, and circumstance. And through your daily times with the Father, He also provides the knowledge you need for a *lifetime* of devotion to Him—a life that is ultimately fulfilling and productive. Likewise, through your time in the Word, you gain the assurance that your all-powerful, all-wise, and unconditionally loving God withholds nothing that would be beneficial to you. Psalm 84:11 promises, "The LORD gives grace and glory; no good thing does He withhold from those who walk uprightly."

Certainly, God is worthy of praise! But you cannot discover His will for your life or for the trial you're experiencing apart from time with Him. So today, devote yourself to studying His Word with a notepad and an open heart.

*Jesus, as I read Scripture, reveal Yourself and*
*Your will to me. Lead me, my Savior. Amen.*

> My hope is in Jesus because
> He leads me in the path of life.

# OPEN TO HIM

*If I have found favor in Your sight, let me know*
*Your ways that I may know You.*

EXODUS 33:13

It's a principle of the Christian life: the more you know God, the less you will want to hide from Him. And the less you conceal, the more He will reveal Himself to you.

We see this in the story of Moses. When Moses first stepped into the Lord's presence, we read that he "hid his face, for he was afraid to look at God" (Exodus 3:6). However, by Exodus 33, Moses responded very differently. Verse 11 states, "The LORD used to speak to Moses face to face, just as a man speaks to his friend." And we find Moses proclaiming, "Show me Your glory!" (v. 18).

You may be in a situation where you need God's guidance but are still hiding parts of yourself from Him. You open His Word, but everything remains confusing. If you're having trouble, it could be because of something in your life that needs to be addressed, but that you're unwilling to allow Him into. Don't shut Him out. Open your heart to Him—be honest, transparent, and obedient. He will certainly guide you in a way that you understand.

*Jesus, You know the area that's difficult to turn over.*
*I open my heart to You. Heal me. Amen.*

My hope is in Jesus because He handles
my open heart with healing truth and love.

# MATURING CHALLENGES

*"I will teach you what you are to do."*
EXODUS 4:15

Are you feeling confounded today—confused because of the issues you face? Often, this will be the case if God is going to reveal Himself to you in a new way. He has a special plan for your life—so the choices, questions, and trials before you have been selected for the purpose of developing you into what He created you to become. They've arisen so you'll depend on Him in a manner that you haven't known before and grow in your character and faith.

Of course, you may be wondering, *I thought these trials were in my life as a punishment because I've made so many mistakes.* But remember: when Jesus is your Savior, God forgives you completely. You may be facing the consequences of your mistakes, but He isn't punishing you. On the contrary, the challenges you're facing are actively preparing you for the future so you can enjoy all the blessings He has planned for you.

So analyze the questions, decisions, and struggles before you today. In what new way is God asking you to rely on Him? This is your opportunity to respond in a manner that honors Him and to grow in the purposes for which He created you.

*Jesus, thank You that everything in my life is*
*working toward Your good purposes. Amen.*

My hope is in Jesus because He
develops me for His purposes.

# A GREATER PLAN

*Hosanna to the Son of David; blessed is He who comes
in the name of the Lord; hosanna in the highest!*

MATTHEW 21:9

When Jesus entered Jerusalem during the last week of His life, the crowds received Him as the Deliverer-King they'd been waiting for—with palm branches and praises. He was the One they thought would restore their nation to them. So they joyously welcomed Him with the messianic greeting from Psalm 118:25–26, "LORD, save us! . . . Blessed is he who comes in the name of the LORD" (NIV).

Sadly, just a few days later, those crowds would disperse. With Jesus in the grave, and their hopes buried with Him, the disciples went away disheartened because they didn't really understand God's purposes. It was not until three days later, when Jesus rose from the dead, that they'd see that the Lord had an even greater plan than they had imagined.

Always remember this when opportunities—things you praised God for—seem to be destroyed. He has a greater plan for you. Continue to trust your Savior regardless of how things appear. He has a way of resurrecting your dreams in a manner far beyond your imagination that is bound to make you truly joyful.

*Jesus, I know that no matter how my circumstances may
appear, You are breathing life into my dreams. Amen.*

My hope is in Jesus because He has
the greatest plan for my life.

# POWERFUL DELAYS

*"This sickness is not to end in death, but for the glory of God."*
JOHN 11:4

Today you may be tempted to see the painful things that happen to you—especially the postponements—as God's rejection. But don't. Instead, consider how Jesus expressed His love for Lazarus, Mary, and Martha.

If you recall, Jesus was told that Lazarus was very sick, but He delayed His journey to see Lazarus by two days. By the time Christ arrived in Bethany, Lazarus had been in the grave four days. But because Jesus had them wait, Mary and Martha saw what very few people have ever witnessed—they saw Lazarus *raised from the dead.* They saw a preview of Jesus' power over the grave (John 11:25)!

Jesus understood it was far more beneficial for this family to see the mighty power of God at work than to spare them their momentary distress. The same is true for you. If He allows some difficulty in your life, it is because He can bring forth some good purpose from it. So don't imagine that the trials and delays you're experiencing are because of the Father's contempt for you. Rather, be glad that this is the perfect platform for you to witness His glorious intervention on your behalf.

*Jesus, thank You that Your delays are not denials. I*
*await Your intervention with hope. Amen.*

My hope is in Jesus because He demonstrates resurrection power on my behalf.

# STABILITY IN THE CHAOS

*"In the world you have tribulation, but take
courage; I have overcome the world."*

JOHN 16:33

It is natural to feel fearful when everything appears chaotic. No one likes the feeling of being out of control—without a firm place to stand or something solid to hold on to. However, when those times come, we must remind ourselves of the one fact that can stabilize us: *God has a plan, and He is in control.* When we're reminded that nothing we experience is a surprise to the Lord, we can cling to hope.

Just before His arrest and crucifixion, Jesus told His disciples, "Behold, an hour is coming, and has already come, for you to be scattered. . . . These things I have spoken to you, so that in Me you may have peace" (John 16:32–33). In other words, everything will look chaotic, but remember that God already knows about it and will bring stability out of the chaos. And certainly, three days later, they saw the greatest victory they'd ever witnessed—the resurrection.

Friend, God is in control of all that's happening to you today. So take heart. He has a plan for you. Cling to Him, and you will see His awesome purposes for you fulfilled.

*Jesus, I cannot see my way through this, but I am grateful
that You have a plan that will be accomplished. Amen.*

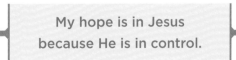

My hope is in Jesus
because He is in control.

# THINK SALVATION

*When He had taken some bread and given thanks, He
broke it and gave it to them, saying, "This is My body
which is given for you; do this in remembrance of Me."*

LUKE 22:19

The night before the crucifixion, Jesus celebrated the Last Supper
with His disciples. During that historic meal, He gave them a visual
illustration of what He was doing for them—so that whenever
they would break bread, which was a daily occurrence, they would
remember the salvation He'd provided. He knew they would need
such a reminder in the days ahead.

It is interesting to note that when doing spiritual battle, the
armor that is given to protect the mind is the helmet of salvation
(Ephesians 6:17). Recalling what Jesus has accomplished for us on
the cross is crucial for us as we live the Christian life, and even more
as we encounter trials. Why? Because thinking about our salvation
helps us focus on what is really important, how God has already
provided for us, and who it is who unfailingly helps us.

So today, remember Jesus—recall the great salvation He has
given you. And rejoice that the One who triumphed over sin and
death is the One who helps you in all your battles.

*Jesus, thank You for this great salvation—especially the hope and
assurance it brings me in every circumstance of life. Amen.*

My hope is in Jesus because
He is my Great Provider.

# The Struggle of Gethsemane

*"Keep watching and praying . . . the spirit
is willing, but the flesh is weak."*

MATTHEW 26:41

Matthew 26 tells us that in the Garden of Gethsemane, Jesus prayed, "Father, if it is possible, let this cup pass from Me; yet not as I will, but as You will" (v. 39). Verse 42 says, "He went away again a second time and prayed." Again, verse 44 reports, "He left them again, and went away and prayed a third time, saying the same thing." Because of the overwhelming burden on His soul, He went back to the throne of grace repeatedly to find comfort.

This tells us something that's very important. If the perfect, sinless Son of the living God found it necessary to pray repeatedly, then there's nothing wrong when we must do so as well. We may often struggle terribly, wondering how we'll survive the trials we experience. There may be sleepless nights when all we know is to cry out, "God, please help me!" But take comfort. Your Savior understands how you feel and has been there Himself. Go to Him for comfort and consolation. But also, take His example and don't leave His presence until you're able to say, "Not as I will, but as You will."

*Jesus, thank You for understanding me. Help
me always to do Your will. Amen.*

My hope is in Jesus because He
always welcomes me into His presence.

# Forsaken to Free

*About the ninth hour Jesus cried out with a loud voice,*
*saying, . . . "My God, My God, why have You forsaken Me?"*
MATTHEW 27:46

It was the ninth hour, right when the slaughter of the Passover lambs would have commenced in the temple. As priests made the offering memorializing Israel's deliverance from slavery in Egypt (Exodus 12), another Lamb—the Lamb of God—was being sacrificed on the cross for a much more enduring liberation: our eternal release from the bondage of sin and the penalty of death.

Yet, we are wise to note the words Jesus said as He became our sin offering: "My God, My God, why have You forsaken Me?" In that moment, He felt the full consequence of our sin and how it makes us feel—alienated, isolated, helpless, and utterly hopeless. But Jesus took that penalty on Himself so that you wouldn't have to endure it any longer—you could be liberated from the painful separation from God caused by your failings.

So whenever you feel rejected, hopeless, or alone, remember that Jesus has been where you are and welcomes you with love and compassion. Your God has not forsaken you. Rather, He's given everything so you can know Him, have the eternal assurance of His presence, and be free.

*Jesus, thank You for paying such a high price for my salvation*
*and for always—eternally—being with me. Amen.*

My hope is in Jesus because He sets me free.

# Our Focus in Heartbreak

*The women . . . saw the tomb and how His body was laid. . . . And*
*on the Sabbath they rested according to the commandment.*

LUKE 23:55–56

The quiet moments after a devastating loss are often the most heartbreaking. You take care of what needs to be done and attempt to understand what's happened to you.

For Jesus' followers, that meant observing the Sabbath. They kept doing what God had called them to do regardless of their circumstances. But it also means we know what they were doing from the moment they saw Jesus crucified, to when they knew He had risen from the dead. Every element of the Sabbath—the prayers, blessings, and rituals—would have reminded them of Jesus. Of course, from the foundation of the world, God knew this would happen. Why would He have set it up this way? Because of how important it is to keep focusing on Him when all hope seems lost.

It isn't in burying your feelings that you find meaning and triumph—it's in taking them to Him. Even when you don't know how things will turn out, He will give you comfort, hope, and peace that transcend your understanding.

*Jesus, I need Your help to make sense of all that's happened. Please*
*give me Your comfort, hope, and peace as I process all of this. Amen.*

> My hope is in Jesus because He
> gives meaning to my heartbreaks.

# RESURRECTION HOPE

*Understand the incredible greatness of God's power*
*for us who believe him. This is the same mighty*
*power that raised Christ from the dead.*

EPHESIANS 1:19–20 NLT

If you need hope today, there's nothing like remembering the resurrection. The most impossible battle any of us will ever face is against death. If there's anything that leaves us feeling powerless, it's the grave. That is, until Jesus was victorious over it.

Jesus is alive! Don't let that thought just pass by—really think about it. He's paid the penalty of sin and brought forth everlasting life for you from the seemingly unyielding grip of death.

Of course, this is extremely important in the eternal sense, but don't allow the message of the resurrection to stop there. Apply it to your daily struggles—the seemingly unbearable battles where all hope seems gone, buried in the grave of devastating circumstances. The resurrection tells you that no matter how difficult and impossible the trial, you have hope as long as you have Jesus!

Could your situation possibly need more power than the resurrection? Yet, that's the provision promised to you. The challenges before you today are no match for the Lord. So rejoice and be assured that He will faithfully help you regardless of what you face.

*Jesus, thank You for the hope that the resurrection*
*gives me. Nothing is impossible for You. Amen!*

My hope is in Jesus because
He has defeated death!

# MORE TO THIS LIFE

*"He who has lost his life for My sake will find it."*
MATTHEW 10:39

The cross was not the end of Christ's life. We know that three days later, He rose again from the dead—demonstrating His victory over sin and death. Likewise, His ministry was not completed at the crucifixion. An important part still lay ahead—working through believers by the indwelling power of His Holy Spirit and ultimately returning as the reigning King of kings.

But we need to understand that the cross is not an end for us either. We may be tempted to think of the Christian life as losing our life here so we might gain heaven—that we walk around as limited, self-sacrificing, dead people so we can experience the life to come. But that's not the picture Jesus gives us. No, we relinquish our imperfect and limited earthly existence so that we can gain Christ's powerful resurrection life (Philippians 3:10–11). And that eternal life starts right now (John 17:3).

You have life—real, unmatched, everlasting, resurrection life. And just as Jesus is working in more powerful ways than ever, so you can have an even more fulfilling and eternally impacting existence. So start living, know Jesus, and discover all you were saved to enjoy.

*Jesus, live Your powerful, eternal, resurrection life through me! Amen.*

My hope is in Jesus because
in Him is true life.

# A Better Life

*Others trusted God and were beaten to death, preferring*
*to die rather than turn from God and be free—trusting*
*that they would rise to a better life afterwards.*

HEBREWS 11:35 TLB

We are called to bear the image of Jesus (Romans 8:29). That is glorious news because we serve a Savior who has been raised from the dead and gives us eternal, resurrection life. But it also means that just as this world hated Him, it may be difficult on us (John 15:18). In fact, we may endure intense persecution as Christians all through the ages have.

In today's passage, we read about believers who were told they had only one choice: *reject Christ and live.* Yet they preferred to be beaten and executed rather than deny the One who saved them.

Friend, have you decided that Jesus means more to you than your earthly life or anything it offers? That He's worth all the pain that bearing His name may bring you? If you haven't, I suggest you make that choice once and for all. Make the commitment. Not only will it influence all the lesser decisions you have to make, but then your treasure really will be in heaven. And it will grow your love for Him exponentially.

*Jesus, You are the goal of my life and the One my*
*soul loves. I commit to You forever. Amen.*

My hope is in Jesus because He is
the Way, the Truth, and the Life.

# Expressing Reverence

*The fear of the Lord is a fountain of life.*
PROVERBS 14:27

Part of experiencing the fullness of the Christian life is having an exalted view of God—such as was exhibited by the scribes who recorded Scripture. Every time they'd come to passages containing the Lord's name, they would lay down their styluses and wash their hands. Why? Because of God's sovereignty and holiness. The scribes did not feel worthy of printing His name without first cleansing themselves. This kind of godly fear may seem foreign to us today. Yet we miss a great blessing when we fail to give the Lord His rightful place.

So consider: Do you fear God? Have you truly pondered His authority, power, and wisdom? This doesn't mean you're frightened of Him, of course, but that you respect Him, acknowledge His holiness, and express humility before Him. Because in every aspect of your life, He is available to you. The unfathomably great Ruler of all creation hears you when you call and is aware of everything that concerns you. This understanding can give you assurance in the uncertainties and strengthen you to face difficulties with courage. It can help you *endure.* So today, consider how awesomely almighty your God truly is.

*Jesus, I am in awe of You. Help me to exalt You*
*with my life as You truly deserve. Amen.*

My hope is in Jesus because He is GOD.

# ENABLED TO DO GOD'S WILL

*It is God who is at work in you, both to will*
*and to work for His good pleasure.*

PHILIPPIANS 2:13

At times, it may seem that God's will is a difficult mystery to grasp—and even more impossible to accomplish. Yet, Scripture promises that He is constantly at work in you. In his book *The Person and Work of the Holy Spirit*, R. A. Torrey explained:

> Some . . . are not distinctly conscious of His indwelling, but He is there nonetheless. What a solemn, and yet what a glorious thought, that in me dwells this august person, the Holy Spirit. If we are children of God, we are not so much to pray that the Spirit may come and dwell in us, for He does that already. We are rather to recognize His presence, His gracious and glorious indwelling, and give to Him complete control of the house He already inhabits, and strive so to live as not to grieve this holy one.

God is always able to communicate His will and enable you to accomplish it because He indwells you. Even when you don't think you hear Him, He's in you—transforming you as you read His Word and leading you as you pray in submission to Him.

*Jesus, thank You for Your Holy Spirit! Help me to be aware*
*and obedient to Your glorious presence. Amen.*

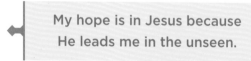

My hope is in Jesus because
He leads me in the unseen.

# CONTROL AND PEACE

*May the Lord of peace Himself continually*
*grant you peace in every circumstance.*
2 THESSALONIANS 3:16

Who is in control of your life? It's a crucial question if you desire to live a life of peace. Think about it. If you allow *situations* to govern how you feel, you can't have lasting tranquility, because at any second, your circumstances can spin out of control.

If *another person* defines your happiness, you may have harmony for a while, but eventually that individual may disappoint or hurt you in some way, which will bring a quick end to your peace.

You may even think *you're* in control—believing you can guarantee yourself a tranquil existence. But the moment a big trial comes along, you'll find that's not the case at all.

But what if you allow God to direct your life? What if you entrust your future to your almighty, unfathomably wise, and unconditionally loving Creator, who is constantly looking out for your best interest? Certainly, with Him in control, there's every reason to hope and to move forward in faith. Why? Because you know He has promised to work *all things* for your good.

So if you lack peace today, search your heart and make sure you've entrusted all things to Him.

*Jesus, I want the peace that transcends*
*understanding. Rule in me, my Savior. Amen.*

My hope is in Jesus because He is my peace.

# The Futility of Sin

*"Repent and live."*

**Ezekiel 18:32**

Have you considered what happens when we sin? We attempt to meet our needs apart from the Lord. Because of this, we become self-centered and drift away from God and His plan. We move further away from Him until, eventually, we may reject the idea that we need His presence at all.

The natural result of this is that we face pain, loneliness, and frustration. Why? Because we don't have the inner resources to bring peace to our troubled hearts, having shut out the only One who can provide them to us—God Himself. He created us to soar like eagles, but instead we become earthbound creatures who have lost the capacity to be who He made us to be. We've clipped our own wings by denying His leadership—which means we won't find the purpose and meaning He created us to enjoy. However, this empty restlessness is actually a good thing because it opens the door for our loving Father to make contact with us again.

If you're feeling the inner warning signals of suffering, purposelessness, uselessness, or frustration, examine your heart. You may be attempting to satisfy your needs apart from God. Thankfully, He wants you back. Don't deny Him. Repent and live.

*Jesus, please reveal my sin so I can repent*
*of it and experience Your peace. Amen.*

My hope is in Jesus because
He leads me to peace.

# WORTHY OF YOUR TRUST

*"Blessed are those who have not seen and yet have believed."*

JOHN 20:29 NKJV

Are you overwhelmed by fears and doubts today? You may think yourself full of faith, but if you're ever frightened by what *could* happen or what the future *may* hold—then your trust in God may not be as strong as you believe it to be.

It's important that you realize that genuine faith means knowing that the Father *will* provide His best for you as you walk with Him. Although what He perceives as most beneficial for you may be different from what you envision, you can be confident that He understands what you really need. The One who created you ultimately knows what will truly satisfy your soul—even better than you do.

So what is it that's making you anxious today? Is there something you fear you'll never receive or achieve? Does it seem as though He's taking a long time answering some important request? Trust God. You may not see what He is doing, but that's the essence of faith— not seeing, but still believing. The Lord *will* provide what you need. And if God does not give you what your heart presently longs for, it's certainly because He has something far better planned for you.

*Jesus, I trust You will provide Your best*
*for me. Thank You for leading me. Amen.*

My hope is in Jesus because
He's worthy of my trust.

# SPEAKING LIFE

*Death and life are in the power of the tongue.*

PROVERBS 18:21

Have you ever considered the power of your words? With them you can either draw others to Christ or push them away. One of the classic examples of this is the Samaritan woman at the well, who undoubtedly felt incredible shame (John 4:7–39). She went to the well during the hottest part of the day, so as to, most likely, avoid the condemnation she usually received from others.

Think about that. She was a woman who yearned for love so desperately that she went from relationship to relationship. Yet, she felt completely alienated from the people who could lead her to God—the One who could truly satisfy her deepest needs of acceptance. What a tragedy!

Thankfully, instead of rejection, Jesus spoke forgiveness and hope into her life. And she received His message so gratefully that she immediately became an evangelist for Him!

Those trapped in sin know their failings—they don't need to feel more shame. And their eternity is at stake. So do as Jesus did: accept them as individuals sacrificially loved by God, while refusing to validate their sin. Have compassion on their needful hearts and lead them to the One who can heal them.

*Jesus, I want to speak Your words of life to others.*
*Help me to be Your ambassador through what I say. Amen.*

My hope is in Jesus because
He sets people free.

# THINK TRUTH

*"You will know the truth, and the truth will make you free."*
JOHN 8:32

What can you do when disheartening thoughts continually plague your mind—when all you can think is: *God doesn't want me. I'm a hopeless failure. He will never answer my prayers*? Understand, when you're bombarded by such false, devastating messages, it's likely you are under attack by the enemy. He knows what most depresses you and will twist how you see your circumstances to undermine your security in Christ.

This is the time to remember that the enemy is "the father of lies" (John 8:44). What he says may appear to be true because it coincides with what your eyes see and ears hear. But don't give in to his onslaught. Those demoralizing messages are absolutely false and do not take into account what God is doing in the unseen. So reject what the enemy tells you and immediately fill your mind with the truth of Scripture.

And what is true about you? The Father loves you with an everlasting love (Jeremiah 31:3). He enables you to accomplish all He calls you to do (2 Corinthians 3:5). And He always answers when you call (Jeremiah 33:3). So wait on God and trust Him to help you.

*Jesus, please root out the enemy's lies and replace them with Your truth so I may walk in Your freedom. Amen.*

> My hope is in Jesus because
> His truth sets me free.

# MAY

We give thanks to God always for all of you, making mention of you in our prayers; constantly bearing in mind your work of faith and labor of love and steadfastness of hope in our Lord Jesus Christ in the presence of our God and Father.

1 THESSALONIANS 1:2–3

# DON'T COMPROMISE

*We want to make it clear to you, Your Majesty, that we*
*will never . . . worship the gold statue you have set up.*
DANIEL 3:18 NLT

In life, there will always be people who intimidate you, whether because of their position, power, or tactics. In order to please them, you may be tempted to do whatever they ask—even when their requests are clearly contrary to God's commands.

This was the situation for Shadrach, Meshach, and Abed-nego. King Nebuchadnezzar issued a decree that everyone must bow in worship before his immense gold statue or be executed by fire (Daniel 3). However, the three men understood that the only One truly worthy of such veneration was the Lord (Exodus 20:3). They could either obey God and be sentenced to death, or pay homage to Nebuchadnezzar and dishonor their Lord.

Thankfully, they made the right choice. And though they were thrown into the fire, God miraculously delivered them out of it.

You'll always lose when you obey others in doing what is clearly contrary to Scripture. Don't compromise to protect yourself. Standing strong for God may cause you trouble, but He always honors the one who places Him first.

*Jesus, help me to honor You whether in submission*
*to authority or in standing firm for You. Amen.*

> My hope is in Jesus because He
> defends those who honor Him.

# AVOIDING SHIPWRECK

*Fight the good fight, keeping faith and a good conscience, which
some have rejected and suffered shipwreck in regard to their faith.*

1 TIMOTHY 1:18–19

Paul understood what it was to be shipwrecked—to experience
such a long and terrible buffeting by a storm that the ship you're
on comes apart beneath you. You're left floating in the turbulent
waters, wondering if you'll survive or be dashed against the rocks.

Of course, Paul's was a literal storm and ship. However, he
understood that many believers have faced similar circumstances
in their walks with God. They encounter tempests, and instead of
trusting the Lord through them, they turn to their own means of
riding out the trials—whether it's through addictive substances or
any number of sins. Deep inside they know they're not honoring
God, and eventually the storms shake apart their security—leaving
them to sink between the swelling tides.

Friend, if you're tempted to compromise God's principles
because of a hurricane of adversity that's developed in your life—
don't. You risk running aground spiritually. Any other ship will fail
you. But this storm has arisen to strengthen your faith in Christ. So
do not abandon your Savior—stay with Him.

*Jesus, I know that You bring me safely through
the storms of life; help me to trust You more. Amen.*

> My hope is in Jesus because
> He has never let me down.

# BLESSED ASSURANCE

*Let us draw near with a sincere heart in full assurance of faith.*
HEBREWS 10:22

Where there is no assurance of God's acceptance, there's no peace. Where there is no peace, there's no joy. Why? Because a person with no assurance is by definition partially motivated by fear—and anxiety and peace cannot coexist. One will always override the other.

In other words, if you're doubtful of God's love and provision today, you won't be able to "be anxious for nothing," as Philippians 4:6 commands. You can't be because you'll always be motivated to wonder if you've done enough. This will be especially true when things don't go your way.

This is why whenever you aren't experiencing the peace Jesus promises you, you need to check if your relationship with Him hinges on *anything* other than His finished work on the cross. If you feel you have *any* part in maintaining your relationship with Him, you won't have much assurance. Hope, maybe; assurance, no.

So today, search your heart for any trace of anxiety and ask the Father to reveal its root. Then ask Him to give you promises from His Word that will reassure you of who you are in Him.

*Jesus, root out my fears and replace them with Your promises so I may live in confident faith. Amen.*

> My hope is in Jesus because
> He keeps me safe in His hand.

# FIGHTING ENVY

*Where jealousy and selfish ambition exist,*
*there is disorder and every evil thing.*

JAMES 3:16

It hurts to see someone else receive something you desire—especially if you think that person is less deserving of it than you are. You may wonder why God would bless that individual and overlook you—and some bitterness toward Him may surface because of it.

But be warned: those jealous thoughts only lead to emotional bondage—it's never worth the pain it inflicts on you. You will never find peace by pondering why God has favored them and not you.

Rather, what can lead your heart back to hope, tranquility, and joy is remembering that God is sovereign and always does what's absolutely best for you (Romans 8:28). He has promised to meet all your needs above all you could possibly ask or imagine (Ephesians 3:20), and is waiting for the optimal moment to bless you with what's most beneficial for you (Isaiah 30:18).

So stop focusing on what you don't have and begin to praise the Lord for all He's already given. And trust that if there's something He hasn't blessed you with yet, His motivation for withholding it from you for now is love.

*Jesus, I don't understand Your timing, but I trust You. Thank*
*You for always providing what's best for me. Amen.*

My hope is in Jesus because He
always provides what's best for me.

# LOVE LIKE JESUS

*If possible, so far as it depends on you, be at peace with all men.*
ROMANS 12:18

Is there someone who just doesn't want to be your friend? Regardless of how nice you are to them—or even how you attempt to adjust your behavior to their preferences—they continue to dislike you and may even badmouth you to others. How should you respond?

First, realize that there were people who rejected Jesus—the most loving, wise, and wonderful Person who ever lived (John 15:18). Don't take it personally. At times, what will bother others about you is something within themselves; it's not you at all. There are any number of things beyond your control that may cause others to feel uncomfortable, vulnerable, or even jealous when you are present—such as their past experiences, personal sins, and failures.

But second, realize that you *never* have the right to be cruel to them—even when they are unkind to you. You still have a duty to represent Jesus and be forgiving regardless of what is done to you or how you're rejected (Luke 23:34).

Why? Because your ultimate responsibility is to honor God, and there are always others judging *Him* by how you respond.

*Jesus, please help me to be kind even when I'm mistreated
so that others may see Your love in action. Amen.*

My hope is in Jesus because
of His unfailing love for me.

# THE BATTLE IS HIS

*I know that the LORD saves His anointed; He will answer him*
*from His holy heaven with the saving strength of His right*
*hand. Some boast in chariots and some in horses, but we will*
*boast in the name of the LORD, our God. They have bowed*
*down and fallen, but we have risen and stood upright.*

PSALM 20:6–8

Is there a battle before you today—one that seems impossible to win? Then fight it on your knees in submission to the One who can triumph in it for you. Don't depend on your own weapons, strategies, or resources; you already know your abilities in this situation are insufficient. Rather, allow Him to be your Commander-in-Chief. In order to achieve the victory He has for you, you must surrender yourself to Him fully.

What does this mean for you? God may call you to let go of some of your goals in order to accomplish the plans He has for you. Likewise, you may need to step out in faith when it's uncomfortable or even frightening to do so. But no matter how challenging His commands may seem, obey Him anyway. Trust His direction. He is a skilled and mighty Warrior who has never lost a battle. He will never let you down.

*Jesus, I trust You as my Commander-in-Chief.*
*Lead me to victory! Amen.*

My hope is in Jesus because
He always triumphs!

# So We Will Know

*"For this reason I have allowed you to remain, in order to show you My power and in order to proclaim My name through all the earth."*

EXODUS 9:16

It's one of the most famous stories in Scripture—how God used ten plagues to free the people of Israel from slavery in Egypt. Why did He choose this as His strategy? In a stunning revelation, the Lord declared to Pharaoh, "By now I could have lifted my hand . . . to wipe you off the face of the earth" (Exodus 9:15 NLT). In other words, He could have freed the Israelites from Egypt immediately. Instead, however, He chose to demonstrate His power. Why?

Repeatedly in Exodus we read it was because He wanted the Israelites—as well as the Egyptians and the rest of the world—to see Him at work. He wanted everyone on earth to know Him as the one and only God.

This should be instructive to you today. The trials in your life have been allowed to tarry because your heavenly Father wants you—and others—to see Him in action. So you will *know Him*—that He is all-powerful, all-wise, and unconditionally loving toward you. So do not despise the difficulties. Rather, see them as the platform for Him to reveal Himself to you.

*Jesus, You are mighty and wise! Thank You for the opportunity to know You better. Amen.*

My hope is in Jesus because
He is the one true God.

# MAKE THE DECISION

*"I am the LORD your God, who upholds your right hand,*
*who says to you, 'Do not fear, I will help you.'"*
ISAIAH 41:13

Today, make a decision that you are going to trust God. Choose not to be fearful of whatever challenges arise or trouble confronts you. This may seem difficult because of the emotions you're experiencing. But you can do it by focusing on the reality that your Savior is with you—He is your Sustainer, your Protector, your Provider, and the Preserver of your life. He is always loving and willing to forgive you of your sin. He ensures that you are eternally secure in Him.

The Lord's desire for you is always good, so you can be certain that whatever He allows to touch your life will lead to some important and eternal benefit. So do it—make the choice to have faith in God, who loves you, provides for you, cares for you, is always available to you, and is in control of your life at all times. And voice your decision to trust Him with prayer, praise, thanksgiving, and worship.

Because as you do, I have no doubt that your Savior will melt away any fears you might have and fill you with His wonderful peace that transcends understanding.

*Jesus, I trust You! Thank You for being my Savior, Sustainer,*
*Protector, Provider, and the love of my life. Amen.*

> My hope is in Jesus because
> He is always with me.

# LEARNED CONTENTMENT

*I have learned to be content in whatever circumstances I am.*
*I know how to get along with humble means, and I also know*
*how to live in prosperity; in any and every circumstance I*
*have learned the secret of being filled and going hungry,*
*both of having abundance and suffering need.*
PHILIPPIANS 4:11–12

The apostle Paul had to *learn* to be content—it was a discipline he had to acquire. And this was accomplished by trusting God in the internal and external struggles of his life. Not only through the beatings, imprisonments, shipwrecks, dangers, and other physical trials he experienced, but also in his own personal struggles against sin, fear, and discouragement.

In our world, we're often told that certain products or experiences will make us happy. But the truth is that true contentment is *learned*. And just like Paul, we learn it through trusting God with all our struggles.

You have the power to *respond* to any situation, not merely *react* to it. You can choose to be content by expressing your confidence in God's sustaining provision and perfect plan no matter what happens. The Holy Spirit in you will always enable you to confront a problem with faith and wisdom if you will trust Him.

*Jesus, I want to learn to be content as Paul did. I will*
*trust You with whatever today brings. Amen.*

My hope is in Jesus because
He truly satisfies my soul.

# RECEIVING THE PROMISE

*Do not throw away your confidence, which has a great reward.*
*For you have need of endurance, so that when you have done*
*the will of God, you may receive what was promised.*

HEBREWS 10:35–36

No matter what promises you are claiming from God, you have three responsibilities when it comes to those promises being fulfilled in your life: you must exhibit faith, endurance, and obedience as you wait for the Lord.

*Faith*—you must hold on to your confident conviction that God will do as He's promised. All of your senses, understanding, even the way your circumstances appear may seem to contradict what He's said—but trust Him anyway. *Endurance*—you must not stray from the course that Jesus has set for you, regardless of the obstacles and trials. Make the choice to stay in the center of God's will no matter how long it takes for Him to act. *Obedience*—you must submit to Him, allowing God to guide you step-by-step to your desired destination. Whether you understand His direction to you or not, you trust He knows the best way forward.

Be victorious in this time of waiting by actively allowing God to do things in His way. Certainly, He will provide for you faithfully, just as He has for all who've gone before you.

*Jesus, help me to have faith, exhibit endurance,*
*and be obedient to You always. Amen.*

My hope is in Jesus because
He keeps His promises.

# IN EVERY PART

*"They will be My people, and I will be their God, for*
*they will return to Me with their whole heart."*

JEREMIAH 24:7

Are there places of emptiness and pain in your life that you just can't seem to get rid of? If there are, then consider: Are there parts of yourself that you've denied God access to? Are there dreams, desires, sins, issues, or areas of unforgiveness you haven't surrendered to Him?

Some people limit God's work by saying that they feel what they feel or want what they want—it's just who they are. But what's crucial to understand is that as long as there are aspects of yourself that you withhold from Christ, the yearning in your heart will persist. You were created to know Him with your *entire* being—not just a part.

So as you read this, is there something God is reminding you of that hasn't been relinquished? If the Holy Spirit has brought it to mind, it is most likely the reason you continue to struggle. Don't deny Him; let it go. Whether it seems minor or constitutes the foundation of all your hopes—give it freely to Jesus. He is faithful and just to help you and give you what is truly best for you.

*Jesus, this is difficult, but I turn myself over to*
*You completely so You can set me free. Amen.*

My hope is in Jesus because
He heals me completely.

# TRANSFORMING RELATIONSHIPS

*Do not merely look out for your own personal
interests, but also for the interests of others.*

PHILIPPIANS 2:4

What effect does your faith have on your relationships? The way you respond to others—especially those who mistreat you—can be a powerful witness to the world.

This means that at times, God may allow you to experience conflicts so He can demonstrate His mercy, love, and forgiveness through you. This is why the apostle Paul wrote, "Walk in a manner worthy of the calling with which you have been called, with all humility and gentleness, with patience, showing tolerance for one another in love, being diligent to preserve the unity of the Spirit in the bond of peace" (Ephesians 4:1–3). He instructs you to behave as a representative of Christ regardless of the situation so that His light can shine through you to those who desperately need His message of hope.

With every conflict, you have an incredible opportunity to exalt the Lord. So allow God to transform the difficult relationships in your life into a blessing by responding with the humility, compassion, and kindness that draws others to Jesus.

*Jesus, I want to be a peacemaker. Please help
me to see others with Your eyes, have compassion
for them, and love them as You do. Amen.*

My hope is in Jesus because
He is a worthy example.

# PLANS FOR YOUR POTENTIAL

*The LORD will work out his plans for my life—for*
*your faithful love, O LORD, endures forever.*
PSALM 138:8 NLT

Do you realize that your heavenly Father sees more in you than you can ever perceive in yourself? In fact, from the time you were in your mother's womb, He had full knowledge of your potential (Psalm 139:13–16) and engineered the circumstances of your life so you could know Him and experience the purposes for which you were created (Acts 17:26–27).

Your life may be less than what you expected at the moment, encumbered by seemingly insurmountable obstacles, or even falling apart. But know for certain, you are not alone, this is not an end, and there is a great future hope for you.

Friend, the Lord is with you through every trial of life and has fantastic plans for you. He will never leave you or forsake you, and He gives you the wonderful assurance that you are indeed accepted, loved, respected, and worthwhile in His sight. So overcome whatever happens by having faith in God and confidence that He will carry out His purposes for you. Certainly, He will lead you on paths you've never imagined.

*Jesus, I trust that You have wonderful plans for me even when*
*I cannot see them. Lead me in the way I should go. Amen.*

My hope is in Jesus because
He created and empowers me.

# Direct Communication

*This is my comfort in my affliction, that Your word has revived me.*
PSALM 119:50

If you need special direction from God today, understand that the primary way He will communicate with you is through His Word. Through it, His Holy Spirit can speak straight to your heart regarding whatever concerns you.

How does He do so? Often, you'll find that God will lead you to a particular passage just when you need it most. He may remind you of what you already know so you will be able to practice His truth in the hours or days ahead. Sometimes, certain words, phrases, or verses will seem to leap off the page, you will see principles that you haven't noticed before, and He will convict you of what you need to apply to your life. In such instances, it is best to ask, "Father, how would You have me obey You in this?"

The wonder of God's Word is that it holds countless layers of insight and meaning, and is always applicable to your situation. The more you grow in your relationship with the Father through His Word, the more insights you have into His character and His will for your life—including the issues that presently concern you.

*Jesus, lead me through my time in Your Word so I*
*may know You better and obey You. Amen.*

> My hope is in Jesus because He
> leads me in the way I should go.

# THE RIGHT WORDS

*"Do not worry about how or what you are to speak in your defense, or what you are to say; for the Holy Spirit will teach you in that very hour what you ought to say."*

LUKE 12:11–12

Do you know how to respond to people who ask you questions about your faith? Do you know how to lead another person to Jesus or how to defend your beliefs?

The first thing you must realize is that it's not up to you to convict people of their sins—the Holy Spirit will do that.

Second, realize that the Holy Spirit of the living God is in you to help you know what to say in a manner that will resonate with the listener. In such moments, it is wise to pray, "Lord, help me to speak to this person as You would. Give me Your words to say." Then, speak freely as He leads you.

Friend, you can trust that if you are walking with God and are genuinely open to what He has to say through you, He is faithful to help you. He will prompt you to speak what needs to be said, and He will cause the other person to hear what he or she needs to hear.

*Jesus, I know that as I lift You up, You will draw others to Yourself. Speak through me. Amen.*

My hope is in Jesus because
He empowers me to exalt Him.

# FACTS AND TRUTH

*Lead me in Your truth and teach me, for*
*You are the God of my salvation.*
PSALM 25:5

What can you do when you need to make a decision but don't know what to do? The choices you have involve their own sets of facts, but which direction is truly right and best?

First, understand there's a big difference between *facts* and *truth*. The facts of your situation are details such as the who, what, when, where, and how, and they can differ depending on perspective. That's what usually makes decisions difficult.

The truth, however—which fully encompasses the facts—ultimately finds its source and full expression in God. He knows the truth of why and how you were created. And in order to make the best decision, you must understand how your choices fit into His truth—into the context of His eternal purposes for your life.

Thankfully, as you seek God, He promises to guide you into truth (John 16:13). So when you face puzzling circumstances or difficult problems, always ask Him to lead you and to show you what He's accomplishing through the situation. Because certainly, the right decision will become clear as you do.

*Jesus, thank You for leading me into truth and*
*revealing the way I should go. Amen.*

My hope is in Jesus because
He knows the right path for me.

# GIVE UP AND GO FORWARD

*"Whoever seeks to keep his life will lose it, and
whoever loses his life will preserve it."*

LUKE 17:33

Knowing God and having a growing relationship with Him will often mean that there are mind-sets and habits in you that need to change. As you progress in your interactions with Him, He may often reveal certain behaviors and attitudes that no longer fit who you are and which actually hinder you from truly knowing Him. When God brings these to mind, understand that you really have only one choice—and that's to give them up.

Perhaps you're facing this today. The Lord has revealed what's preventing your spiritual growth, but you fear what you'll have to give up because of the security it offers you or the pain you may experience. This is where many people get stuck and refuse to change. Sadly, they don't experience the fullness of the Christian life—the joy and power God created them to enjoy.

It's important to realize that—though the sacrifices may be difficult—the Father truly wants what's best for you. Don't stagnate. Make the choice to move forward with Jesus and let Him show you all your life can be.

*Jesus, I want my relationship with You to be as strong as possible.
Please help me to be brave, let go, and move forward. Amen.*

My hope is in Jesus because
in Him is the fullness of life.

# ADEQUACY THROUGH DEPENDENCE

*Our adequacy is from God.*
2 CORINTHIANS 3:5

Did you have circumstances early in life that made you feel like less than enough? Do you wonder if you have what it takes to be successful in the challenges before you? The Father may have brought you to a place where you feel inadequate so that you will place your trust completely upon Him. Because only then will you trust Him enough to step out in faith in the power of the Holy Spirit.

Why? Because He wants us to live every single day of our lives in complete dependence upon Him. We may imagine ourselves to be ineffective and insignificant, but the Father wants us to rest in His ability and presence so we'll see that "the surpassing greatness of the power" and the victory we experience is because "of God and not from ourselves" (2 Corinthians 4:7).

It is the Lord at work in and through you today. And He has a wonderful plan for you that is as unique as your fingerprints and designed to give you profound fulfillment and joy. So trust Him—especially when what's before you seems too big to handle.

*Jesus, thank You for being my adequacy for every trial and challenge. Help me to exalt You in everything I do. Amen.*

> My hope is in Jesus because He empowers me for every challenge.

# DEPEND ON YOUR HELPER

*"It is the Spirit who gives life."*
JOHN 6:63

You will never outgrow the need to depend upon the Holy Spirit. In fact, the more mature you grow in your faith, the more you will need to rely on His indwelling presence.

I say this to you because He is who you need for all you face. If you have been depending on your own resources, wisdom, or strength, it's no wonder you become tired, overwhelmed, and frustrated, possibly even feeling somewhat hopeless. What is before you is often greater than you can handle so you will learn to rely on Him.

It is the Holy Spirit who guides you on the right path, convicts you of sin, reminds you of God's truth, and teaches you to apply Scripture to your life. But even more importantly, it is the Holy Spirit who works to conform you to the image of Christ and who empowers you to serve Him and others.

This is why the lesson all believers must learn is how to experience and live daily in the power of the Holy Spirit. No matter where you are in your journey with Jesus, this is the key to being a truly successful, fulfilled, productive, and joyful Christian.

*Jesus, thank You for Your Holy Spirit, who guides and empowers me. Help me to depend on You more every day. Amen.*

> My hope is in Jesus because
> He leads me by His Spirit.

# WORK FOR HIM

*Do your work heartily, as for the Lord rather than for men,*
*knowing that from the Lord you will receive the reward.*

COLOSSIANS 3:23–24

At times, you may have thankless and unpleasant tasks to accomplish. You may feel as if no one really understands the stress you feel or cares about how hard you have to work.

Though this can hurt, understand that what's really important is not that others see your efforts, but that God does—and you should do every job you're given as if it's exclusively for Him. Whatever your hands find to do, work with enthusiasm, diligence, and perseverance to the best of your ability. The Lord takes note of everything you do and rewards you according to His riches.

But even more important, God is seeing if you're trustworthy with small tasks in order to see if He can entrust you with greater assignments (Matthew 25:14–30). Scripture promises that those who use their talents to please the Lord will see their gifts multiplied and their efforts rewarded.

So today, it doesn't matter what your vocation may be or what task you're given. If you will do your work unto God and trust Him to reward your faithfulness, you'll certainly be blessed.

*Jesus, help me to do everything with excellence,*
*wisdom, and passion—as unto You. Amen.*

My hope is in Jesus because
He is worthy of my best efforts.

# YOU CAN!

*Faithful is He who calls you, and He also will bring it to pass.*

1 THESSALONIANS 5:24

Do you realize that once you trust Jesus as your Savior and receive His Holy Spirit, you can never again say, "I can't do that," when God calls you to do something? Why? Because the Holy Spirit in you says, "You *can!*" and enables you to accomplish His plans. Therefore, there's only one right response when the Lord gives you an assignment, and that's to say, "Yes!"

Of course, you may be thinking, *But I'm not adequate to serve Him.* Friend, none of us is sufficient in our own strength and wisdom to carry out God's will. But in Christ, all of us are empowered by the Holy Spirit. So any time you are feeling inadequate, here are four things you should do:

*First, acknowledge your need for Him.* Admit to the Lord that you need His help, wisdom, strength, power, resources, protection, and provision. *Second, rely upon Him.* Trust God to faithfully provide what you need. *Third, take a step of faith and act upon what He has called you to do. Fourth, choose not to be afraid.* God is fully committed to the fulfillment of His plans. He will always help you as you walk in obedience to Him.

*Jesus, I will rely on You—accomplish Your plans through me. Amen.*

> My hope is in Jesus because He accomplishes great things through me.

# STRATEGY FOR DISCOURAGEMENT

*"I have given you authority to tread . . . over all the power of the enemy, and nothing will injure you."*

LUKE 10:19

Do you ever feel discouraged? One way the enemy works to defeat you is through feelings of disheartenment. He knows if he can cause you to doubt God's goodness, love, timing, or provision, you may become fearful and give up.

So what do you do when the going gets rough and frustrations, feelings of inferiority, and external pressures assail you? How do you take a stand and resist the enemy?

*First, ask the Lord to strengthen and encourage you for the battle.* He is your greatest source of help, so go to His throne of grace frequently in prayer. Likewise, all of God's greatest saints have had to learn how to withstand heartaches, disappointments, and all kinds of evil. So *second, read about their victories in Scripture for insight and hope* (Romans 15:4). *Third, fill your arsenal.* You know the messages the enemy uses to discourage you, so find promises from God's Word that you can use to fight him (Matthew 4:1–11; Ephesians 6:17).

You can trust the Lord on all battle fronts because He is faithful. Whatever concerns you concerns Him. So trust Him and witness His power at work in your life.

*Jesus, thank You for fighting for me and leading me to spiritual victory!*

My hope is in Jesus because
He is my Defender and hope.

# FROM END TO BEGINNING

*He gives strength to the weary, and to him*
*who lacks might He increases power.*

ISAIAH 40:29

Do you ever feel weak and limited? That's actually a good thing. You see, the unlimited God of creation has chosen to indwell in you. And when you reach the end of who you are, you begin to see who He is and what He can accomplish through you.

*God is omnipotent.* He has all power. When you run out of your natural strength, you start to see all He's capable of. *God is omniscient.* He is all-wise. When your imagination, mental ability, and understanding run dry, His knowledge, wisdom, and creativity flow forth. *God is omnipresent.* Everything is in His presence at every moment. While you may run out of time and reach, He is always where you cannot be. *God is unconditionally loving.* While you may grow weary of others, He never fails to extend His mercy and loving-kindness to all who open their hearts to receive Him.

The Lord your God can energize your body, enlighten your mind, be where you're not, and make His love flow through you. So if you're feeling limited today, rejoice! And invite Him to be everything you're not.

*Jesus, I know that when I am weak,*
*You are strong. Glorify Yourself in me. Amen.*

My hope is in Jesus because He provides
me with the strength and wisdom I need.

# NO MORE DETOURS

*O LORD my God, I cried to You for help, and You healed me.*

PSALM 30:2

We all have a desire to avoid pain. Because of that, when we're hurt emotionally, we often find ways of evading our distressing memories. We take mental detours—we don't allow ourselves to think about certain topics, and we change the subject when they're brought up. We even take physical detours—avoiding people and situations that stir our damaged emotions. In other words, we find paths of escape rather than dealing with our wounds.

Sadly, this desire to avoid past hurt motivates many people to drink, become addicted to drugs, or engage in destructive behaviors. They're unable to cope with their pain, so they drown it. But this was never God's plan. No, His promise is to heal (Isaiah 53:5).

If you're living with memories that are excruciating even to think about, please accept by faith that it's worth the pain to be set free. God wants to perform spiritual surgery and root out all the bitterness and hurt you feel. Yes, it will be uncomfortable and even painful at times, but He *can* and *will* heal you. And He will turn your worst memories into an avenue of victory for you (Romans 8:31–37).

*Jesus, this is difficult, but please heal my deepest wounds and set me free of the pain. Amen.*

> My hope is in Jesus because
> He is my Great Physician.

# A PLATFORM FOR HIS POWER

*I come to you in the name of . . . the God of the*
*armies of Israel, whom you have taunted. This day*
*the LORD will deliver you up into my hands.*

1 SAMUEL 17:45–46

The famous battle between David and Goliath wouldn't have been very noteworthy if the two had been the same size or had possessed similar skills. However, because David was merely a boy with no armor or experience in battle and Goliath was a nine-foot, bronze-clad, seasoned warrior, it was a match to be remembered.

Of course, no one present would have bet on David for the victory. It was obvious that God's intervention was David's only hope. So David proudly proclaimed his trust in the Lord, as we see in today's verse. And God gave him the victory.

But this illustrates the principle of 2 Corinthians 12:9, that God's "power is perfected in weakness." And so, at times, you may experience challenges that are too big for you to handle. But this is so that the Father can show His supernatural power through you. The important thing is that you honor God as David did. Have no fear. Run forward in faith and trust the Lord to empower you.

*Jesus, nothing is too difficult for You! Triumph in the*
*challenges before me so everyone will see You are God. Amen.*

> My hope is in Jesus because
> He is my all-powerful help.

# HE IS AT WORK

*Eye has not seen and ear has not heard, and which have not entered the heart of man, all that God has prepared for those who love Him.*

1 CORINTHIANS 2:9

Do you realize that even at this moment, God is working out what concerns you? It may seem from your perspective as though He is silent or even unconcerned with your life. But He is actively engineering circumstances on your behalf.

Of course, this is something we all know in theory, but at times it is so much harder to put into practice because of how impossible our situation may seem. We absolutely cannot work out how God will deliver us, and we grow disheartened waiting for Him.

And the truth is, you've probably gone to Him with your troubles so many times before that you wonder if He's really listening to you. He hasn't answered yet—so why should you continue to go to Him?

Yet, understand that this uncertainty is meant to build your faith—He works in *all* of His people this way. He hasn't abandoned you, and you aren't alone. Just because you don't perceive His activity at the moment doesn't mean anything. Your God is working it out. Don't doubt Him; cling to Him.

*Jesus, I don't see Your activity, but I trust You are working all things for my good and Your glory. Amen.*

> My hope is in Jesus because
> He has never let me down.

# DON'T REACT; RESPOND

*Be careful how you walk, not as unwise men but as wise,
making the most of your time. . . . Do not be foolish,
but understand what the will of the Lord is.*

EPHESIANS 5:15–17

Today consider: God does not just ask us to *react* to what happens to us; we're called to *respond* to it—to know His will and act in accordance. And there's a big difference.

Most people *react* to their circumstances—they fire back out of emotion. They strike out unthinkingly at others due to the fear or anger they feel welling up without considering the consequences. As a result, their reactions cause deeper problems.

This is why God calls us to *respond* to life by being careful how we walk. We are called to be peacemakers—people who infuse situations with the tranquility of the Lord's love and presence. And this means that whenever anything happens—whether conflict or tragedy, we immediately go to God for wisdom. We allow Him to shape our view of circumstances rather than our emotions.

So today, as situations arise, don't just react; rather, take a moment to pray. Ask God what to do. What is He teaching you and who does He want you to minister to? Actively look for opportunities to glorify Him.

*Jesus, I want to respond wisely. Help me to
walk in Your will in every situation. Amen.*

My hope is in Jesus because
He teaches me to be godly.

# STOP HIDING

*I was afraid because I was naked; so I hid myself.*
**GENESIS 3:10**

When we picture Adam and Eve crouched behind bushes in an attempt to hide from all-knowing God, we may chuckle at the futility of their act. Of course, they knew that eventually they would have to face Him and that He already knew what they'd done. But where we can empathize is in that feeling of fear that God can really see us—that He knows all the shame we bear and all the ways we've failed.

Maybe you aren't hiding behind bushes, but perhaps you understand what it is to conceal your most private thoughts, faults, and failures out of embarrassment. Afraid that their deepest hurts will be exposed—naked for all to see—most people hide behind defensive responses. However, this does absolutely no good for anyone. Those coping mechanisms only end up isolating you further from others and from the One you need most—from God Himself.

Friend, understand that today, the Father is calling you to come out of concealment so you can be free of those shameful places. Will you blame your past and keep covering yourself with ineffective methods? Or will you open yourself to His healing presence? Don't act ineffectively, like Adam and Eve. Stop hiding and be free.

*Jesus, You know what I keep hidden.*
*Heal me, my Savior. Take away my shame. Amen.*

My hope is in Jesus
because He heals me.

# REJOICE ALWAYS!

*Rejoice in the Lord always; again I will say, rejoice!*
PHILIPPIANS 4:4

If anyone understood the amazing power of praise, it was the apostle Paul. As he wrote his letter to the Philippian church, no doubt he remembered being in the prison of that same city with his coworker Silas (Acts 16:16–26). Unjustly incarcerated, beaten, and in chains, the two men of God sang hymns to the Lord—demonstrating that their joy came from *Him* and not their circumstances. It was then that the doors of the prison flew open and they were freed.

That is why Paul knew that his admonition to rejoice would be meaningful to the Philippians. They had seen it all firsthand, and some had even been saved as a result (Acts 16:27–34).

It should be meaningful for you as well. Whatever your difficult situation, it does not control you. Your joy comes from God, and giving thanks to Him is one of the most powerful things you can do as a believer. So rejoice! Acknowledge you're dependent upon His provision and strength because that's exactly the attitude necessary for Him to exhibit His power through you. Soon He will fling open the doors of your situation and set you free as well.

*Jesus, my joy comes from You—so I will continue to praise You and give You thanks regardless of what happens. Amen.*

My hope is in Jesus because
He is my strength and my song.

# FULFILLED IN HIM

*If the Spirit of Him who raised Jesus from the dead dwells in you,*
*He . . . will also give life to your mortal bodies through His Spirit.*

ROMANS 8:11

That place of unrest in you is one that only Jesus can fill. Until you invite Him in, you will continue your futile search for fulfillment in that area. Your human instinct is to turn to what you can see and touch in the physical realm, but it will never really satisfy you. It can't. Inherently, your need is spiritual—and can only be appeased in places unreached by earthly methods.

This is why when the Holy Spirit indwells you, He begins the process of transforming how your desires, needs, and innermost goals are met. He doesn't necessarily *eliminate* them, but He *changes* your understanding of them.

Of course, old habits die hard. Most of us have developed patterns of thinking and responding that take time and intentional effort to change. And really, only the Holy Spirit can do so effectively. So what can you do to help the process? Submit to Him. Acknowledge that God knows more than you do and can satisfy your soul. And obey what He calls you to do. In this way, you'll embrace the abundant life and supernatural peace He has for you.

*Jesus, only You can meet my deepest needs.*
*Help me submit in every way. Amen.*

> My hope is in Jesus because
> He is everything to me.

# OBEY THE SPIRIT

*Do not quench the Spirit.*

1 THESSALONIANS 5:19

God has been speaking to you. The Holy Spirit—who came to indwell when you accepted Jesus as Savior—is continually leading you to grow in your faith. He communicates God's will and plan to you. But often, you'll find that what He's saying requires faith and is therefore difficult to accept. This is why today's verse admonishes you not to quench how He's working in your life.

To *quench* means "to extinguish," such as when there's a fire. You stifle the work of the Holy Spirit when you reject His plan because it doesn't make sense to you or doesn't fit your priorities. For example, one of the ways you quench God's Spirit is when you ignore His call to spend time with Him. You feel Him drawing you, but instead you say, "I'll do it tomorrow—there's too much to do today."

But understand, that causes the feelings of unrest you cannot get rid of—you're actually experiencing the battle between your will and the Holy Spirit. And if you want your peace to return, the only choice is to conform your will to His. You must obey His leading. So do it! Agree with God in faith and embrace the plan He created you to enjoy.

*Jesus, bring to mind all the ways I've quenched the Spirit that I may obey You now. Amen.*

My hope is in Jesus because He leads me by His Spirit with perfect wisdom.

# JUNE

"Not by might nor by power, but by My Spirit," says the Lord of hosts.

ZECHARIAH 4:6

# UNCONDITIONAL SURRENDER

*I urge you . . . present your bodies a living and holy sacrifice,*
*acceptable to God, which is your spiritual service of worship.*

ROMANS 12:1

In yesterday's devotion, we talked about the necessity of submitting to the Holy Spirit. When you lack peace, it's often because you refuse to accept how God is calling you to respond to Him in faith.

The Lord's goal is ultimately to teach you how to be unconditionally surrendered to Him in every area of your life because this is when He does the truly miraculous work through you. Of course, when you read about the biblical saints, you'll find that they had as much trouble doing this as we do. It is indeed difficult. But you will also find that it is *not only possible*, but *absolutely blessed* when you do so. You are conformed to the image of Jesus, who, yes, became a sacrifice for us, but who is also honored above every other name (Romans 8:29; Philippians 2:5–11).

Therefore, don't fear submitting to God's will because of what He might require of you. Instead, surrender your life to the One who is perfect in His stewardship of all things. He has untold blessings waiting for you as you obey Him. Don't let fear stand in the way of His extraordinary plan for your life.

*Jesus, I surrender completely to You.*
*Make my life a vessel of Your glory. Amen.*

My hope is in Jesus because
He is worthy of my all.

# SPLINTER REMOVAL

*"Why do you look at the speck that is in your brother's
eye, but do not notice the log that is in your own eye?"*
MATTHEW 7:3

Conviction can be a spiritual battleground. In it, God does battle
to set you free by speaking to your heart about the strongholds of
your life. Immediately, however, the enemy will retaliate, whispering, *That rebuke is not for you—it's for someone else.* This is so you
never admit the bondage God wants you to be free of.

Then the enemy takes the next step and gives you another target for the censure. You can probably recall reading a devotion,
hearing a message, or finding a poignant passage of Scripture and
thinking to yourself, *He needs to read this—then he would certainly change.* In other words, the enemy tempts you to wrongfully
assume the role of the Holy Spirit in another person's life. So then,
not only has he stopped you from being free, but he also tempts you
to the deeper, more treacherous sin of taking God's place.

Don't fall for it! Whenever you read something convicting,
apply it to *your own* heart. Let God take the plank out of your eye;
then, in love, you can minister to and encourage others.

*Jesus, please forgive me for playing the Holy Spirit in others'
lives. Convict me, Lord, so I can walk in Your will. Amen.*

> My hope is in Jesus because
> He frees me from sin.

# How God Sees You

*O Lord, You have searched me and known me.*

PSALM 139:1

Whenever you begin to feel low, useless, and hopeless, remember that you're only seeing your life from your limited point of view. Your heavenly Father sees much more than you ever could—and He watches you with eyes of love and forgiveness.

Yes, He knows where you are in life—including the faults and failures that break your heart. But more importantly, He never loses sight of the person He made you to be. God sees all the potential in you and the assignments He created you to accomplish. And because you are in Christ (1 Corinthians 1:30) and He is in you (Colossians 1:27), all things are possible if you'll believe (Mark 9:23).

So do not despair and don't give up. Your heavenly Father knows how to get you from where you are to where you need to be—from feeling low and hopeless to being a vessel through which His glory shines. So continue to align yourself with His purposes for you. Certainly, He will bless you more than you could ever imagine and lead you on the path to life at its best.

*Jesus, thank You for seeing more in me than I see in myself. I will trust Your plans for my life. Amen.*

My hope is in Jesus because He sees my full potential and helps me reach it.

# PLANNING WITH GOD

*You ought to say, "If the Lord wills . . ."*
JAMES 4:15

Most people chart their futures with little thought of God. But as believers, it is important that we include the Lord in all our planning. This is not merely asking, "Will You bless my goals?" Or, "Is it all right if I do this?" But rather, Scripture tells us God has specific objectives to accomplish through our lives (Jeremiah 29:11–13).

So consider: have you ever stopped to ask God about His will, plan, and purpose for you? If you haven't or even if it's just been awhile, spend time seeking Him today. Ask:

- What did You have in mind when You created me?
- What do You want to do in and through my life?
- How are You working through the circumstances I am currently experiencing to prepare me for Your assignments?
- Is there anyone You want me to minister to or anywhere You desire me to go in Your name?

Only God can answer these questions, so wait for Him to speak to you and then obey Him. Because when He sets you on the path of His will, you will be glad you listened to Him.

*Jesus, I want to serve You wholeheartedly.*
*Show me the path of Your will. Amen.*

> My hope is in Jesus because
> He knows why I exist.

# KNOW THE HOPE

*I pray that the eyes of your heart may be enlightened, so
that you will know what is the hope of His calling.*
EPHESIANS 1:18

It is eye-opening and inspiring to catch a glimpse of how God
is working in your life—weaving together who He made you to
be with the things He's prepared you to do and experience. He
intertwines the threads of who you are—your dreams, desires, personality, and talents—with unique challenges, relationships, and
resources to prepare you in every way for the many opportunities
that are ahead, as well as your heavenly inheritance.

When you begin to see the wonderful future that God is unfold-
ing before you, life takes on greater importance and purpose. You
wake up with anticipation and a desire to experience all that He has
planned for you.

However, be warned: you can miss those opportunities to
see God at work if you get bogged down by your trials or become
apathetic to the Christian life. So how do you avoid doing so and
ensure your heart remains open to His presence? By passionately
pursuing your relationship with God every day. Make knowing *Him*
better your priority and everything else will follow (Matthew 6:33).

*Jesus, help me to know You better and love You more so I can
know the great hope of all You've prepared for me. Amen.*

> My hope is in Jesus because He
> has prepared great things for me.

# ENTIRELY

*You will seek Me and find Me when you*
*search for Me with all your heart.*
JEREMIAH 29:13

Do you ever find yourself praying: "God, please draw me to You and help me to know what to do"? If you do, realize that prayer actually originated with Him. The Lord leads you to ask this because He knows that when you reach that place of deep intimacy with Him, you'll experience joy, peace, and an overflowing sense of being loved that nothing in all creation can equal.

"But wait," you might say. "I'm praying that because I *need* to hear Him. I need His guidance, and He is silent." If so, then understand there may be something He is targeting in you—some area or issue that you've refused to relinquish to Him. Perhaps it has come to your mind even at this moment, but you push the thoughts away with the justification, *That can't possibly be what God wants to address.*

But realize that the Lord wants your *whole* heart—yes, even *that thing* He's just brought to mind. Don't shut Him out. Ask Him to reveal how He wants you to proceed in that area. Open your heart to Him fully, and you'll find Him drawing near in ways you never imagined possible.

*Jesus, I want to honor You with my whole heart. Reveal*
*any way in me that isn't submitted to You. Amen.*

> My hope is in Jesus because
> He wants all of me.

# STOP HURTING YOURSELF

*"Saul, why are you persecuting Me? It is hard*
*for you to kick against the goads."*
ACTS 26:14

Unless you raise cattle, what Jesus said to Saul may not make much sense. A goad is a stick with a pointed piece of metal at the end, which farmers would use to prod oxen as they plowed fields. When a rebellious ox would fight back, he would end up kicking the goad—which would actually drive its sharp tip into his flesh. The more he fought, the more he would wound himself.

As a zealous Jew, Saul thought he was living for God because he was persecuting the Christian church. But he was really fighting against the Lord—and hurting his own soul in the process.

This is what we all do. Whenever God guides us in a certain direction and we fight Him, we may think we are asserting our autonomy; but really, we're just wounding ourselves.

If God has asked you to give something up or to head down a particular path—do it! He is good, kind, and wise, and He only wants what's best for you. Don't be afraid. Rather, obey God and leave the consequences to Him. You'll just end up hurting yourself if you don't.

*Jesus, I don't want to hurt myself anymore.*
*Lead me in the way I should go. Amen.*

> My hope is in Jesus because
> He heals my self-inflicted wounds.

# GO TO HIM TO KNOW

*In the day you eat from it your eyes will be opened,
and you will be like God, knowing good and evil.*

## GENESIS 3:5

Did you notice what argument the enemy used to entice Eve? "You will be *like God, knowing* good and evil" (emphasis added). In other words, the temptation was that she'd know all the Lord does and not have to seek Him to learn it.

Aren't we tripped up by the same thing—wanting the knowledge of God without God Himself? How often, when we experience trials that fill us with uncertainty, do we demand that He give us a plan of how to succeed on our own? And when He doesn't, our trust in Him fails.

Yet, Proverbs 3:5–6 tells us what true faith in Him looks like: "Trust in the LORD with all your heart and *do not lean on your own understanding*. In all your ways *acknowledge Him*, and He will make your paths straight" (emphasis added). Like Abraham, who set out "not knowing where he was going" (Hebrews 11:8), we're to trust God to lead us step-by-step.

If you're struggling with knowing what direction to take today, understand this has been humanity's struggle from the very beginning. Stop relying on your own wisdom and go to God for the right path.

*Jesus, I will trust You to lead me step-by-step. Amen.*

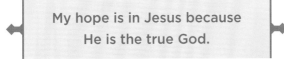

My hope is in Jesus because
He is the true God.

# YOUR PART

*"The LORD will fight for you while you keep silent."*
*Then the LORD said to Moses, "Why are you crying*
*out to Me? Tell the sons of Israel to go forward."*
EXODUS 14:14–15

There are battles that the Father has promised to fight for you. We see an example of this when the Israelites escaped slavery in Egypt and arrived at the Red Sea. Pharaoh reversed his decision to let them go and sent his army after them. Of course, as Moses said, the Israelites could trust the Lord to deliver them. And He did.

You can trust God to take care of what concerns you as well. However, what often happens with trials is that we're so concerned with God's part of our deliverance that we are paralyzed by fear and either unable or unwilling to carry out what He's instructed us to do. This almost happened to the Israelites. They were so frightened that they almost failed to do their part—to walk through the Red Sea—though this was an important part of His plan.

Don't make the same mistake. The Lord has shown you what He wants you to do. So today, go forward in obedience and trust that when you do, you're fulfilling your part of the plan. Don't worry about the rest—God has that completely covered.

*Jesus, help me to focus on my responsibility in Your plan. Amen.*

My hope is in Jesus
because He delivers me.

# CULTIVATE RESPECT

*The centurion said, "Lord, I am not worthy for You to come under
my roof, but just say the word, and my servant will be healed." . . .
When Jesus heard this, He marveled and said . . . , "Truly I say
to you, I have not found such great faith with anyone in Israel."*

MATTHEW 8:8, 10

The centurion didn't need to see Jesus perform the miracle of healing his servant. He had such great respect for Christ, that he trusted it would be done just because Jesus said so.

How instructive this is for us today. The more respect we have for God, the more we'll trust Him to do as He says—even when we don't see Him at work. The more we honor Him as the Lord of creation, the more we'll have confidence that everything He sends into our lives will work out for our good.

If you're worried about some trial today, then this is the perfect opportunity for you to spend time thinking about who God really is—in all His power, majesty, wisdom, glory, and honor. He is the King of kings. If He commands it, so shall it be! The more you realize this, the more you'll have faith like the centurion's—trust that honors God and brings Him joy.

*Jesus, I trust what You say! You are worthy
of all my love, devotion, and respect. Amen!*

> My hope is in Jesus because
> He is worthy of my trust.

# DON'T FEEL ALONE

*"I will not leave you as orphans; I will come to you."*
JOHN 14:18

Today realize that you are not alone. Jesus is one Friend you will always have, who is "the same yesterday and today and forever" (Hebrews 13:8)—always with you and always faithful. So when loneliness engulfs you, the first thing you must do is to turn your focus away from what you don't have to what you *do* have—God Himself with you.

You cannot ever be alone once you've trusted in Jesus as your Savior. His Holy Spirit comes to dwell within you, and He becomes inextricably connected to you. You share with Him the most profound relationship possible—an eternal, spiritual intimacy through which you have access to Him always.

However, understand that the depth to which you enjoy that close fellowship is, to a great extent, up to you and how much you desire to be near the Lord. Are you welcoming Him into your life by spending time with Him? Are you allowing Him to fill you with His presence and reveal Himself to you?

He is always there, desiring to be ever more intimate with you. So really, there's never a good reason to be lonely. Look to the One who remains close to you.

*Jesus, fill up my lonely moments with Your wonderful presence. Help me to know and love You more. Amen.*

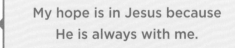

My hope is in Jesus because
He is always with me.

# BE A FRIEND

*A man who has friends must himself be friendly.*
PROVERBS 18:24 NKJV

How many loving, committed, loyal, genuine friendships do you have? Not casual relationships, mind you—but tried-and-true, long-term, devoted friendships that you can really count on. If you are like most people, you may not have many.

But in order to be healthy as believers, we need enduring relationships with others with whom we can share our lives. We need loving relationships that will spur us to grow into the likeness of Christ and the fullness of our potential. We need people who will be honest with us, who will help us grow beyond our limitations, and who will speak the truth to us in love and wisdom.

So if you're lacking friendships today, consider: Are you taking the time to build such friendships? Are you having difficulty finding people who are trustworthy? Have you learned how to build a godly friendship and to resolve the differences of opinion that may occur along the way?

In all these things, God can help you. So seek Him today. Ask Him not only to bring you good friends, but also to make you into a friend that others will want to be around.

*Jesus, help me to identify the friendships that will build my faith and help me to be a loving and committed friend to others. Amen.*

My hope is in Jesus because
He is the ultimate Friend.

# HE SHALL SUPPLY

*God shall supply all your need according to
His riches in glory by Christ Jesus.*
PHILIPPIANS 4:19 NKJV

You have the wonderful privilege of approaching God with every need you have. He is your unfathomably wise and all-powerful heavenly Father—who loves you so much He gave His Son for your salvation. Everything you possess is from Him (James 1:17). So you can certainly trust Him to provide what you need to live (Romans 8:32).

Unfortunately, we often believe just the opposite—we trust in what we have as our security and blame the Lord for what we lack. But realize, that's not the reality. Rather, all things belong to God, and in His generosity, as your loving Father, He has graciously made His resources available to you. And He invites you to approach His throne of grace for whatever else you may need (Hebrews 4:16).

This is why you can be sure that God will supply your needs—because it is His character to be faithful, and His nature doesn't change.

So when you're in need, remind yourself of Jesus' words in Luke 12:30, "Your Father knows that you need these things." Trust God to be the Source of your supply and praise Him for what He gives you.

*Jesus, You know my need. Thank You for
providing for me in Your loving-kindness. Amen.*

My hope is in Jesus because He is
the Source of every good thing.

# GUIDANCE FOR THE FUTURE

*Live in the fear of the LORD always. Surely there is
a future, and your hope will not be cut off.*

PROVERBS 23:17–18

Are you trusting God for your future? Only He knows with certainty what tomorrow holds, and only He can lead you to a path that's guaranteed to be beneficial to you. He promises, "I will instruct you and teach you in the way you should go; I will guide you with My eye" (Psalm 32:8 NKJV). For God to direct you with His eye, you need to be focused on Him.

Think about it. You know what it means to take a nonverbal cue from someone—how an individual can motion you to turn in one way or another with just a look. To receive that direction, however, you must be watching him or her. The same holds true for the guidance you receive from the Lord. He can't lead you if you're focused on someone or something other than Him.

Friend, God is not only infinite in His wisdom; He's also unfailing in His love for you. Undoubtedly, He knows the best path for you to follow. So trust Him to lead you successfully into the wonderful plan He's prepared for you. Because with Him, you know for certain your future is secure.

*Jesus, I trust Your plans for my life.
Thank You for leading me. Amen.*

My hope is in Jesus because He
knows the end from the beginning.

# THE BLESSING OF RELATIONSHIP

*The LORD God said, "It is not good for the man to be*
*alone; I will make him a helper suitable for him."*
GENESIS 2:18

When God created the world, He saw that each thing He'd made was good. In fact, the first time He declared that something *wasn't* good was when He saw that Adam was alone.

This is a principle of the Christian life: it's not good when you isolate yourself from others. The Lord's desire is not only that you have an intimate relationship with Him, but also that you have edifying relationships with other believers (Hebrews 10:24–25). This is why when you're lonely, you're instructed first to seek the Lord, and then also to turn to friends and loved ones.

In fact, one of God's great blessings in life is godly friends. This is especially true in times of intense grief and heartbreaking loss. Friends can comfort you, give you godly counsel, and help you heal.

In other words, loneliness is remedied by interaction and involvement—with the Lord and with others—not by withdrawal into fantasy, entertainment, drugs, or other escapist activities. So when you're lonely, don't turn to things that can't satisfy. Go to God or to someone He has given you to love, and find what you really need.

*Jesus, help me grow closer to You and*
*those You've given me to love. Amen.*

My hope is in Jesus because
He satisfies my soul.

# BE HIS EXAMPLE

*"Let your light shine before men in such a way that they may see
your good works, and glorify your Father who is in heaven."*
MATTHEW 5:16

Whether you realize it or not, you're an example. It doesn't matter
if you think you're too weak or inadequate to be one—there are
people who look up to you and are watching to see how you live.
And God wants you to be His representative to them.

Jesus came into this world as a Servant, humbly giving His life
so that we would be reconciled to the Father. And God's will is that
we imitate what He did for us by serving others. We perform loving
acts of service that meet the spiritual and practical needs of those
around us so that they'll grow closer to Him.

There are so many people around you in need today—not just
physically or financially, but emotionally and spiritually as well.
Everyone you meet needs someone to encourage him or her. Will
you make time to reach out and show them the awesome, unconditional, sacrificial love of Christ? Remember, God sees everything
you do in His name and will bless you for all you do in obedience
to Him (Hebrews 6:10).

*Jesus, show me where I can serve others with Your love and
compassion. Work through me to draw others to Yourself. Amen.*

My hope is in Jesus because
He is worthy of my service.

# SEE GOD

*"Blessed are the pure in heart, for they shall see God."*
MATTHEW 5:8

Do you want to see more of God's work in your life and experience His presence in a more profound way? Would you like the capacity to perceive His protection and provision in your work, trials, relationships, and in every aspect of your existence? Jesus tells you the way: *pursue purity.*

When you purge your life of all the behaviors and attitudes that displease God, you clear your vision of the impediments that usually obscure His work in you. You receive a clearer understanding of how He's behind every good gift you receive (James 1:17) and how He gives meaning to all your struggles (Romans 8:28). Without sin clouding your thinking and deadening your spiritual senses, you become more aware of how the Father is engineering all circumstances for your ultimate good.

So keep your heart pure by seeking and obeying the Lord. Invite the Holy Spirit to convict you through God's Word and repent of sin as soon as you're conscious of its presence. And in all things, do as He says. After all, obedience always brings blessing, and when the reward is seeing God, you're receiving the ultimate desire of your soul. It's certainly worthwhile!

*Jesus, purify my heart and help me see*
*You in every aspect of my life. Amen.*

> My hope is in Jesus because
> in Him is everything I need.

# TRANSFORMED BY GOD

*Put on the new self, which in the likeness of God has been created in righteousness and holiness of the truth.*

EPHESIANS 4:24

If you've been abused or mistreated—make a choice right now that you're not going to allow the offender to dictate the course of your life or keep you from doing what God has called you to accomplish. First, forgive the person who hurt you—that's imperative. Second, understand that part of moving forward is believing that not only can Jesus help you overcome your wounds, but He can make you more than a conqueror through them (Romans 8:37).

Although behavioral researchers have discovered that those who are wounded by others often go on to repeat the pattern, as Christians, we can choose to be conformed to Christ's image (Romans 8:29). We can say:

*Lord, I choose to be a loving, forgiving person as Jesus is. So Father, please free me from the wounds I've experienced and transform me into Your likeness. Teach me to be godly, wise, and sacrificially loving as Jesus is. And work through everything I've been through so I can be a more compassionate and effective minister to others. Amen.*

*Jesus, this is indeed my prayer. Thank You for turning my wounds into a platform of Your victory. Amen.*

> My hope is in Jesus because He makes me new and victorious.

# RESTLESSNESS

*Give ear to my prayer, O God; and do not hide Yourself
from my supplication. Give heed to me and answer me; I
am restless in my complaint and am surely distracted.*

PSALM 55:1–2

It's the feeling of internal irritation. Something is wrong, but you just can't put your finger on what it is or why it's bothering you. Nothing you do can rid you of the uneasiness in your heart.

Understand that one of the simplest ways God gets your attention is to make you restless. Just as the blast of a warning siren can make you stop in your tracks and take cover, a spirit of unease is God's way of prompting you to seek Him so that He can ready you for what is ahead.

So when that happens, the wisest thing to do is to stop and ask the Lord what He is trying to say to you. Ask, "Father, what are You communicating to me? What is it about Your will that I'm missing?" Do not distract yourself or try to soothe the irritation with anything other than His presence—it won't work. Just continue to seek Him until He shows you what to do and restores peace within you.

*Jesus, I don't know why I feel so restless, but I will seek You
as long as it takes for You to show me Your will. Amen.*

My hope is in Jesus because
He knows how to get my attention.

# CHOOSE TO KEEP HOPING

*Why are you in despair, O my soul? And why have you become disturbed within me? Hope in God, for I shall again praise Him.*
PSALM 42:5

Have you experienced yet another setback? Has some problem arisen that makes your situation seem hopeless? Understand that God allows disappointments to occur so that you'll learn to rely on Him more fully—so you'll walk by faith and not by sight. But never forget this: while disappointments are inevitable, being discouraged is a choice.

You can choose to have hope and joy—you can make a decision to embrace the abundant life God has for you. And you do so by living by one simple rule: circumstances do not control you; Jesus does. You can choose to look to God and trust Him regardless of how your situation looks. And as you do, the scars of old disappointments melt away through His reviving, restoring love.

The Father has many blessings for you to enjoy—blessings you cannot even begin to imagine. So let go of your disappointments and fears. God holds your future in His hands, and you will never lose by keeping focused on Him. So trust Him with all your heart.

*Jesus, I choose not to be discouraged. Thank You for a good future and for showing me who You are. Amen.*

> My hope is in Jesus because He has good things in store for me.

# STRENGTHEN YOUR FAITH

*The Lord stood with me and strengthened me.*

2 TIMOTHY 4:17

Are you facing an overwhelming challenge that seems greater than you can handle? Have you become doubtful that everything is going to turn out all right? If so, how can you keep your faith from failing?

*First, turn to God's Word.* Reading Scripture will not only give you unique insight and courage to move forward with His commands, but also keep you connected to His unfailing love, wisdom, power, and presence. *Second, choose the right message.* Are you thinking about how God has helped you in the past, His unfailing character, and the promises of His Word? Or are you rehearsing your failings? The former leads to peace and courage while the latter leads only to discouragement. So be careful what you think about. *Third, keep your focus on God and not your problems.* Your all-knowing, all-powerful, and ever-present Lord is the One who helps you. He delights in delivering you and can overcome anything you face.

Instead of getting wobbly in your faith, choose to believe God and strengthen your relationship with Him. Place your trust in Him with complete confidence that He has never let you down and never will.

*Jesus, I know You've never let me down. I will focus on and trust You—confident that You're always with me. Amen.*

> My hope is in Jesus because
> He is worthy of my trust.

# UNANSWERED PRAYER

*My prayer is to You, O LORD, at an acceptable time;*
*O God, in the greatness of Your lovingkindness,*
*answer me with Your saving truth.*

PSALM 69:13

Have your prayers gone unanswered? God may be trying to get your attention. As long as your petitions are granted, you can simply enjoy His blessings and provision. But now that you need His help, the Father has your complete attention.

This is an excellent time to conduct a spiritual self-examination. Scripture tells us there are many reasons why the Lord may delay or deny a response. Perhaps you're asking for the wrong reasons (James 4:3), there's disobedience in your life (1 John 3:22), you're asking outside of the will of God (1 John 5:14), or the fulfilled request will become an idol in your life. More often than not, however, the Father's goal is to teach you something. For example, in 2 Corinthians 12, Paul prayed that God would remove his thorn. The Lord did not grant his request, but instead shifted Paul's focus to the constant provision of His grace. In other words, that unanswered prayer brought Paul to a new level of dependence on Christ.

Whatever the reason, make God's will your goal. Keep watch for all He has to reveal to you.

*Jesus, teach me what You desire for me to know. Amen.*

> My hope is in Jesus because He
> is wise and faithful to guide me.

# DIFFERENT WAYS

*"My thoughts are not your thoughts, nor are your ways*
*My ways . . . . For as the heavens are higher than the*
*earth, so are My ways higher than your ways."*
ISAIAH 55:8–9

Although there are exceptions, when God requires something of you, it will often clash with what you consider to be a sensible course of action.

For example, Jesus said that if someone strikes you on one cheek, you should turn and offer him the other (Matthew 5:39). Of course, that's not the usual human response. Normally, we'd either hit back or run away. Likewise, Jesus said, "If anyone wants to sue you and take your shirt, let him have your coat also" (v. 40). In other words, Jesus generally did the opposite of what people usually would. This is because He wasn't setting a natural standard—but one that is *super*natural. He left room for God to work.

If what you think you hear from the Lord seems reasonable from an earthly standpoint, then make sure you're really listening. That's not to say that God doesn't utilize human wisdom—He does. But often, He will ask us to accomplish what seems illogical to our rational minds so that His glory can shine through.

*Jesus, I know what You ask requires faith.*
*Help me to trust You wholeheartedly. Amen.*

My hope is in Jesus because
He operates in the supernatural.

# DON'T RUSH

*It is not good for a person to be without knowledge,*
*and he who hurries his footsteps errs.*

PROVERBS 19:2

Are there choices you must make today? Do you feel the stress of your situation—the pressure to rush? Understand that throughout the pages of Scripture, God never tells anyone to hurry into a decision. He simply doesn't operate that way.

Though there may be times when you need to hear from Him quickly, or when He demands immediate obedience, generally those are after months of preparation where He is already guiding you to the right answer. He will not counsel you to rush into a decision blindly. Of course, the enemy will usually tempt you to act immediately, because that's how he traps you. He knows that if you think about a situation long enough, you'll see that certain choices are not God's will for you at all. This is why Scripture admonishes you repeatedly to wait for the Lord (Psalms 27:14; 37:7; 62:5).

You know the difference between the call of God that is supernaturally saturated with His peace and situations that are cloaked in confusion. If you feel an overwhelming, frenzied urge to rush and act spontaneously, pull in the reins. Let God guide you and show you the right way to proceed.

*Jesus, I need You to speak into my situation clearly.*
*Show me what to do, my Savior. Amen.*

My hope is in Jesus because
He leads me perfectly.

# JUST WAIT

*God is not unjust so as to forget your work and the love
which you have shown toward His name, in having
ministered and in still ministering to the saints.*

HEBREWS 6:10

I often say you reap what you sow, more than you sow, and later than you sow. But at times you may become frustrated because what you've sown doesn't seem to be producing anything at all. This is difficult with whatever you are planting—but especially so when you've invested love, mercy, truth, and kindness into other people's lives and there is no visible harvest.

Don't be disheartened. There are certain seeds that sprout up quickly, and we rejoice at those. But there are others whose roots must reach deep into the ground before they can ever live. And the most wondrous thing about those is that they are often the ones that grow tallest, sturdiest, and most fruitful.

So don't give up. God sees how you are serving Him and your faithful love to His people. Nothing goes unnoticed or unrewarded. Keep nurturing, watering, praying, and watching. And trust God to bring the bounty.

*Jesus, You know who is on my heart today. I know
the love I have shown is not wasted, but will have a
harvest. Do a miracle in my loved one's life. Amen.*

My hope is in Jesus because
He brings even the dead to life.

# STOP COMPARING

*"Before you were born I consecrated you."*
JEREMIAH 1:5

Do you ever look at other people and feel a painful pang in your heart: *If only I were like _____. Wealthy or athletic like him. Beautiful or smart like her?* Or perhaps your comparisons are based on family dynamics, opportunities, education, or social connections. The ways you can compare yourself to others goes on and on.

And the truth is, you're right—you aren't like any other person. You are one of a kind! Likewise, the plan God has for your life is unique and amazing—and no one else has one that matches it. The Father has set a course before you, designed exclusively for *you* to travel; He has planned tasks for *you* that are *yours alone* to complete. And He has given you exactly what He intended for you to have as the gifts, background, and abilities needed to fulfill His purposes for you.

You know that person you keep comparing yourself to? That person would never be able to complete the plan God has *for you.* Because the Father created *you* for that role. So don't let those comparisons be an excuse for disobedience or discouragement. Embrace the reason He created you and triumph in His name.

*Jesus, help me to walk in Your will and be
all You created me to be. Amen.*

My hope is in Jesus because
He formed me for a purpose.

# KEEP GETTING UP

*Though the righteous fall seven times, they rise again.*
PROVERBS 24:16 NIV

Whenever you fail—whether it's in your relationships, business, Christian walk, or whatever the case may be—you may feel as if your world has crashed around you. But what you must understand is that your experience of failure never defines you. It simply reveals your limitations and blind spots. In other words, your failures can instruct you in a powerful way if you'll remain open to the Holy Spirit's guidance.

So the very best thing you can do in the face of failure is say, "Dear God, please show me why I failed. Enable me to get up, move forward, and depend more on You." In fact, this is crucial, because if you refuse to take risks out of fear of disappointment and failure, then you won't experience the full joy and satisfaction that God desires for you.

But if you will get up, focus on the Lord, and continue to obey Him, God will indeed lead you to success. He has built you with the ability to do His will, and He will enable you to fulfill His wonderful purposes for your life. So no matter how many times you fall down—don't get discouraged. Keep getting up and keep going.

*Jesus, thank You that You see more in me than*
*my failures. Lead me to success. Amen.*

My hope is in Jesus because He
lifts me up and transforms my life.

# KEEP IT CLEAN

*If we say that we have no sin, we are deceiving ourselves.*

1 JOHN 1:8

You may feel alone in the things you've done wrong today, but realize: everyone sins. We all do things we shouldn't. Certainly, the longer we follow Jesus, the more we should mature spiritually and walk in increasing freedom from the sin nature. In fact, the Holy Spirit indwells to keep us in the center of God's will and to convict us quickly when we err. So when we sin, our first response should be, "Lord, forgive me and help me never to do that again!"

But realize that at no point in our earthly lives are we ever beyond temptation. As long as we have human bodies, we are subject to physical desires that, if left unchecked, can lead us away from God's best and to destruction. This is why we must *always* be on guard, watchful, and careful.

While you may not be able to eliminate every bad influence, you can and must guard your thoughts and keep them from becoming impure. Refuse to harbor sin in your heart. No dalliance with iniquity is ever harmless, but always results in heartbreak. So ask the Holy Spirit to help you walk in purity and live a life that honors God.

*Jesus, I know the sins I harbor are destructive.*
*Show me how to repent and be free. Amen.*

My hope is in Jesus because
He frees me from sin.

# STOP COMPLAINING AND ASK

*You do not have because you do not ask.*

JAMES 4:2

Do you ever talk with your friends and loved ones about the things you need, but neglect to go humbly before the throne of grace to make your requests?

This happened to the people of Israel as they left their bondage in Egypt. They grumbled among themselves about needing food to eat—even reminiscing about the meat pots they'd left behind. Of course, the Lord was more than willing to provide what they required. He said, "I have heard the grumbling of the Israelites. Tell them, 'At twilight you will eat meat, and in the morning you will be filled with bread. Then you will know that I am the LORD'" (Exodus 16:12 NIV). How sad, however, that instead of taking their need as an opportunity to go to God and know Him, they instead chose the path of ungratefulness and disrespect—complaining about how He was running things.

Don't make the same mistake. The temptation will always be to talk incessantly about your problems with others rather than ask God to help you. But He wants to fellowship with you and be your Provider—that's why He allowed those needs in your life to begin with. So go to Him, know Him, and be filled.

*Jesus, You know my needs. Thank You that they are an opportunity to know You better. Amen.*

My hope is in Jesus because
He answers my prayers.

# PUT IT INTO PRACTICE

*Prove yourselves doers of the word, and not merely hearers.*
JAMES 1:22

You may know a lot about the Christian life, but are you actually living it out? Your walk with Jesus was never intended to be a matter of book learning or head knowledge. God wants you to put into practice the principles He teaches you. The Bible tells us repeatedly to get wisdom and understanding, but then it challenges us to *apply* what we have learned in real-world situations. Your knowledge of God's Word is incomplete until you actually make it an active part of your life.

You will find this is ultimately fulfilled and perfected in your service to God. What you believe and how you behave is truly challenged and developed when you help others in Jesus' name. This is when what you believe is put to the test, and you can see the Lord's power and presence transform lives through your obedience to Him.

So consider: are you serving God? I'm not talking about sitting on committees, but actively pouring your life into others. Have you asked Him, "How would You have me serve You? Who do You want me to minister to in Your name?" If you've never asked Him these things, do so right now and obey what He shows you.

*Jesus, how can I serve You? Who can*
*I minister to in Your name? Amen.*

My hope is in Jesus because
He transforms lives.

# July

Do not throw away your confidence, which has a great reward.
For you have need of endurance, so that when you have done
the will of God, you may receive what was promised.

HEBREWS 10:35–36

# HAVE HOPE

*Do not grieve like the rest of mankind, who have no hope.*
1 THESSALONIANS 4:13 NIV

There is nothing that tests our faith like losing someone we love. I remember the day we buried my mother. What shocked me the most were the thoughts of uncertainty that entered my mind. *Suppose there's no resurrection. Suppose this is the very last time I will be with her.* Those doubts lasted just long enough for me to truly feel their devastating effect. Then all of a sudden, Scripture verse after Scripture verse kept coming to my mind, confirming Jesus' promises about the resurrection and eternal life (John 11:25–26; 14:1–3; 1 Corinthians 15:54–57).

That was a powerful moment—one I'll never forget. Did I really believe there was a resurrection for those who believe in Christ? Yes! Did I have faith that I would see Mom again? Yes! And did I truly have confidence that we would be together again—that I would dwell with her in the presence of God for eternity? Yes! Yes! Yes!

Whenever you experience a loss, it's good to review what you believe as well. Find comfort in who Christ is and what He has promised you. You do not grieve as a helpless person. With Jesus, you always have hope.

*Jesus, thank You for giving me hope, comfort, and assurance even in my worst losses. Amen.*

My hope is in Jesus because
He gives us eternal life.

# INFLUENCE IN THE LIMITATIONS

*He who began a good work in you will*
*perfect it until the day of Christ Jesus.*
PHILIPPIANS 1:6

You have no idea how God is working through you—even in your limitations. Consider Paul and his time in a Roman jail. Certainly, anyone in his situation would feel as if his or her time for effective service had come to an end. Yet during those prison years, Paul wrote the letters that would become such an important part of our New Testament. Do you think Paul knew that those epistles would continue to transform people's lives two thousand years later? Yet, God had a greater plan than the apostle could have imagined.

You may feel limited in your service to God, but there's no way to know how many people you are influencing through your obedience to Him—who is watching, listening, or learning from you, or how they'll affect the world.

But always keep this in mind: every person impacts history in some way—either for God or for the enemy. What you do lives on in the lives of others. So make sure you are seeking the Lord daily and that you're obeying all He calls you to do. Because the good you do in His name continues to bear fruit in eternity.

*Jesus, thank You for working through me,*
*even when I feel limited. Amen.*

My hope is in Jesus because He brings
eternal fruit from my obedience.

# LIGHT ON THE PATH

*The teaching of your word gives light,*
*so even the simple can understand.*
PSALM 119:130 NLT

Do you need direction today—for God to show you what to do? He promises that His Word will be a light to your path (Psalm 119:105). This means He will help you see three things as you follow Him:

*What you carry with you.* Through Scripture, God shows you what is influencing your decisions and the encumbrances that are slowing you down. He also teaches you how to exchange your fears for confidence in His abiding presence.

*What lies on either side.* Through His Word, the Father gives you an understanding of the forces that are trying to pull you off His path and how to keep His will for you central.

*What lies ahead.* Finally, God prepares you for future circumstances with words of warning, wise counsel, and practical advice for dealing with the challenges and pitfalls that are likely to come your way.

The Lord wants to guide you. Seek His wise and all-encompassing direction by going to His Word. He will teach you what to do and strengthen you for whatever you encounter.

*Jesus, You know what I face. Thank You for encouraging*
*me and leading me in the way I should go. Amen.*

> My hope is in Jesus because He leads
> me effectively through His Word.

# HOPE IN GOD

*It is better to take refuge in the LORD*
*than to trust in princes.*

PSALM 118:9

At times, we may either intentionally or unconsciously look to people to make our lives better. We believe if we have a certain relationship, boss, or political leader, everything will be okay. But when we do, we may be missing out on what's much better.

For hundreds of years, the Jewish people watched for the coming of the Messiah. What they expected was a bold king and military leader like David, who would forever do away with the stranglehold of foreign rulers. They believed the Messiah would inaugurate peace and prosperity in the land that had been promised as their inheritance.

But because so many in Israel were so intensely focused on earthly success and security, rather than on God's plan, they missed Jesus—the One they were truly yearning for. Their hope was placed on the wrong goal, and they forfeited a far superior salvation.

Don't do the same thing. Any time you look to a leader to do what only God can, you're asking for trouble and disappointment. People can let you down, but your Savior will never mislead you. Hope in Him—the One who can truly satisfy your soul.

*Jesus, I don't want to miss the fullness of Your blessings*
*because of a misplaced focus. I will follow You. Amen.*

My hope is in Jesus because
He is the true King of kings!

# The Helper

*"I will ask the Father, and He will give you another
Helper, that He may be with you forever."*
John 14:16

You need help. We all do. This isn't a sign of weakness—it's a spiritual reality. And it is why God has given the Holy Spirit to indwell us. In fact, telling us about His provision was Jesus' way of informing us of one of the most profound truths concerning the Christian life—it's impossible. The life Jesus expects from His followers is unattainable apart from His intervention.

This is good news for you today. God doesn't expect you to face what's before you on your own. He knows it's unfeasible in your strength, so He sends His Holy Spirit to do His work in you—empowering you, conforming you to the image of Christ, and guiding you in your daily life.

So what should you do? Be aware of His presence and activity—how He convicts you of sin, prompts you to act, and enables you supernaturally with wisdom, energy, and talent you don't have within yourself. When you know what to look for, you'll be amazed at how real the Holy Spirit will become to you. So accept the help that's been given you and rejoice that the One who accompanies you can handle anything.

*Jesus, thank You for Your Holy Spirit.
Empower me to do Your will. Amen.*

My hope is in Jesus because
He gives me all the help I need.

# FAITH OR SIGHT?

*We walk by faith, not by sight.*

2 CORINTHIANS 5:7

It's something that we're often told, but that's also difficult to grasp in its entirety: *the Christian life is a life of faith.* We usually don't have much trouble accepting that fact in connection with our salvation—we trust God to provide what He has promised. But when it comes to our daily challenges, faith is sometimes conspicuously missing. We take matters into our own hands and do the best we can. Simply put, we walk by *sight.*

In other words, we think: *If I don't see or feel it, it mustn't be true. If I am not aware of God's presence, He must not be with me. If I don't sense how He's engineering my circumstances, then He must be absent from them.* But nothing could be further from the truth.

Faith means that your eyes don't see, your ears don't hear, and you don't have any earthly indication that God is intervening in your situation—but you still trust that He is. You have more confidence in His character than you do in your own senses—in His promises than in your circumstances.

So let go and trust Him. It may feel irresponsible to your earthly sensibilities—but it's the wisest thing you can do.

*Jesus, I don't see Your activity in my situation,*
*but I trust You. Help me to walk in faith. Amen.*

My hope is in Jesus because
He is working in the unseen.

# CHANGE YOUR MIND

*Do not be conformed to this world, but be*
*transformed by the renewing of your mind,*
*so that you may prove what the will of God is.*

ROMANS 12:2

Whether you have just accepted Jesus as your Savior or have grown up in a Christian home, there is something every believer must do—and that's have his or her mind renewed by the work of the Holy Spirit. Why? Because even if you've had a godly upbringing, you've been influenced by the world—a way of thinking that's based on man's reason rather than God's.

The renewal of your mind begins with an act of your will. You must make an active commitment to subject everything you think to the truth of Scripture. And as you submit every thought, attitude, and perception to the Holy Spirit for His examination, your mind will be supernaturally transformed. You will be surprised by how many "Christian" beliefs have absolutely nothing to do with God, and how they're actually undermining your walk with Him.

Friend, nothing changes the quality of your life and relationship with God like allowing Him to shape your thinking. You can rely on Him completely to lead you to the truth (John 16:13).

*Jesus, examine my thoughts, purge what isn't of You,*
*and renew my mind with Your truth. Amen.*

My hope is in Jesus because He leads
me to the truth that sets me free.

# THINK ABOUT HIM

*Whatever is true, . . . honorable, . . . right, . . . pure, . . .
lovely, . . . of good repute, if there is any excellence and
if anything worthy of praise, dwell on these things.*

PHILIPPIANS 4:8

Yesterday, we discussed the importance of renewing your mind. Through Scripture, the Holy Spirit cleans out the thoughts that no longer fit who you are as a believer. But perhaps you're wondering, *What* should *I be thinking about?*

The apostle Paul gave you the answer: "Set your mind on things above, not on things on the earth" (Colossians 3:2 NKJV). Focus on what matters in eternity and what will give your life the greatest meaning and fruitfulness here on earth. And nothing will help you more than thinking about Jesus and His example.

At the start of each day, ask Christ to reveal Himself more to you and live His life through you. Declare your desire to walk according to His ways. Likewise, think about how He would respond to every situation you encounter. Stop dwelling on the negative ways of the world—the what-ifs and the worst-case scenarios. Instead, pursue godly wisdom and apply it to your life. Seek the Savior's perspective, and His thoughts will certainly become yours.

*Jesus, fill my mind with Your thoughts and help me
be a living testimony of Your goodness. Amen.*

> My hope is in Jesus because
> He is worthy of my full attention.

# TRUST HIS PRESENCE

*They tested the Lord, saying,*
*"Is the Lord among us, or not?"*
EXODUS 17:7

After God sent ten plagues to convince Pharaoh to release the Israelites from Egypt, parted the Red Sea, provided water at Marah, gave them manna to eat—the Israelites still doubted Him. In Exodus 17, we again find them grumbling about water.

We might be tempted to judge them, but their concerns were *real*. Think about not having anything to drink for days and not having any relief in sight. Consider what it would do to your body—the headaches, nausea, and pain. Certainly, watching their children and elderly suffering would have tried even the strongest heart.

It takes less for us to complain, doesn't it? Like the Israelites, we encounter a trial and cry out, "God, where are You?" We doubt that the Lord is God or that He cares for us.

But He does. And for the Israelites, He did yet another miracle—He brought forth *water from stone* (v. 6). The same is true for your situation. It's come to a desperate point so He can show You His incredible power and provision. So stop grumbling. Trust Him, and be confident of His presence and supernatural deliverance.

*Jesus, I will trust You when my situation appears impossible. Amen.*

> My hope is in Jesus because
> He never fails or forsakes me.

# HIS STRENGTH

*The LORD is my strength and shield. I trust him with all*
*my heart. He helps me, and my heart is filled with joy.*
PSALM 28:7 NLT

Whenever you feel weak and inadequate, choose to think about the power of God. He's in control of all things and reigns over heaven and earth with His awesome ability.

Then, open Scripture and read how hopeless and ordinary most of the biblical saints were before they were used by the Lord to accomplish great things. David was just a shepherd in the fields. Joseph was a slave and a prisoner. And Nehemiah was a servant in the court of a foreign king. Really, it was as they stepped out in faith and trusted God that their lives took on greater meaning and importance.

They are no different than you are—they had the same fears, doubts, and failings. But the good news is that the same God who helped them works through you today.

So when you doubt that you're able to face some challenge, remember His promise that He'll never leave you nor forsake you (Deuteronomy 31:8). Choose to think about His faithfulness, power, and wisdom. Then praise Him that the great provision He made for David, Joseph, and Nehemiah is available to you as well.

*Jesus, thank You for helping me as You did them! I exalt You. Amen!*

> My hope is in Jesus because
> He gives me strength.

# FIND YOUR FUNCTION

*As each one has received a special gift, employ it in serving
one another as good stewards of the manifold grace of God.*

1 PETER 4:10

Do you know what the Lord created you to do? Are you functioning within the spiritual gifts He's given you? Do you realize that using those talents is central to finding the fulfillment you long for?

Any good workman knows you need the right tool for the job. When tools are used properly, brilliant work can be accomplished. But when they're used improperly, the results can be disastrous. This same principle applies to the way God works through you.

Through the Holy Spirit, He has gifted you to build up the kingdom in a unique way. But if you're working outside your giftedness, or if you're using your abilities in ways contrary to His will, you may find yourself filled with anxiety and frustration.

Your Creator has given you your talents so that you may use them for His glory. So when you use them in His name to serve other people in love, great things can be accomplished. Therefore, today, ask Him if you're using your gifts the way He desires. If the answer is no, ask Him to provide opportunities so you can become everything He created you to be.

*Jesus, thank You for the gifts You've given me.
Help me to honor You with them. Amen.*

> My hope is in Jesus because He
> does great things through me.

# RECOGNIZE YOUR GIFT

*Since we have gifts that differ according to the grace given
to us, each of us is to exercise them accordingly.*

ROMANS 12:6

As we said yesterday, God has given you a gift to glorify Him and serve others. Today, take a moment and consider which you may possess.

*Prophesying* is proclaiming God's truth. *Ministering* is serving and meeting needs in others' lives. *Teaching* is presenting God's Word and explaining how the Lord desires us to apply it to our lives daily. *Exhorting* is appealing to others to live out the Christian life and showing them how to do so. *Giving* involves practical expressions of time, treasure, and talent that are marked by generosity and faithfulness. *Leading* may also be called *administration*, and it includes being accountable, diligent, and consistent over time. The gift of *mercy* involves expressing compassion that points to God's loving-kindness and His free offer of forgiveness, which is made possible through Jesus.

This list is brief, but it's important that you recognize the gift you've been given, embrace it, and then seek to grow in it. If you don't know how God has gifted you to serve Him, talk to a member of your church's staff or find a spiritual gifts inventory online.

*Jesus, thank You for the gift You've given me. Show me how
to serve in the most effective manner possible. Amen.*

My hope is in Jesus because
He equips me for service.

# TRUST BEYOND SIGHT

*Faith is the assurance of things hoped for,*
*the conviction of things not seen.*

HEBREWS 11:1

Any time you choose to trust God, even when your circumstances appear contrary to your hopes, you are exercising and establishing your faith.

I've had many times when the Lord spoke to me about what He was going to do in my life. But then, as troubling challenges arose, I would think, *How in the world can this happen?* Then the Lord would say to me, "Are you going to believe what you see, or are you going to trust Me?" So, as difficult as it was, I would make the decision to believe Him rather than what I could see. To "walk by faith, not by sight" (2 Corinthians 5:7). And every time, I was blessed to experience the Father's astounding presence and provision.

I can say without a shadow of a doubt that you will never go wrong waiting on God. You will never be disappointed when you trust Him to make a way for you, regardless of how your circumstances appear. And when you make the choice to believe Him, He will grow your faith in awesome ways.

*Jesus, it's difficult to believe when my circumstances look so*
*impossible. But I will believe You—that it will be as You say. Amen.*

> My hope is in Jesus because
> He always keeps His promises.

# Choose the Bridge

*Although the Lord has given you bread of privation and
water of oppression, He, your Teacher will no longer hide
Himself, but your eyes will behold your Teacher.*
Isaiah 30:20

We all carry heavy burdens at one point or another. We all experience difficult things in life that shape who we are. And the truth is that when those trials happen during our childhoods, they often become an excuse for us to give up, treat others badly, and be negative. How often have you heard someone justifying their wrong behavior because of the adversity they experienced in their youth?

But understand that *you have a choice* about how to respond to trials—both the ones in your past and those you face today. You can see them either as a burden or as a bridge—as weights that weaken and discourage you or as conduits the Lord uses to develop your character, strengthen your faith, and deepen your relationship with Him.

Of course, no one wants to experience hardships and afflictions. But when you do, always remember that they can be paths to a deeper relationship with Christ. So don't try to handle them in your own strength. Turn to God in faith and allow your adversity to take you to a place of deeper intimacy with Him.

*Jesus, use what I face today to draw me closer to You. Amen.*

My hope is in Jesus because He
works through everything for my good.

# CHOOSE GODLY FRIENDS

*He who walks with wise men will be wise, but*
*the companion of fools will suffer harm.*

PROVERBS 13:20

Are your friends and associates godly people? If you spend time with people who are walking with the Lord, it will help you to grow closer to Him. This is because the company you keep influences how you view the situations and circumstances of your life. On the other hand, when you fail to fellowship with other strong believers, you will almost surely drift away from your heavenly Father.

So consider: Do the people you associate with meditate on God's Word? Do they have a Christ-centered lifestyle? Do they have humble spirits and seek godly solutions to their problems? If not, then you may need to reexamine the time you spend with certain people and how they influence your daily decisions, behaviors, and opinions. Because what 1 Corinthians 15:33 teaches is true: "Bad company corrupts good morals."

God wants you to be wise, and one way He trains you to become so is through other believers who are actively glorifying and serving Jesus. So choose your influences carefully, because it will shape the path of your life in astounding ways.

*Jesus, help me to walk with godly people who will*
*teach me to draw closer to You. Amen.*

My hope is in Jesus because He
works through my relationships.

# REMEMBER WHO HELPS YOU

*Seek the LORD and His strength; seek His face continually.*
*Remember His wonders which He has done.*

PSALM 105:4–5

Your difficulties may seem enormous today, but that's what happens when you focus on something—it seems to intensify and get larger. This is why it's so utterly important to keep your attention on God. That is the only way to put your problems in their proper perspective, so that they no longer overwhelm you.

So think about the Lord—reflect on His greatness, grace, and goodness. Consider His names and character: He is *Yahweh*—the existing One and the Great I AM. *Elohim*—the One who is infinite in power and absolutely faithful to keep His promises to you. *El Shaddai*—the almighty God, the Most High over all, who is always victorious. *Yahweh Yireh*—your perfect Provider, who perceives your needs and faithfully supplies what will fulfill them. And *Yahweh Rapha*—the One who heals you both inside and out.

Is there anything you need that He cannot handle? Of course not! Certainly, your gigantic troubles will shrink in comparison to your great and mighty God. In the light of His presence and power, nothing will be impossible for you.

*Oh, Lord, You are GOD! Thank You for being greater*
*than all my troubles and always helping me. Amen.*

> My hope is in Jesus because He
> can overcome anything I face.

# INFLUENCE

*The eyes of the LORD move to and fro throughout the earth that
He may strongly support those whose heart is completely His.*

2 CHRONICLES 16:9

You've probably heard me say, "Your intimacy with God determines the impact of your life." The more profound your fellowship with Him, the more powerful your influence—regardless of who you are or where you come from. It's your relationship with God that makes all the difference in what kind of effect you have on the world.

So how do you achieve a deep and transformative relationship with Him? *First, spend time meditating on Scripture.* Don't just read the Word, but ask questions such as, "God, what are You saying to me?" "How does this apply to my life?" "How do You want me to respond to You in obedience?" *Second, pray.* Make your life one long conversation with God—one in which you share all the joys as well as the sorrows. *Third, realize how important it is to actively listen to Him.* Train your ears to hear Him so you can have the Lord's direction, wisdom, and power.

God can do astounding things through your life. So read His Word, pray, and listen to Him. And allow Him to make your life a platform of His glory.

*Jesus, draw me closer so my life will shine with
Your presence, wisdom, power, and glory. Amen.*

My hope is in Jesus because He
does powerful things through my life.

# BE TRANSFORMED

*As obedient children, do not conform to the evil*
*desires you had when you lived in ignorance.*
1 PETER 1:14 NIV

Are you afraid of allowing God to transform your life? Perhaps your immediate answer is no. But if you're having trouble doing what He asks of you, then you are. Of course, what He commands is never easy because it means giving up ungodly thought patterns and behaviors or confronting wounds and beliefs that you've held since childhood. You may also need to relinquish your desires or the possessions you depend upon for security and worth. So it may appear far more agreeable to live in the same defeated status quo than to experience the extraordinary life God has planned for you.

Certainly, it's a discipline and sacrifice to let go—it's not easy for anyone. Our fleshly nature holds on and opposes the liberating work of the Holy Spirit at every turn. Even so, when you allow Him to change you, you will experience joyous liberty and assurance. Be confident that if the Father asks you to surrender something, it is because He has something better for you. He is faithful to do what's in your best interest and lead you to the freedom He created you to enjoy.

*Jesus, help me to do as You ask—no matter how*
*difficult. I trust You to lead me to freedom. Amen.*

My hope is in Jesus because
He transforms me.

# NEED FOR THE BODY

*Encourage one another day after day, as long as
it is still called "Today," so that none of you will
be hardened by the deceitfulness of sin.*

HEBREWS 3:13

When you're hurting emotionally, do you isolate yourself from others? Do you avoid church or other godly activities? Understand that eventually, a lack of encouragement and support from fellow Christians will take a toll on your spiritual life.

Why? Because without other believers, you'll find it difficult to counteract the ungodly messages of the world and will become an easy target for the enemy—whose goal is to discourage you and undermine your effectiveness. This is why it's so important for you to invest in godly relationships with Christlike friends and mentors who inspire you, hold you accountable, and challenge you spiritually.

It's in relationship with other believers that you discover and fulfill God's will for your life. And when you have godly, Spirit-filled people loving you, building you up, cheering you on, and ministering to you as you serve them—well, that's when you're positioned to experience the fullness of the Father's grace, power, and plan. That's a blessing you certainly don't want to miss.

*Jesus, thank You for other believers and
the encouragement they give me. Amen.*

My hope is in Jesus because He
gives me support through His body.

# SPIRITUAL VICTORY

*Let us lay aside the deeds of darkness*
*and put on the armor of light.*

ROMANS 13:12

Today understand that the enemy is trying to prevent you from having an intimate relationship with the Lord. So, for example, he will try to get you to sin so that you'll feel so much shame that you'll avoid the Father altogether. But remember, Jesus is the One who makes you worthy. Another way the enemy tries to derail your devotion to God is by filling your time with so many distractions that you're prevented from meditating on His Word.

Why does the enemy go to such lengths? Because he knows that the more you spend time with God, the more impactful your life will be for His kingdom. You will discover the joy, peace, wisdom, strength, security, and blessing of being with Jesus and be prepared for life's difficult challenges. You will also discern the truth about the enemy—who is a deceiver—and you'll be set free of his bondage. In other words, you'll be a threat to him.

So don't let anything stand in the way of your time with God. If you've sinned, then confess and repent. If you've a lot to do, make Jesus your priority anyway. This is the way to a strong, fruitful life and victory over the enemy.

*Jesus, thank You for being my steadfast*
*defense against the enemy. Amen.*

My hope is in Jesus because
He leads me to spiritual victory.

# SPIRITUAL TREASURE

*Wisdom is better than jewels; and all
desirable things cannot compare with her.*

PROVERBS 8:11

If I gave you a box with a million dollars in it and said you could do whatever you wanted to with the money, would you put it on a shelf and forget about it? Of course you wouldn't. More than likely, you already know what you'd do with it. You would use it.

Of course, Scripture is exceedingly more valuable than anything this world can offer. In its pages are treasures money cannot buy: freedom for your soul, security in God's promises, comfort, guidance, contentment, and—most important—the revelation of God Himself. And yet many leave it on a shelf, untouched. So why is it that people put more value on money than on the wonderful gift of Scripture? I'm convinced that it's because most people don't understand how spiritually impoverished they are.

No matter how spiritually mature you've become, there are *always* more blessings God has provided through Jesus for you to enjoy (Ephesians 1:3). Don't miss out. Every day, continue to embrace the treasure of God's Word and take hold of the spiritual inheritance He has for you.

*Jesus, thank You for all You've provided for me.
Help me to take hold of it all. Amen.*

My hope is in Jesus because He has
given me extraordinary blessings.

# RELY ON GOD

*Who is among you that fears the LORD, that obeys the voice
of His servant, that walks in darkness and has no light? Let
him trust in the name of the LORD and rely on his God.*

ISAIAH 50:10

There will be times in your life when you've done all you can—
you've obeyed the Father, you've stayed close to Him through Bible
study and prayer, and you've sought out godly influences. But you'll
still find that there are details of your situation that require faith—
soul-stretching trust that God is willing and able to help you.

These are the Father's divine appointments for you—doors He
closes in order to grow your faith. Circumstances that He engineers
to take you down the road you're supposed to be on. God will do
that—He will allow everything to look like a dead end so that the
only way through is if He makes it.

But it is then that He puts people and opportunities in your path
that you know could only come from Him. And when He does—
when He arranges those unseen details to make the impossible
possible for you—it is absolutely awesome. So have faith in Him.
Trust in the Lord and rely on your God.

*Jesus, my situation looks bleak, but I know it's the
perfect platform for Your intervention. Amen.*

**My hope is in Jesus because He
always provides a way for me.**

# PREPARED FOR THE PROMISE

*Our soul waits for the LORD; He is our help and our shield.*

PSALM 33:20

Sometimes we believe that if God would just give us the desires of our hearts, we would be okay. But just because you get to the border of the Promised Land, that doesn't mean your problems will suddenly disappear. In fact, more often than not, the opposite is true.

This was the mistake the Israelites made as they approached Canaan. They thought the worst of their struggles was over—left behind in Egypt. But when they got to the territory God had promised their forefather Abraham, they discovered "the people who live in the land are strong, and the cities are fortified" (Numbers 13:28). In other words, it wasn't just waiting there for them. It would take faith to drive out the inhabitants and conquer the land.

You may be growing weary of waiting for the desire of your heart to come to fruition, but realize, you're going to need real faith to take hold of it, and God is preparing you for what it will require. So wait with trust in His timing. He knows what He is doing and is making you strong to receive what your heart most longs for.

*Jesus, thank You for preparing me for the desire of my heart and that my hopes are safe in Your hands. Amen.*

> My hope is in Jesus because He prepares me for His provision.

# GIVE AND RECEIVE

*"Give, and it will be given to you. They will pour into
your lap a good measure—pressed down, shaken
together, and running over. For by your standard of
measure it will be measured to you in return."*
LUKE 6:38

When God makes you aware of a need, it is because He is inviting
you to take part in His supernatural work. His opportunities to
give are like train tracks through which He sends you blessings.
You get on board with Him by doing as He asks, and that creates
the path by which you see His provision and join in His victory.

We see this with David, when he invited the people of Israel to
contribute to building the temple. David wanted them to experience
the overflowing joy of seeing God do a mighty work through them.
But first, it would require them to trust the Father more than their
own resources and make the sacrifices He directed. If they clung to
their possessions instead of to Him, they would miss the blessing.

Likewise, when God calls you to give your resources, you must
pour them out as an offering and embrace those great assignments
out of obedience to Him. Then you will see Him work supernaturally through your gift and supply all that you're lacking.

*Jesus, thank You for inviting me to be part of
Your work and blessing my giving. Amen.*

My hope is in Jesus because
all I have is from Him.

# HIS HEALING TOUCH

*"Your faith has made you well; go in*
*peace and be healed of your affliction."*
MARK 5:34

Jesus cares about every part of you—your spirit, soul, and body. A good example of this is found in Mark 5, when He cured a woman who had suffered with hemorrhaging for twelve years. It's hard to imagine how she maintained her hope for healing, especially after so many doctors had failed and her finances had been spent.

The emotional toll would have been terrible as well. According to Jewish law, she would have been considered perpetually unclean (Leviticus 15:19–30) and would not be permitted to touch others or be embraced by them. Imagine doing without anyone's loving caress for twelve years! But not only does Jesus heal her physical disease; He heals her spiritually and emotionally as well by accepting her touch and blessing it.

Understand that Jesus does this for you as well. No matter how complex and disillusioning your life may appear, Jesus refuses to turn His back on you. And just like the woman in today's text, if you will reach out to Him, He will comfort you not only in your outward needs but in those that are inward as well.

*Jesus, thank You for meeting my deepest needs—spirit, soul,*
*and body—and for healing me in profound ways. Amen.*

My hope is in Jesus because
He heals my deepest wounds.

# DRIVE IT OUT

*"If you do not drive out the inhabitants of
the land . . . they will trouble you."*

NUMBERS 33:55

As Israel entered the Promised Land, she was instructed to drive out the other nations because they worshiped other deities. The Lord understood that Israel would be vulnerable to idolatry and would stumble in her devotion to Him should the other nations remain. Unfortunately, we know that the people of Israel did not obey God. While many of her enemies were defeated in battle, Israel didn't drive them out completely. Eventually, the Israelites intermarried with those other tribes and pursued their false deities—destroying their relationship with God.

There's a reason the Lord demands obedience, and it's because He sees our future, and He knows that sin—if we allow it a place in our lives—will keep us from experiencing His blessings and lead us into terrible bondage. So today, whatever God tells you to expel from your life—drive it out. If you're tempted to disobey because you think He's asking too much, consider the love and wisdom He's always shown you. He knows what's best for you, and He understands that there's really only one way to deal with stumbling blocks: eliminate them. So do it, and rid yourself of unneeded temptations.

*Jesus, help me to rid myself of anything that would
compromise my obedience to You. Amen.*

My hope is in Jesus because He
knows what's dangerous to my future.

# BATTLE READY

*You have girded me with strength for battle.*
PSALM 18:39

Beneath the waters of the Savannah River lies the wreckage of the CSS *Georgia*. Protected with railroad iron and armed with heavy cannons, this gunboat was thought to be unassailable—incapable of being defeated by Union troops during the Civil War.

Unfortunately, this floating fortress proved useless because of her hidden internal weaknesses. First, she was too heavy for her own steam engines to propel, so she never made it past the entrance to the port. Likewise, she leaked terribly. Pumps were often stretched to the limit just to keep her from sinking. In the end, she barely obstructed enemies from moving up the Savannah River—a far cry from the defensive force she was created to be.

Sadly, this can be a picture of the Christian life. Too many believers focus on how they look on the outside, while inside there are major weaknesses—sin, woundedness, and self-sufficiency.

Don't be shipwrecked. Ask God to make you fit for battle by making you strong in Him. Strengthen your inner person by allowing Him to repair what's broken and by empowering you through His unfailing Holy Spirit. Then you will be the unassailable power-house He created you to be.

*Jesus, make me strong and whole in You, with the power and energy to move forward in Your will. Amen.*

> My hope is in Jesus because
> He makes me strong.

# THE SOURCE OF UNBELIEF

*"The seed is the word of God. Those beside the road are those who have heard; then the devil comes and takes away the word from their heart, so that they will not believe and be saved."*

LUKE 8:11–12

When Jesus told the parable of the sower, He did so in order that we may know the condition of our hearts. Of course, Jesus began at the most basic level—with unbelievers. They heard the truth but just could not accept it, so the word was taken from them.

As believers, we don't have to worry about this because we are indwelt by the Holy Spirit, who will "bring to your remembrance" everything Jesus said (John 14:26). But we should take note of *who* takes the truth from the unbelievers' hearts: "the father of lies" (John 8:44). This reveals the enemy's goal—to prevent people from embracing the Word and thereby cause unbelief.

Remember this when the thought crosses your mind, *Lord, I'm having a hard time believing You.* Your doubt doesn't originate with God's promise or character, which are unassailably steadfast and good. Rather, it comes from the author of unbelief—your enemy. And he is not worth listening to. So grab on to God's Word and hold it fast.

*Jesus, thank You that I can always trust*
*Your character and Word. Amen.*

My hope is in Jesus because
His Word is sure.

# HITTING ROCK

*"Those on the rocky soil are those who, when they hear, receive the word with joy; and these have no firm root; they believe for a while, and in time of temptation fall away."*

LUKE 8:13

Yesterday, we saw that Jesus told the parable of the sower so we can examine our hearts and understand how we're progressing in the Christian life. The next condition Jesus addressed is when there are rocks impeding our growth. Although we may have a saving faith, our trust is shallow—it has no root because of stony areas beneath the surface. So when there's trouble, we doubt God.

We can liken that rocky soil in our hearts to the internal issues we wrestle with—the wounded areas, coping mechanisms, and places we've learned that we cannot trust *anyone*. We may not even realize how deep they go. But every time there's a trial in that area, we doubt God and struggle terribly.

Friend, is this you? Are you hitting a wall in your relationship with Him? Think about the challenge you're facing right now—what old wounds does it bring up? You may have learned not to trust others in that area, but God is *always trustworthy*. Break through that stony hindrance by resolving to have faith in Him regardless of the pain or your fears.

*Jesus, I want to trust You! Break through the rocky places and heal me. Amen.*

My hope is in Jesus because He is always trustworthy.

# CHOKED UP

*"The seed which fell among the thorns, these are the ones who have heard, and as they go on their way they are choked with worries and riches and pleasures of this life, and bring no fruit to maturity."*

LUKE 8:14

As we continue studying the parable of the sower, we see that the next impediment Jesus addressed is the thorns that choke the effectiveness of His Word. The realities of life—the worries, riches, and pleasures—can suffocate what He tries to accomplish in us.

In essence, thorns are the external things we turn to as our earthly security or comfort other than God. They can be anything: money, relationships, addictions, even escapist entertainment—whatever you rely upon for self-esteem, safety, worth, or even just a brief getaway from the pressures of life. The point is, however, that you're turning to these things instead of to the Father. And because they're a priority to you, God's Word always comes second. Ultimately, because of them, you choose your wisdom over His. And that never works out well.

So consider, when bad news or stressors hit, where do you run for comfort? If it's anything other than Jesus, it's impeding you from pressing on to maturity. Remove its chokehold and turn to Him.

*Jesus, it'll be difficult to let go of what You're bringing to mind. But with Your help, I can. Amen.*

My hope is in Jesus because
He leads me to maturity.

# THE FRUITFUL HEART

*"The seed in the good soil, these are the ones who have heard the word in an honest and good heart, and hold it fast, and bear fruit with perseverance."*

LUKE 8:15

In the parable of the sower, we learn how important it is to be truly receptive to Scripture, because it produces "a crop a hundred times as great" (Luke 8:8). In other words, God's Word makes us spiritually successful.

Jesus tells us that fruitful hearts *hear the word*—they don't just let the truth pass by, but they really listen to and apply it. They are *honest*—they are open, transparent, and genuine with God. They are *good*. The good heart is turned toward the Lord—accepting all He says and cleansed of what opposes Him. These individuals *hold fast* to the Word—literally, they keep possession of it. They never let go of God, even when they don't understand what He's doing. Likewise, they *bear fruit*—they're always productive and careful to examine what comes from their lives. Finally, they *persevere*—they stay the course regardless of what happens.

That's how you become spiritually successful. So become truly effective for the kingdom of God by allowing His Word to be planted deep in your heart.

*Jesus, make my heart truly productive for You. Amen.*

> My hope is in Jesus because He leads me to eternal fruitfulness.

# AUGUST

May our Lord Jesus Christ Himself and God our Father, who has loved us and given us eternal comfort and good hope by grace, comfort and strengthen your hearts in every good work and word.

2 THESSALONIANS 2:16–17

# OVERCOMING ANGER

*Be kind to one another, tender-hearted, forgiving each
other, just as God in Christ also has forgiven you.*
EPHESIANS 4:32

When you're hurt, how do you handle your anger? Do you vent it openly? Do you stuff it down deep and continue to seethe? Or do you actively defuse it by turning to Jesus and asking for His wisdom? It shouldn't surprise you that the only healthy way to deal with your resentment is to turn it over to Christ.

This doesn't mean your anger is intrinsically wrong—far from it (Matthew 21:12–17). You may be experiencing anger in response to sin, which is often referred to by Christians as *righteous indignation*. Unfortunately, when your ire becomes bitterness or a spirit of vengeance, it no longer honors God.

Therefore, a key principle for keeping anger from destroying you is through forgiveness. When you let go of your desire for revenge by forgiving those who hurt you, you're on the road to experiencing true freedom.

When offenses are not addressed, they work their way into your innermost parts—affecting everything about you, including your health and spiritual well-being. Don't let that happen. Turn your feelings over to Jesus and let Him show you how to respond.

*Jesus, I don't want anger to control me.
Help me to forgive as You forgave me. Amen.*

My hope is in Jesus because
He empowers me to forgive.

# WHERE'S YOUR JOY?

*May the God of hope fill you with all joy and peace in believing,*
*so that you will abound in hope by the power of the Holy Spirit.*

ROMANS 15:13

Jesus often instructed those He healed to go to the temple and offer a sacrifice to God. By doing so, He helped them acknowledge the Lord's provision to them in a tangible way. In other words, He directed their attention to where it should be—on the *Giver*, rather than the gift.

Of course, the Lord God should *always* be our focus—whether things are going our way or not. Whether we're receiving the desires of our heart or not. This means that even when we fail to see His miraculous hand working in our lives, we can and should be joyful simply because *He is with us.* And because of His presence in our circumstances, we know that He is working all things together for our good even in times of disappointment, heartache, and personal loss (Romans 8:28).

So consider: have you become so focused on what you want that you've forgotten Who is with you? If so, then take a sacrifice of praise to Him. And base your joy—not on your circumstances—but on your unfailing Savior, the Lord Jesus Christ.

*Jesus, You are my joy! Thank You for*
*leading me in the way I should go. Amen.*

My hope is in Jesus because
He never fails me.

# TRUST AND OBEY

*"I will do as You say."*
LUKE 5:5

Is there something God has asked you to do that seems unreasonable? Don't allow the fear of failure, desire to control your own life, or even others' expectations to hinder you from submitting to Him.

Peter learned this important lesson one day as Jesus spoke to the crowds by the Sea of Galilee. The people pressed in so insistently that Christ was forced to get into Peter's boat in order to continue teaching. When He was finished instructing them, Jesus said to Peter, "Launch out into the deep and let down your nets for a catch" (Luke 5:4 NKJV). Peter was reluctant, of course—he had toiled all night without catching *any* fish and was terribly weary. And Jesus was not a fisherman. What did this Teacher know about fish?

Eventually, however, Peter chose to obey. The result was that he witnessed a miracle—he caught so many fish that his nets began to break.

This is why it's so important to obey God even when He doesn't make sense. Because He knows best and has blessings for you that you'll not experience any other way. So every time the Father asks you to do something, do it and trust He has something good in store when you obey.

*Father, help me trust You in everything, knowing*
*You'll bless my obedience. Amen.*

> My hope is in Jesus because He does the miraculous through my obedience.

# DEMONSTRATE REVERENCE

*Who is the man who fears the LORD? He will*
*instruct him in the way he should choose.*

PSALM 25:12

At times, the decisions you'll have to make will be important but difficult. Thankfully, the Lord is willing to give you clear guidance about every choice in your life. So why don't more Christians take advantage of this astounding privilege?

Although the promise of God's direction is an incredible gift, it will not really make a difference to us unless we truly believe that God is perfect in knowledge, all-sufficient in strength, unfailing in character, and unconditionally loving toward us. This is key to trusting Him for our futures because He requires us to respect Him *as God*. We must honor what He says because of who He is.

Reverence to the Lord means you hold Him in higher esteem than you do yourself. You "trust in the LORD with all your heart and do not lean on your own understanding" (Proverbs 3:5). In other words, you acknowledge that He has greater authority and wisdom than you do, and you trust Him to the point of obedience.

Are you facing a difficult situation? Analyze your attitude toward the Lord. Do you really have reverence for Him? Then respect Him as God and do what He says.

*Jesus, I humble myself before You. I will*
*obey You fully—show me what to do. Amen.*

My hope is in Jesus because He is God.

# FORGIVE FREELY

*"Forgive us our sins, for we ourselves also
forgive everyone who is indebted to us."*
LUKE 11:4

Can you imagine how horrible it would have been if—at salvation—God had stopped at a particular sin and had said, "No, this one isn't pardoned because it's just too terrible. There is no way I could ever forgive that"? That one transgression would have kept you separated from Him forever. Thankfully, the Lord didn't do that to you—and He wouldn't pick and choose which sins to forgive once you've repented (1 John 1:9). This is because at the cross, Jesus forgave *all* you've done—past, present, and future—and once you accept Him as Savior, every transgression is pardoned.

However, that's what you do whenever you refuse to forgive others—you put yourself in God's place, but without His mercy and provision. Instead of releasing them completely as Jesus did for you, you choose to hold on to your hurt, resentment, and hostility.

Don't do that! In everything you do, imitate Christ. Rid yourself of unforgiveness—letting go of resentment, laying down your desires to get even, and allowing God to deal with the person who's hurt you. Choose forgiveness so you can be a disciple who both honors Jesus and draws others to Him.

*Jesus, please forgive me for my bitterness.
Please help me to forgive fully. Amen.*

My hope is in Jesus because
He freely forgives me.

# THE NAME OF JESUS

*There is no other name under heaven that has been*
*given among men by which we must be saved.*

ACTS 4:12

There is power in the name of Jesus. We see it throughout the book of Acts. By His name, people were saved (2:37–40), the lame walked (3:6–7), the disciples preached with boldness, the sick were healed, and wonders were performed to His glory (4:29–31).

Even the council of Jewish leaders recognized the power of it, commanding the disciples "not to speak in the name of Jesus" (5:40). But regardless of the persecution they encountered, the disciples not only spoke His name, but embraced His lordship and carried out His mission. And Christ blessed them for it.

Friend, you bear the name of Jesus, and His mighty power is available to you as well. Are you still clinging to the reins of your life and hoping that somehow God will bow to your will and make *your* name great? Understand that when you do so, you're missing out. Nothing but Jesus will ever satisfy your deepest longings, and only the name of Jesus will ever bring fruit that lasts in eternity. So bear His name and do His will with joy. Because then you'll experience the power that's available to you.

*Jesus, I praise Your holy name! Help me*
*to serve You faithfully. Amen.*

My hope is in Jesus because
His name is above every other!

# LOVE AND FORGIVENESS

*If someone says, "I love God," and hates his brother, he is a liar; for the one who does not love his brother whom he has seen, cannot love God whom he has not seen.*

1 JOHN 4:20

Today's verse hits straight to the heart, doesn't it? It helps us remember that the trials God allows into our lives—including the conflicts we have with others—are opportunities for Him to reveal His faithfulness to us. So if you despise someone because the Lord is teaching you something through them, then you really loathe God Himself and the purposes He has for your life. That's both heartbreaking and convicting, isn't it?

If you hate someone, the simple truth is that you need to repent. Confess the unforgiveness and assume responsibility for your resentment. Lay down your anger at God's altar and ask Him to provide a way for godly reconciliation. Then pray for the person who hurt you. If the individual is no longer alive or is unaware of your feelings, then seek the Lord's healing for your emotional wounds and His wisdom about how to be free of the bitterness and hatred you feel. In this way, you show you truly love God.

*Jesus, I want to love You. Help me to forgive the person who hurt me. Amen.*

My hope is in Jesus because He loves me unconditionally.

# ETERNAL PERSPECTIVE

*Each will receive his own reward according to his own labor.*

1 CORINTHIANS 3:8

How frequently do you think about eternity? Often, people talk of time as passing too quickly or of not having enough of it to do the things they want to. But how often do they fix their thoughts on how life will be in heaven and the responsibilities they'll be given there because of their faithfulness here on earth?

Yet, the apostle Paul instructed, "Be careful how you walk, not as unwise men but as wise, making the most of your time, because the days are evil" (Ephesians 5:15–16). What did Paul mean when he said "the days are evil"? He understood that most people have their minds set on things that are fading or that contain little eternal value.

Learning how to manage your time in a way that honors Christ comes down to a matter of discipline and wisdom. Are you focused on the things God has given you to do—the things that are eternal—or are you being drawn away by other, less-meaningful activities? Refuse to yield to the pressures around you. Focus your life on what matters to the Lord, and you will find that it is, indeed, time eternally well spent.

*Jesus, teach me how to invest my time wisely—in a*
*manner that will count in eternity. Amen.*

My hope is in Jesus because He
understands what's eternally important.

# RADIANT

*They looked to Him and were radiant,*
*and their faces will never be ashamed.*

PSALM 34:5

Do you like how you look? Do you see the attractive qualities that God created you to bear? Or do you only see your flaws? Cosmetics and weight-loss companies all claim to have what will help you. However, understand that what is truly powerful, compelling, and appealing about you comes from the Lord God Himself (Zechariah 4:6). This is why it helps you to understand what Jesus does in you as you grow in your relationship with Him: "You were formerly darkness, but now you are Light in the Lord; walk as children of Light (for the fruit of the Light consists in all goodness and righteousness and truth)" (Ephesians 5:8–9). There is something irresistible about you when you shine with His radiance.

Can you remember what you were like before you accepted Christ as your Savior? No matter what your story, you can certainly recall areas of darkness that were made new by Jesus. And the good news is that it continues—He is persistently conforming you to His brilliant image. He is the help of your countenance, so look in the mirror and rejoice at how He shines through you.

*Jesus, thank You for making me more like You—*
*my most beautiful Savior. Amen.*

My hope is in Jesus because
He brings out the best in me.

# FROM FEAR TO FAITH

*Moses said, "If you don't personally go with us, don't make
us leave this place. . . . For your presence among us sets your
people . . . apart from all other people on the earth."*
EXODUS 33:15–16 NLT

What makes the difference between a timid, fretful life and one
that's strong, fruitful, and rewarding is faith in the presence of the
living God. Moses understood this, which is why he asked the Lord
to be with him and the Israelites. He knew that nothing would be
impossible if God provided for and protected them.

Likewise, you'll undoubtedly feel anxious if you try to face the
overwhelming troubles of life in your own strength. But once you
embrace the truth that God is indeed in control of your circumstances, has equipped you for every challenge, and will give you
the victory as you obey Him, your outlook will change. You won't
see life as a continuous series of trials, but as an ongoing adventure
with your Creator.

Certainly, life isn't risk-free. But God has set a divine course
for you that He oversees with perfect wisdom and love. So trust
Him and enjoy your exciting journey with your Savior. Certainly,
He won't ever let you down.

*Jesus, I know that You're directing my path, so I will not fear. Amen.*

My hope is in Jesus because
He is my Defender and Provider.

# THE LONG LESSON

*It is for discipline that you endure;*
*God deals with you as with sons.*
HEBREWS 12:7

Endurance is not just the ability to bear difficulties; it's the capacity to triumph in and over them. You've probably had seasons of adversity when you've experienced trouble in remembering the basic truths of God's Word. Ironically, those times demanded you hold on to His truth the most. And so, as you've clung to His promises, you've found that not only did they become more real to you, but they've actually become a vital part of your life.

Likewise, your difficulties have probably helped you view your situation from God's perspective. For example, when the apostle Paul was imprisoned, from an earthly viewpoint it looked as though his ministry was over. However, he realized that God had put him there to evangelize one of the most impenetrable sectors of Roman society—the praetorian guards. Hopefully, God has shown you how He is working through your trials as well.

The point is, no matter how long the trials, trust that God is bringing good out of them. Such lessons take time to work into your soul. So endure and be victorious by understanding that what He's achieving in and through you is worth it.

*Jesus, please give me Your divine perspective on my troubles*
*and make Your Word even more real to me. Amen.*

> My hope is in Jesus because He
> is teaching me important truths.

# SPORTSMANLIKE CONDUCT

*Everyone who competes in the games exercises self-control in all things. They then do it to receive a perishable wreath, but we an imperishable.*

1 CORINTHIANS 9:25

Athletes who compete in the Olympics must be singularly focused and disciplined. So they practice continually—diligently running through the foundational principles related to their sports. Then, when they finally get to compete, they must block out the taunts of opponents and the cheers of enthusiastic spectators and center their attention on the goal. Why? Because losing focus can mean the loss of their dream.

As a believer, you are called by God to the same intensity of focus in spiritual matters. In addition to training your mind with Scripture, you're instructed to remain vigilant to the traps that can undermine your effectiveness. In other words, there's really never a time when you can drop your guard and just let loose. That doesn't mean you should be fearful—you're also told not to be anxious about anything (Philippians 4:6–7).

Rather, you understand that Christ wants and deserves your full attention. And when your focus is fixed on Him, He will lead you to the victory.

*Jesus, help me to become a disciplined, watchful, effective, and fruitful athlete for You. Amen.*

> My hope is in Jesus because
> He is my focus and my victory.

# BEYOND IMAGINATION

*To Him who is able to do far more abundantly beyond
all that we ask or think, according to the power
that works within us, to Him be the glory.*

EPHESIANS 3:20–21

Have you ever considered the overwhelming hope of today's verse? God can take us places we could never dream of going. His wisdom and power open doors we may have thought permanently locked. God has a way of providing opportunities and blessings that exceed our imaginations. The problem with this, however, is that when we don't see what we want come to pass, we often fail to trust Him. Although He may be providing something far better than we've been requesting, we may be tempted to think He's failed us, especially if we've been waiting a long time.

Yet Jesus told His disciples to seek God first, and whatever else they needed would be given to them (Matthew 6:33). This is because when you focus completely on Him, He plants His own outstanding desires in your heart.

God's blessings are wonderful, satisfying, and able to exceed your hopes. So don't fret. Wait for Him to provide abundantly beyond what you can imagine, and the blessing He gives you will certainly fill your heart with boundless joy.

*Jesus, I want Your desires for me! Thank You for
providing beyond what I can imagine. Amen.*

My hope is in Jesus because
He exceeds all of my hopes.

# ASK FOR WISDOM

*If any of you lacks wisdom, let him ask of God,*
*who gives to all generously and without reproach.*

JAMES 1:5

Take heart in this truth: God loves it when you go to Him for direction. He *never* listens to your prayers for His guidance with the attitude, "You're foolish for asking this." He would never shame you for seeking His wisdom. Rather, your heavenly Father always answers you as a patient Teacher instructing His cherished student. He wants you to know His will and enable you to carry it out.

Of course, you may be worried about hearing the Lord. But understand that His ability to communicate can always overcome any inability you have to hear Him. So if you don't understand God clearly, He will continue speaking to you—using various methods (Hebrews 1:1)—to get His message across to you.

Likewise, as long as you follow God's guidance, He will continue to give you His wise counsel. And He will tell you not only *what* to do, but also *how* and *when* to do it.

So be sure to wait for the Lord to give you His full counsel on whatever matter concerns you. And once you've heard from Him, do what He tells you to do and without doubt or hesitation.

*Jesus, I need Your wisdom.*
*Teach me the way I should go. Amen.*

My hope is in Jesus because He
always provides the wisdom I need.

# USABLE

*I was shown mercy because I acted ignorantly in unbelief;*
*and the grace of our Lord was more than abundant.*

1 TIMOTHY 1:13–14

You may feel that because you've sinned or failed in a certain area, God can no longer use you. That's not the gospel of Jesus Christ. The Lord always wants to work through those who love Him.

Think about the biblical saints. Moses killed an Egyptian, but the Lord used him to deliver the people of Israel from Egyptian bondage. Jacob was a deceiver—tricking his father, brother, and father-in-law; but God still made him the father of the twelve tribes of Israel. Saul was a vicious persecutor of the church, even consenting to the death of Stephen; yet Christ transformed him into the apostle Paul, who took the gospel to the Gentiles and wrote a good portion of the New Testament.

The difference in their lives was this: when they encountered God, they said yes to Him. They were willing to turn from doing things their way to doing things His way. They didn't remain the people they once were. They chose instead to order their lives after God and to follow His plan for them. And today, you can do the same.

*Jesus, I want my life to glorify You. Work*
*through me to draw others to You. Amen.*

My hope is in Jesus because He can
use me to bring glory to His name.

# UNCHANGING

*Jesus Christ is the same yesterday and today and forever.*
HEBREWS 13:8

The Lord doesn't change—He is absolutely consistent. As loving, powerful, wise, and trustworthy as He was throughout the Old and New Testaments, He is the same today.

Of course, many people don't believe God functions that way anymore—at least not the way He did with Moses, Gideon, David, or Paul. True, things are different because of Jesus' provision of salvation. We also have the Word of God to live by and His Holy Spirit living within us to show us His will. But many people believe there's no longer any place for God's miraculous intervention.

Yet those who put the Lord in a box do so to their own detriment. Like the biblical saints, when we're in an intimate, growing relationship with the Lord, we'll have moments when we are surprisingly and supernaturally aware of His holy, almighty presence. No, there may not be a literal burning bush or a parted Red Sea, but during those times we realize we're truly on holy ground before the living God. He provides for us, defends us, addresses us in a manner that we'd never expect, and it changes our lives completely. And we realize that truly, the One who was miraculously available to them continues to defend and provide for us today.

*Jesus, thank You for being so trustworthy,*
*consistent, and available to me. Amen.*

> My hope is in Jesus because
> He doesn't change.

# ON TIME

*From days of old they have not heard or perceived*
*by ear, nor has the eye seen a God besides You,*
*who acts in behalf of the one who waits for Him.*
ISAIAH 64:4

There will be times when the enemy tries to get you to doubt God by whispering, *If He doesn't hurry up and make a way for you, the desires of your heart will slip away forever.*

In such instances, it's crucial for you to remember that the Father owns the clock and knows a great deal more about the right schedule than you ever will. Likewise, throughout Scripture, you're repeatedly admonished that His timing is *going to be* different from yours. But that in your seasons of waiting, He's orchestrating your circumstances in the unseen so His promises to you can be fully accomplished. Therefore, if you run ahead of His timing—as the enemy is tempting you to do—you will miss His best blessings.

So right now, commit yourself to living by His schedule.

Friend, the Father knows what He is doing in your situation. His delays are not denials; rather, they offer divine opportunities for you to know Him better. So don't be discouraged. Rather, be patient and wait, knowing He has a great plan for your life and that He is already acting on your behalf.

*Jesus, the waiting is so difficult, but I will trust Your plan. Amen.*

My hope is in Jesus because
His timing is perfect.

# EXULT IN SALVATION

*My soul shall rejoice in the LORD; it shall exult in His salvation.*

PSALM 35:9

In 1 Thessalonians 5:8, the apostle Paul instructed believers to put on salvation as a helmet. In other words, thinking about the great gift God has given us protects us from spiritual onslaughts.

So today, consider: have you ever truly thought about all your salvation entails? Yes, Jesus has forgiven your sins, and you have everlasting life in heaven. That's an extremely important aspect of our redemption. But many believers stop there in their understanding. Even worse, that definition of salvation can be repeated so often that we become numb to all it really means.

You were spiritually dead and separated from God. Now you are spiritually alive and united with Him so intimately that His Holy Spirit inextricably indwells you. You have a new eternal purpose, identity, and family. You now possess the incredible capacity to receive God's wisdom, strength, and power, and to be a conduit of His glory. Knowing that should make a tremendous difference in your life!

Ephesians 1:3 affirms that you've been "blessed . . . with every spiritual blessing . . . in Christ." So today, protect your mind and encourage your heart by considering all that Jesus has done.

*Jesus, help me to realize the fullness of what You've done in salvation. Thank You for redeeming me. Amen.*

My hope is in Jesus because He saves me in ways too numerable to count.

# The Certainty of His Word

*It is impossible for God to lie. Therefore, we who
have fled to him for refuge can have great confidence
as we hold to the hope that lies before us.*

Hebrews 6:18 nlt

There is absolutely nothing more certain in this world than a promise God has given. Whatever He says He'll do *will be* accomplished—regardless of the obstacles, setbacks, and seeming impossibilities.

Take heart in this truth today. Repeatedly in Scripture we are told, "Not one word has failed of all His good promise" (1 Kings 8:56). This is because it is impossible for God to lie, which means His holy character prevents Him from deceiving you.

But also realize that though people may unintentionally fail us because of their lack of ability, God never will because He is not subject to our weaknesses. His power is always enough to achieve His every goal. Because of His great wisdom, He plans not only *a* way to get you there but the *best*, most *beneficial* way. Nothing catches Him by surprise or is able to foil His ultimate objectives.

The Lord your God is completely trustworthy. So keep obeying Him no matter how difficult the road seems. Have faith in the promises He's given you and never, ever give up your hope in Him.

*Jesus, thank You for fulfilling Your promises.
Help me to trust You always. Amen.*

My hope is in Jesus because
He is absolutely trustworthy.

# He Is Enough

*God is my helper; the Lord is the sustainer of my soul.*
PSALM 54:4

No matter how lonely you feel—regardless of how others have used, abandoned, battled, deceived, or failed you—you are not alone. Even in the deepest moments of utter rejection or betrayal, you always have Christ.

Of course, Jesus may not feel like what you need. In our humanity, we rely on audible voices to love us, direct us, and affirm we're worthy. We long for arms and hands to hold, and bodily presence to comfort and support. But if we truly understand where our hurt resides, we realize that Jesus is the only One who can truly reach it. Often, after the human encouragement, expressions of condolence, and even loving embraces end, we find that the pain remains because it does not have its root in these outward places. The emptiness we feel can only be healed by the inward working of the Holy Spirit.

Spend time in the presence of the One who will never leave, forsake, betray, or lie to you. He is enough to fill the emptiness you feel and to provide hope regardless of your situation. You are not alone, and He is sufficient for what you need.

*Jesus, I need You. You know how deep my hurt goes, but I know You are enough and will love me through it. Amen.*

> My hope is in Jesus because
> He never leaves me.

# FAITH CHALLENGE

*"The righteous man shall live by faith."*

ROMANS 1:17

It is a certainty in the Christian life: you *will be* challenged to rely on God more with every aspect of your being. This is the purpose of the sacrifices you will be called on to offer, the seasons of waiting, and the leaps of faith you'll be pressed to make. You will be placed in situations where you must make a choice: *Do you trust the Lord's wisdom or your own? Is He God or are you?*

Hopefully you'll acknowledge: "*He* is God!" But it does come at a price. It will mean trusting Him when life hurts, nothing makes sense, you cannot see the path ahead, and the burdens appear more difficult than you can bear. But in every instance He is saying, "Trust Me, and experience the powerful and eternal things I've planned to accomplish through you."

This is the process by which your faith grows. You obey Him above your own wisdom, fears, insecurities, and natural senses, and He readies you for a more profound relationship with Himself and a more meaningful and impactful life. So listen to God and say yes to Him no matter what. Don't spend the rest of your life constrained by your own limitations. Trust and obey Him.

*Jesus, You are God. I step out in faith knowing You*
*always lead me in the best way possible. Amen.*

My hope is in Jesus because
His wisdom surpasses my own.

# POSSIBLE THROUGH YOU

*"He who believes in Me, the works that I do, he will
do also; and greater works than these he will do."*

JOHN 14:12

The idea that nothing is impossible for God should be very comforting to us. We can consider the parting of the Red Sea, the collapse of Jericho's walls, or the resurrection and realize that the Lord can overcome any problem for us. However, when it comes to God doing the miraculous *through* us, we may be more skeptical.

Yet when God formed you, He did so with a special design in mind. Jesus commanded believers to make disciples of the whole world (Matthew 28:18–20). He died on the cross so that people from every nation, tribe, and tongue can be saved. And He has a unique way He wants to work through you to achieve this.

British evangelist Henry Varley once said, "The world has yet to see what God can do with and for and through and in a man who is fully and wholly consecrated to Him."[1] God seeks believers who know that nothing is impossible with Him—who willingly follow Him with full trust and commitment. Friend, this can and should be *you*. You can have an astounding impact on the world. So obey Him and allow Him to do the impossible through You.

*Jesus, please work through me to
accomplish Your awesome will. Amen.*

My hope is in Jesus because
nothing is impossible through Him!

# SETTING YOUR IMAGINATION

*The mind set on the flesh is death, but the
mind set on the Spirit is life and peace.*

ROMANS 8:6

Our imaginations are a blessing from God. Unfortunately, because of humanity's fallen nature, they're susceptible to being corrupted by sin. We visualize what we want and imagine what we lust after. And then, when the Lord does not give us what our minds construct, we become frustrated and even angry with Him.

But the truth is, there's no legitimate place in our minds for ideas or fantasies that are contrary to His truth and will. To entertain such thoughts for even a moment is to set our minds on the flesh and therefore pursue sin. Understand, this is spiritual warfare at its most fundamental level—the enemy influences you through what you think (2 Corinthians 10:4–5). So when any deceitful, lustful, flesh-centered thought pops into your mind, the best thing you can do is recognize it for what it is. Call it a lie, refuse to think about it, and reset your mind on what is true. And do it immediately!

To win the battle here makes all the difference. So don't focus on sinful fantasies. Set your mind on the Spirit, and dedicate your imagination to bringing praise to His name.

*Jesus, purge my imagination of its fleshly fantasies
and help me to focus on You. Amen.*

My hope is in Jesus because He
is better than all I can imagine.

# ALL THINGS?

*God causes all things to work together for good to those who*
*love God, to those who are called according to His purpose.*

ROMANS 8:28

Have you ever experienced a difficulty that's utterly confounded you? You can't make sense of what's come to pass. Why in the world would the Lord allow what's happened, especially when you're trying to be faithful?

As you wrestle with such circumstances, here's a truth that can give you hope: the Lord is actively involved in everything you experience. Now, this does *not* signify that God always *instigates* the problems you face. Rather, it means He only permits adversity if there is some divine, eternal purpose He can achieve through it. You may not be able to see what His reason is, but you can fully trust that if you'll continue following Him in faith, eventually you'll see some worthwhile good come from your suffering.

God can work through all things that happen to you for your good and His glory. That's right—*all* things. There's nothing you can experience that He won't use to teach you something important. Therefore, take your hurts and confusion to the Lord. He wants to give meaning to your life, so allow Him to reveal His great purposes to you.

*Jesus, help me to understand all You wish to teach me. Amen.*

My hope is in Jesus because He uses
all things for my good and His glory.

# He Sustains

*On the glorious splendor of Your majesty and on
Your wonderful works, I will meditate.*

PSALM 145:5

Have you experienced the amazing, sustaining power of God's awesome presence? Have you waited before Him in silence, meditating on His strength, greatness, wisdom, and majesty? Have you learned how important it is to spend still, quiet moments before Him to give you strength for today and hope for tomorrow?

This is why David remained strong in every circumstance of life, no matter what happened—because of his abiding relationship with God. Throughout his life, David was able to cope with the extremely challenging and heartbreaking situations he faced because he experienced the power of being in the Father's presence daily. He wrote, "The LORD is near to all who call upon Him. . . . He will fulfill the desire of those who fear Him; He will also hear their cry and will save them" (Psalm 145:18–19).

So today, focus on Christ. Discover who He is and how much He loves you. Through uninterrupted times of sitting before Him, He will strengthen you, help you overcome, mature your faith, and use the trials you are experiencing for good. And that's exactly what you need to keep going.

*Jesus, help me to focus on You so I can experience
Your sustaining power. Amen.*

My hope is in Jesus because
He powerfully sustains me.

# DIRECTION

*"I do not seek My own will, but the will of Him who sent Me."*
JOHN 5:30

There are four questions we are wise to ask God daily:

1. *What do You want me to do?* God desires to reveal His will to you, so ask Him to show you His goals for the day. Be open to the promptings of the Holy Spirit and trust Him to guide you.
2. *How do You want me to act?* For everything that God desires to accomplish, He has a plan that is detailed and specific. So ask Him how to proceed with the objectives He has given you.
3. *When do You want me to act?* We often fail because we get ahead of God, so ask Him to help you stay on His schedule.
4. *How can I best represent You today?* The Lord will work through you to influence others, so ask Him to mold you into an even greater likeness of Christ as you carry out His will.

Listen closely for God's answers to your questions and then begin to act. In this way you know you are making the most of your day.

*Jesus, please show me what You want me to do and how, when, and in what manner You desire me to act so I can glorify You. Amen.*

My hope is in Jesus because
He leads me with wisdom.

# UNTO HIM

*"Well done, my good and faithful servant. You have been faithful in handling this small amount, so now I will give you many more responsibilities. Let's celebrate together!"*

MATTHEW 25:21 NLT

Many people promote themselves so that others will compensate them with raises, better job titles, or greater benefits. But as a believer, you can rest in the confidence that God is the One who rewards you in His timing and in the way that's right for you.

This means you don't have to be concerned about whether or not others see your good works or efforts. Jesus observes how you are serving and the attitude of your heart, and He will reward you in a way that brings you personal fulfillment and greater usefulness in His kingdom. And any responsibility you have or item on your job description—no matter how great or small—can be done "as for the Lord" and for His glory (Colossians 3:23–24). So do every task you're given as if you are doing it exclusively for Him.

Whatever your hands find to do, work with diligence, perseverance, and to the best of your ability, knowing your faithfulness and devotion are never wasted. Rather, you know God will see your work and reward you according to His riches.

*Jesus, knowing that You are the One who rewards me brings me hope. Thank You that my effort isn't wasted. Amen.*

> My hope is in Jesus because
> He sees me when others don't.

# OVERCOME FEAR

*When I am afraid, I will put my trust in You.*
PSALM 56:3

Today, don't deny your anxieties—you cannot just put them away as if they don't exist. Every one of us fears something at one time or another. Even the great saints of Scripture were afraid on occasion: Moses and Jeremiah feared their call to leadership (Exodus 3–4; Jeremiah 1). The psalms openly reveal David's concerns and apprehensions (Psalms 3; 27; 34; 55; 56). Timid Timothy had to be exhorted by Paul to continue his ministry (2 Timothy 1:6–8).

Notice that in today's verse, David said, "*When* I am afraid" (emphasis added). Fear *will* come. And when it does, confess it to God. Rather than refusing to admit your fears, acknowledge them and place your trust in God. Turn your gaze to your Rock, Jesus Christ.

A healthy fear of God—reverence, respect, and reliance upon Him—is your foremost weapon against worry. He is always trustworthy. He is always faithful. He will not fail or forsake you. You can count on Him. So place your trust in God's powerful presence. His great wisdom, power, strength, and love are your confidence. Dwell on Him—not your fears. And confess that no matter what comes against you, it is no match for the Lord your God.

*Jesus, I will trust You in all of my overwhelming and fearful circumstances because You overcome them all. Amen.*

My hope is in Jesus because
He is greater than all my fears.

# OVERCOME REGRET

*I acknowledged my sin to You . . . and*
*You forgave the guilt of my sin.*
PSALM 32:5

Are you wracked with misgivings about your past and fearful about your salvation? Do you wonder if God really forgives you? It's possible for believers to feel that they need to continually earn God's favor because of their remorse—possible, but not right. Is this your experience? Do you constantly feel guilty?

Understand, this is not God's will for you. He wants you to be free of guilt. And the way out of your misery is to receive His grace and extend it to others. Realize that when you beat yourself up, it doesn't add anything to your already perfect standing with your heavenly Father. Rather, you must believe once and for all that your faith in Christ's sacrifice on the cross has settled your sin debt— past, present, and future—forever. Your salvation is sure.

But then take one more step. As you have received His forgiveness, pass it along to all those who have offended you. Embracing God's grace to you and extending it to others will destroy guilt's destructive cycle—replacing it with an unceasing celebration of Christ's amazing, unconditional love.

*Jesus, thank You for forgiving me fully and taking away my*
*guilt. Help me to show the same grace to others. Amen.*

My hope is in Jesus because
He forgives me completely.

# OVERCOME JEALOUSY

*Where jealousy and selfish ambition exist,*
*there is disorder and every evil thing.*
JAMES 3:16

It is very painful when another person receives what you've been asking God for. And when jealousy surfaces, it can also stir up feelings of unworthiness, fear, and even rage. However, the emotional stranglehold of jealousy can be prevented when we understand God's principle of contentment.

Biblical contentment means we are grateful that God has given us everything we truly need. Others may be promoted while we wait. Others may have intelligence, strength, beauty, or talents, while we feel we are plain and mediocre. But we know that God, our Creator and Provider, has supplied us all we really need to carry out His eternal purposes for us.

Are you envious of others? Do you feel as if you have been given a raw deal while others seem to have an unending flow of God's favor? Your Savior gives you the full measure of grace needed for a productive, joyful life in the center of His will. So instead of comparing, start to embrace what He has given you and trust that the best is still ahead.

*Jesus, thank You for loving me specially and uniquely.*
*I will rejoice in Your specific will for my life. Amen.*

My hope is in Jesus because
His favor abounds to me.

# TRUST HIS TRUTH

*Set your mind on the things above,*
*not on the things that are on earth.*

COLOSSIANS 3:2

Perhaps the deepest yearning of your heart is to know God—to worship, serve, and please Him with everything in you. But before you trusted Jesus to be your Savior, you had trouble with anger, fear, lust, greed, or some other sin. Now, even with the great victory Jesus has given you, you are easily depressed because of the failings of your flesh.

So what can you do? You commit yourself to Bible study, prayer, memorizing Scripture, and reading books about your struggles, but nothing works. Temporary triumphs almost always lead to eventual relapse. It's a very frustrating circle of resolve and regret.

Understand that your struggle isn't just about improving your behavior but is about renewing your mind—changing how and what you think. God must completely replace your thought-life with His own. That takes not only time, but acknowledging that God is right even when you disagree with Him.

Do not be wise in your own eyes. Trust Christ's truth to set you free from your bondage to sin. Examine your response to the Lord and submit yourself to whatever He shows you.

*Jesus, forgive me for deciding that I am right and You*
*are wrong. Help me to accept Your truth fully. Amen.*

> My hope is in Jesus because
> He sets me free from sin.

# September

Let us hold fast the confession of our hope without wavering,
for He who promised is faithful.

Hebrews 10:23

# FREE THROUGH TRUTH

*Be renewed in the spirit of your mind.*

EPHESIANS 4:23

There may certainly be areas in your life where you want freedom, and as John 8:32 promises, "The truth will make you free." So how can you build truth into your life?

*First, rely on the instruction of the Holy Spirit.* The Spirit of truth alone can reveal the wounds in your life and bring transformative healing (John 14:17). He guides you to understand the otherwise inscrutable ways of God and how He meets your innermost needs. *Second, be committed to your study of Scripture.* From Genesis to Revelation, God's Word is your guide to abundant living—so do not neglect it. *Third, spend time in prayer.* It is through interaction with your heavenly Father that the Spirit and Word do their transforming work. Through prayer, He sifts your needs and desires, makes sense of your trials, and gives you His guidance. *Fourth, have the courage to act.* Truth can never be left on the table—it must be applied if you are to benefit from it.

In cultivating the disciplines explained above, your entire thought process can be conformed to God's pattern for living. You can learn the truth and be set free.

*Jesus, teach me Your truth and help me to walk*
*in the liberty You've provided for me. Amen.*

My hope is in Jesus because
He teaches me how to be free.

# CONTINUE IN THE LIGHT

*Continue in the things you have learned.*

2 TIMOTHY 3:14

Why is it we can be open to the truth but still walk in darkness—not having victory in key areas? Often it's because we fail to continue in the light that first brought us to an awareness of God's redemptive plan—simple faith in Him. Spiritual darkness encroaches when we grow indifferent to Him. And it can be so subtle that we're unaware of it happening through these almost imperceptible means:

*A shift from devotion to performance.* We move from trusting Jesus to work in us to dependence on what we do for Him.

*A gradual change from devotion to convenience.* We lose our commitment to honor Christ regardless of the cost. We make excuses and get stuck in our fleshly ways.

*A move from repentance to tolerance of sin.* As our love for and commitment to Jesus wanes, it becomes easier to settle into our sins instead of rejecting them.

Such shifts always frustrate our growth. So examine your life and make sure you haven't strayed from your simple faith in what God says. Then you will be certain to continue in His light and take hold of the victory He has for you.

*Jesus, please identify the areas where I have strayed*
*so I can continue to walk in Your light. Amen.*

> My hope is in Jesus because He
> shines His light in my darkness.

# VANQUISHING YOUR GIANTS

*The battle is the LORD's and He will give you into our hands.*

1 SAMUEL 17:47

Do you have a giant in your life—a problem bigger than you can possibly overcome in your own strength? Does it mock you in much the same way Goliath taunted the army of Israel? Then take this truth to heart today: *giants are given by God to show His power in your life.* And they were made to be vanquished.

How do you do so? *First, confront that giant.* David did not shrink from the challenge but rose up to meet Goliath. No victory is possible until you stop expecting defeat. *Second, realize your giant stands in opposition to the Lord.* Goliath wasn't just David's adversary; he was disparaging God's people—and therefore the Lord Himself. And He doesn't tolerate what opposes His will. *Third, since your giant is God's enemy, the battle is His.* You won't win this with your resources—you must depend on His weaponry: the armor of God, His Word, and the power of the Holy Spirit.

Do not fear your giant—it is nothing for your Mighty Warrior. So trust Him, and in His time and power, He will overcome your Goliath and give you the joy of victory.

*Jesus, thank You that my Goliaths are nothing to You.*
*You always win the battle and give the victory. Amen.*

> My hope is in Jesus because
> He overcomes all my giants.

# DEVELOPED FOR THE PROMISE

*You, O Lord God, have spoken; and with Your blessing*
*may the house of Your servant be blessed forever.*

2 SAMUEL 7:29

David was anointed by Samuel to be the next king of Israel, but he spent most of the next ten years fleeing from the sitting king, Saul. Why would God promise such great things to him and then allow him to experience such adversity?

Thankfully, we know that the Lord eventually fulfilled His promises to David. And as we face doubts about our own futures, we can trust God to operate on the same principles He used with him.

*First, God is in control.* No matter how far from the promises David seemed to be, the Lord was always orchestrating His details in the unseen. The same is true for you. *Second, He is working through all things for your good and His glory.* As with David, God understands what character qualities your future will require— and He allows circumstances that will strengthen you. *Third, God will bless others through your wilderness experiences.* Just as you can draw encouragement through David's story, God will hearten others through your testimony of His faithfulness.

So don't despair as you wait, but trust that just as He did with David, God knows what He's doing with you.

*Jesus, thank You that these challenges*
*are part of the process. Amen.*

My hope is in Jesus because He knows
how to prepare me for His great plans.

# SERVE LIKE JESUS

*"The Son of Man did not come to be served, but to serve."*
MARK 10:45

One of the most wonderful and impactful things we can learn through Jesus' earthly ministry is His unceasing commitment to servanthood. Though He is God, Christ humbly submitted Himself to minister to us. We should take note of this, especially since we are called to be conformed to His image. This means we should reflect these characteristics:

*Abiding*—If we are to serve others, we must have something to give them. As I often say, our intimacy with God determines the impact of our lives. Spend time with the Lord so you'll have something to contribute to others. *Awareness*—Are we alert to the needs of others and sensitive to their hurts, dreams, and troubles? *Acceptance*—One reason we may find it difficult to serve is we focus on others' faults. Instead, concentrate your efforts on loving them as Christ would. *Availability*—Do we make time for others?

Jesus taught that if man is to find his life, he must lose it (Matthew 10:39). That means giving yourself away in His name. So pour out your concern for others, because when you do, you'll certainly be conformed to His image.

*Jesus, help me to abide, be aware, accept, and be available so that I might help others and glorify You. Amen.*

> My hope is in Jesus because
> He is the best example.

# OUR GENEROUS GOD

*Every good thing given and every perfect gift is
from above, coming down from the Father.*

JAMES 1:17

The Lord our God has many wonderful attributes: He is loving, patient, merciful, gracious, forgiving, kind, good, and much more. Yet we would never know of any of those astounding qualities without Him demonstrating one very important trait—and that is *generosity*. Our magnificent God is astounding in how He freely gives us all good things.

Think about it—we have life because the Lord has created us by an exercise of His loving will. We can receive salvation only because He has graciously given it through Christ on the cross. And He explained in Ephesians 2:7 that He's given our redemption, "so that in the ages to come He might show the surpassing riches of His grace in kindness toward us in Christ Jesus." In other words, He saves us so He can give us even more throughout eternity.

So if you are struggling with your resources and needs today, remember that your God is the preeminent Giver. Look to Him— seek His face and His provision—and trust that He will supply not just your needs, but beyond your imagination (Ephesians 3:20–21).

*Jesus, thank You for giving so freely to me. I trust
Your loving and generous provision. Amen.*

My hope is in Jesus because He holds
nothing back when it comes to my good.

# TIME TO GO FORWARD

*There is a time for every event under heaven. . . .*
*A time to be silent and a time to speak.*

ECCLESIASTES 3:1, 7

You know that everything will be right in God's perfect timing. That when He calls you to wait, the wisest thing for you to do is be patient. And when He commands that you act, you must go forward in faith. But how can you know for certain when to tarry and when to launch out?

If you have done everything you know to discern God's leadership—being diligent in prayer, searching the Word, obtaining wise counsel, and submitting yourself completely to Jesus' lordship—and a decision arises that must be made, then you can go forward. Don't be anxious. Have faith that God "is at work in you, both to will and to work for His good pleasure" (Philippians 2:13). If you sincerely desire to honor the Lord, but make the wrong decision out of ignorance, trust that He will forgive you and steer you in the right direction.

When you must chart a course, place your confidence in the God who knows your future. Wait on Him until He makes the way clear, and then act boldly in faith by entrusting yourself to your faithful God.

*Jesus, thank You for showing me clearly when I*
*must wait and when I should go forward. Amen.*

My hope is in Jesus because
He is faithful to lead me.

# PRAY FOR OTHERS

*Devote yourselves to prayer.*

COLOSSIANS 4:2

Prayer is not only the wonderful way we communicate with God, but it's also how He develops our sense of mission—He gives us genuine compassion and burdens for the needs of others. We are admonished to intercede for leaders (1 Timothy 2:2); Christian workers (Matthew 9:38); the whole body of Christ—especially the persecuted church (Ephesians 6:18–20); Israel (Psalm 122:6); our enemies (Matthew 5:44); and the lost (Romans 10:1).

Perhaps most of our prayer time is usually spent on personal needs, but it is important to labor in prayer for the wisdom, welfare, and strength of those mentioned above because this is where the spiritual battles are won. That is why—when we begin earnestly interceding for others—we may find an increase in the spiritual warfare we experience. But we will also find a shift in our focus and how we perceive our own challenges. With less time spent on ourselves, prayer becomes the spiritual scalpel that lifts off the stifling layers of self-preoccupation. We are freed to heed Jesus' great command: "Love one another, just as I have loved you" (John 15:12) and develop His heart for this lost and dying world.

*Jesus, I pray for all these listed above, but specifically the lost. Lord, give me opportunities to share. Amen.*

> My hope is in Jesus because He empowers me to minister to others.

# THE RIGHT REASONS

*Many of His disciples withdrew and were*
*not walking with Him anymore.*

JOHN 6:66

In the beginning of Jesus' ministry, many people followed Him as He preached, ministered, and did miracles. But as the cross neared, only a few remained by His side. Most of the people returned to their everyday routines because they had sought Him for their own reasons—for healing, provision, or deliverance from Rome.

Of course, Jesus did cure their illnesses, but the real healing was achieved on the cross. Jesus did feed the hungry, but His ultimate purpose was to satisfy our spiritual hunger and thirst. Jesus did come to deliver us—but from Satan's grip, rather than earthly authority. We need to make sure we are following Jesus today, not just for His blessings, but because He is God, who truly knows what we need. Because there will come a time when there will be no visible sign of blessing—when every comfort may be removed and tribulation may come because of our faith in Him.

If you've followed Christ for any other reason than because He is the promised Messiah, you will be sorely disappointed. He is Lord and King of all creation, and He is worthy of your love, respect, and devotion. That is what will sustain you when the difficulties arise.

*Jesus, You are God and deserve my*
*full respect and devotion. Amen.*

My hope is in Jesus because
He is the living God.

# FIX YOUR GAZE ON THE GUIDE

*For Your name's sake You will lead me and guide me.*

PSALM 31:3

Do you ever fear that finding God's will for your life is like walking a spiritual high wire—one misstep and disaster awaits? That if you don't hear Him right, you'll suffer irreversible consequences?

Anxiety about discerning the Lord's path for your life can be paralyzing. But this isn't His intention. Certainly there is no evidence for it in Scripture—we never see Moses, David, or Paul panicking because they were unsure of His will. Rather than focusing on the need for direction, they fixed their gaze on their God and trusted His guidance. You are wise to do the same.

This is because even after meditating on Scripture, seeking counsel, and gathering facts, you will still be incapable of forecasting the future. But God knows what is ahead. And when you focus on Him, you will know He leads you well.

So today, view God's will in the context of your relationship with Christ. Seek to know Jesus in daily obedience and dependence, trusting Him as your Source and Sustenance. And as you draw near to your constant Guide and Companion, you will find direction and wisdom sufficient for every need.

*Jesus, I will fix my gaze on You, knowing You always lead me perfectly in every decision. Amen.*

> My hope is in Jesus because He leads me faithfully as I focus on Him.

# PRAY FOR THEM

*"Love your enemies and pray for those who persecute you."*
MATTHEW 5:44

Is there someone who has hurt you or irritated you? If so, have you prayed for that person? Usually the last thing we do for such individuals is intercede on their behalf. The temptation is usually to gossip or backbite. But have you ever considered why that's true? Of course, this is the natural response of our fallen nature, but there's actually an even more ominous force at work.

Our adversary, the devil, wants to keep strife brewing in the lives of believers. The enemy realizes that intercessory prayer is the supernatural weapon that can tear down strongholds of anger, bitterness, and hurt. As long as we refuse to pray for those who wounded us, he continues to have a foothold and can undermine your effectiveness for God's kingdom. By making sure you don't pray for the offender, he keeps you mired down and unlikely to grow in Christ's likeness.

So rather than attacking those who hurt you, mount an assault on the evil one through regular, sincere, forgiving, and loving intercession. Your petitions can spell the difference between freedom and bondage—for you and for them.

*Jesus, I pray for those who hurt me. Help me understand where they're coming from and how to minister to them. Amen.*

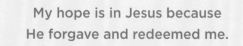

My hope is in Jesus because
He forgave and redeemed me.

# TRUE PROSPERITY

*"Sell your possessions and give. . . . For where*
*your treasure is, there your heart will be also."*
LUKE 12:33–34

In Luke 12:16–21, Jesus told a story about a rich farmer who hoarded his grain, accumulating his wealth for his own pleasure. This is the world's way to handle money. However, Jesus pointed out that the formula for true blessing is very different, and it's summed up with one word—*give*.

This may not make much sense. How can a person gain by giving away what he or she has? But in the Lord's eyes, giving is the key to true prosperity. This is because giving declares our dependence upon God as our only true Source. The person who greedily hoards wealth almost always sees his stockpile as his security. The open-handed person must instead trust in the Lord.

Giving is also the key to blessing because being generous reflects God's character. Our heavenly Father is lavish toward us— always providing what we truly need, even at great cost to Himself (Romans 8:32). When we give of our time, money, or love, we are providing a living example of His wonderful love to others.

So give. Show that Christ is your true treasure. Minister to others lavishly. And trust that God will provide you with true prosperity (Luke 6:38).

*Jesus, help me to be generous so others will believe in You. Amen.*

My hope is in Jesus because He is my treasure.

# PUTTING ON HIS CHARACTER

*Put on the new self who is being renewed to a true knowledge according to the image of the One who created him.*

COLOSSIANS 3:10

Throughout the New Testament, we are told that when we receive Jesus as our Savior, we are given a wonderful new identity that He's provided for us. We are accepted in His sight, belong to His family, and are competent for His every assignment.

So with this in mind, we are to put on the qualities that reflect His nature: compassion, kindness, humility, gentleness, patience, forgiveness, peace, and love (Colossians 3:12–15). Each virtue is a part of our new wardrobe of righteousness—given to us as gifts from God. However, we must decide whether or not we'll wear this heavenly attire. This is why Paul told us to "put on the new self" (v. 10). These spiritual garments are useless unless we choose to wear them.

How do you do that? You must trust that they are already yours and seek to honor God in your walk. You are "complete in Christ" (Colossians 1:28)—everything you need is provided by the indwelling Holy Spirit. So accept this, by faith, by thanking God for giving you His attributes. Choose to put them on and walk in a manner that honors Him.

*Jesus, I choose to reflect Your likeness.*
*Help me to walk in Your ways. Amen.*

> My hope is in Jesus because He clothes me with His righteousness.

# EMPOWERED TO TESTIFY

*Having obtained help from God, I stand to this day testifying.*
ACTS 26:22

Do you realize God can use you powerfully to proclaim the gospel and make disciples? Perhaps this is a somewhat intimidating thought to you—especially when you see other Christians who are fruitful in their ministries. But understand that the effectiveness of the gospel isn't about human talent, personality, or skill. Rather, it's about the power of God working through you.

This is why an effective ministry depends on a complete reliance upon the power of the Holy Spirit. People are born again by the Spirit of God, not the oratory of men. Only the Spirit of God can reach into people's souls, convict them of sin, regenerate them, and transform them.

Effective ministry also requires a focus on the Person of Jesus. The good news is His death, burial, and resurrection through which He bore the penalty for our sin and secured our pardon. When you share the gospel, you exalt Christ. And as He said, "I, if I am lifted up . . . will draw all men to Myself" (John 12:32).

The power of God is what brings people to salvation and helps them grow in their faith. So don't fear. Trust in Him to empower you and to lead others to know Him through you.

*Jesus, I exalt You. Help me to testify about You effectively. Amen.*

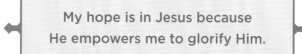

My hope is in Jesus because
He empowers me to glorify Him.

# IN JESUS' NAME?

*"Whatever you ask in My name, that will I do."*

JOHN 14:13

Why do we pray "in Jesus' name"? Some may use this phrase as the standard conclusion to their prayers and not really realize the significance of it. Praying in Jesus' name, however, represents the foundation of our prayer to and relationship with the Father. When we pray in His name, we pray according to:

*Jesus' access.* Christ's death atoned for our sins and ushered us into the presence of the Father. We can approach the Lord because He made us spiritually alive and able to interact with Him. *Jesus' advocacy.* Like an appointed court attorney, Christ represents us wisely and intercedes for us before the Father in a way that honors Him and blesses us. This isn't a blank check, but a call for His wise leadership. *Jesus' authority.* Our prayers are influential because Christ's sovereign power is at work on our behalf. The voice that spoke the universe into existence provides the way for His will to be carried out in our lives.

You pray in Jesus' name because it represents His access, advocacy, and authority. There is wisdom and power in your prayers because He carries them. So the next time you pray, remember that—and make sure to give Him the praise.

*Jesus, thank You for Your access, advocacy,*
*and authority in my prayers. Amen.*

My hope is in Jesus because
His name is above all others.

# WHOM YOU'RE TALKING TO

*"Your Father who sees what is done in secret will reward you."*
MATTHEW 6:4

Do you ever wonder what it is you should say to God? Of course, it's important to listen to Him and not just rattle off a laundry list of requests. But how can you engage Him respectfully when you approach Him?

In Matthew 6, Jesus provides you with a wonderful pattern for prayer. He begins with whom you're talking to: "Our Father who is in heaven" (v. 9). The focal point of prayer is intimate, loving fellowship with God—who is unfathomably wise, powerful, and loving.

Likewise, Jesus reminds you that He is to be respected: "Hallowed be Your name" (v. 9). Our relationship with the Father is one of reverence and adoration.

Therefore, as you approach God, show your love and respect for Him by listening; committing to what pleases Him; and sharing your innermost hurts, needs, and desires. God longs for companionship with you, and prayer is how you build your relationship.

So when you pray, start by focusing your attention on God's character: His love, mercy, holiness, power, and grace. Worshipping Him sets your heart to honor Him—magnifying His ability and presence, while diminishing the size and scope of your problems.

*Lord Jesus, I honor and worship You. Lead me into*
*a deeper relationship with You. Amen.*

My hope is in Jesus because
He is worthy of my respect.

# TRUSTING HIM FOR THE PATH

*"Your Father knows what you need before you ask Him."*
MATTHEW 6:8

Yesterday we discussed how Jesus' pattern of prayer has a God-centered focus—with reverence for the Lord of creation. Today we see that this attitude must continue when thinking about His will.

Jesus said, "Your kingdom come. Your will be done" (Matthew 6:10). As the Architect of our lives, God has eternal plans for us, and He communicates those through prayer. Once our minds and wills are in tune with God's, our focus can turn to our practical needs. "Give us this day our daily bread" (v. 11). This includes food, resources, and direction for our careers. We present our needs to the Father so He can reveal His will for receiving His provision.

Finally, Jesus' turns our hearts to our relationships: "Forgive us our debts, as we also have forgiven our debtors" (v. 12). Debts are our failures to obey God—either deliberately or unconsciously. So as we pray, we humble ourselves before Him to restore our fellowship and to extend mercy to others who have hurt us.

In all things, the Lord leads us to obey Him. And as our paths are molded to God's perfect pattern, we see His plans for us are formulated in perfect wisdom and love.

*Jesus, show me Your will for my life and*
*help me obey in every area. Amen.*

My hope is in Jesus because
He knows the path I should take.

# NOT INTO TEMPTATION

*Let no one say when he is tempted, "I am being
tempted by God"; for God . . . does not tempt anyone.*
JAMES 1:13

These last two days we've been discussing the Lord's pattern for prayer. The next point in Jesus' instruction is: "Do not lead us into temptation, but deliver us from evil" (Matthew 6:13). Of course, this may seem confusing, especially in light of James 1:13. Why would Jesus tell us to ask the Father not to guide us into situations where we would be enticed to sin when He'd never do so in the first place?

But the Greek word used here for *temptation, peirasmos*, means "to put to the test" or "to try one's character." It carries the idea of having our virtue, faith, and integrity proven genuine through adversity. So what Jesus is really instructing us to do is pray that the Lord will prevent us from going the wrong direction when we face tribulations—that God would stop us from responding to stressful situations in sinful ways that will harm us. Jesus is telling us to ask Him to uphold, strengthen, and protect us so that we won't fail Him. Certainly, this is a wise and worthy thing to pray. And as always, our Savior, who knows our failings, is looking out for our best interests.

*Jesus, thank You for instructing and upholding
me in times of trial and temptation. Amen.*

My hope is in Jesus because He
strengthens me in the difficulties.

# REMEMBER TO PRAISE HIM

*Sing praise to the LORD, you His godly ones,*
*and give thanks to His holy name.*

PSALM 30:4

In concluding His pattern for prayer, Jesus reminds us to always exalt God, saying, "Yours is the kingdom and the power and the glory forever. Amen" (Matthew 6:13). This is a declaration recognizing the Lord's supremacy and sovereignty. We give Him thanks, expressing all the ways He has been faithful to care for us. We declare our gratefulness that He is powerful, all-knowing, ever present, loves us unconditionally, and is always willing to lead us. And we give Him all the honor and glory for our successes.

This is His due as our God, but it is also vital to our well-being. Praise reminds us of our dependence upon Him, and the fact that no matter what issue we're facing, He is able to lead us to triumph in it. In fact, the Father already knows everything we need, and He is already at work delivering us. And if we respond with faith and trust in Him, the obstacles we face will result in our blessing and edification.

Therefore, like the apostle Paul, we can and should declare: "Thanks be to God, who gives us the victory through our Lord Jesus Christ" (1 Corinthians 15:57). So take time to praise Him today!

*Jesus, I praise You, recognizing Your supremacy and*
*sovereignty and how You always provide what's best. Amen.*

My hope is in Jesus because
He deserves my praise!

# THE PRIORITY

*"I will be found by you," declares the LORD.*
JEREMIAH 29:14

A sea captain was convinced the wreckage of an ancient, treasure-laden ship lay somewhere off the coast of Florida. Finally, after many years and setbacks and thousands of unsuccessful dives, the ship was located, abounding with priceless medallions and riches.

Seeking God requires similar convictions. We must be convinced that nothing is as valuable as our relationship with Jesus. He is the King of glory—worthy of any sacrifice He asks of us.

Until we recognize the incomparable worth of our life in Christ, we will seek other things before God—wealth, relationships, pleasure, or whatever it might be. So ask yourself: How important is your relationship with Jesus really? Do you hunger and thirst for Him?

Decide that God is the preeminent desire of your life and pursue Him. Daily, ask the Lord to speak to you through His Word. Pray without ceasing. Don't turn back from God, regardless of the disappointments or frustrations. And always obey faithfully.

That determination will set your spiritual sail even when the winds of circumstance are contrary.

*Jesus, You are my heart's desire, and I delight in You.*
*Reveal Yourself and Your will to me. Amen.*

My hope is in Jesus because He is
the King of glory and my God.

# SEEK FIRST

*"Seek first His kingdom and His righteousness,*
*and all these things will be added to you."*
MATTHEW 6:33

Why does God require us to seek Him? Why doesn't He just make Himself known without so much effort on our part? While it's not difficult for anyone to know the Lord, we must seek Him for two important reasons.

*First, seeking God is a demonstration of our faith in Him.* Because God wants an intimate relationship with you, He will place you in situations that require you to look beyond yourself for help and guidance. Hebrews 11:6 explains, "He who comes to God must believe that He is and that He is a rewarder of those who seek Him." When you pursue the Lord, you acknowledge both that He exists and that He has what you need. In other words, that He has the answer to your questions.

*Second, seeking God is a demonstration of your dependence upon Him.* The universe is upheld by His perfect power—He is the Creator and Sustainer of all. And when you diligently pursue Him, you declare your ultimate reliance upon Him for all things. You acknowledge that He is your Provider and that you're willing to relinquish control and lean on Him for your every need.

*Jesus, I believe You exist, have what I need, and*
*provide all I require. Reveal Yourself to me. Amen.*

My hope is in Jesus because
He is worthy of my pursuit.

# WHY WAIT?

*I waited patiently for the LORD; and*
*He inclined to me and heard my cry.*
PSALM 40:1

In our "on demand" age, the prospect of waiting for God to answer us may seem almost irrational. Why delay meeting our needs when we have options right in front of us?

Yet the benefits of waiting upon God far outweigh those of forging ahead apart from His involvement. Why? Because He knows the future and we don't. Our decisions are usually based on an incomplete assessment of our existing circumstances. We cannot see what is still to come or what is outside our influence. But God can. He knows how our choices today impact tomorrow.

Likewise, the Lord has a plan for your life, and His purposes for you far exceed anything you can come up with yourself. For example, rushing headlong into marriage or a business venture may fit your plan, but not His—and it may also be disastrous.

But when you wait for Him, you're demonstrating that you want to do His will above your own. Yes, waiting on God is tough, but that is precisely how your faith is strengthened and your inner character is molded into Christ's image. So regardless of how pressing your need may be today, remember that waiting on God is always well worth it.

*Jesus, I will wait—show me Your will. Amen.*

My hope is in Jesus because
He knows the best path for me.

# ACTIVE WAITING

*Wait for the LORD and keep His way.*
PSALM 37:34

The idea of waiting upon the Lord usually brings to mind the image of a bored person who's sitting restlessly in an uncomfortable reception area. The biblical concept, however, is quite different. Picture the daily, steadfast labor of a ship's captain, who continues doggedly on the course while knowing the journey's end is far away. He is active, committed, and focused on the destination. In other words, waiting on God is anything but idleness. It's doing all we've been given to do, yet trusting fully that God's answer is still to come.

Missionary Jim Elliot said, "Wherever you are, be all there." Be 100 percent committed to God regardless of where you are on the path to receiving His promises. Don't avoid responsibility or give in to despair—continue obeying Him faithfully.

Likewise, take small, trusting steps in the direction you believe God is leading you. For instance, if you think the Lord wants you on the mission field, then plan a short-term trip overseas or host international students. If you've been indifferent or apathetic while waiting for God's direction, begin trusting Him in ways that can ultimately reveal His greater plan.

*Jesus, I will continue faithfully in what You've given me to do—*
*actively waiting upon Your answer and provision. Amen.*

> My hope is in Jesus because
> He will answer me.

# Staying Sensitive

*Today if you hear His voice, do not harden your hearts.*

Hebrews 3:15

After we're saved, our hearts are meant to continually express the life of God—becoming continually more sensitive to Him. Yet we can all recall times when we haven't been able to discern His presence or experience His love and fellowship. This is not unusual, but if it persists, we need to answer three critical questions:

*Are we cultivating a personal relationship with Christ?* So much can get in the way of knowing Jesus intimately. But we were created to have a personal relationship with the Lord Jesus—and we must set Him as our priority. *Are we obeying what we know to do?* If we're not submitting to Christ daily, our spirits may ultimately grow numb to His call, which leads to stunted growth and failing faith. *Are we sincerely repentant of our sins?* When God convicts us of some behavior, attitude, pattern, or problem, we must humble ourselves and agree with Him—trusting Him for victory over it.

So consider: has your heart grown insensitive to Jesus' presence? Examine yourself by pondering these questions and confess any failures. Return to His loving presence with honesty, openness, and trust, and enjoy Him again.

*Jesus, I don't want to have a hard heart. Reveal what's making it insensitive to You and bring me back into Your loving presence. Amen.*

My hope is in Jesus because
He speaks to my heart.

# THE BLESSING OF FOCUSED TIME

*David spoke the words of this song to the Lord*
*in the day that the Lord delivered him.*

2 SAMUEL 22:1

Whether you feel afraid, lonely, hopeless, discouraged, or betrayed, the Psalms are a wellspring of comfort. Why? Because the refreshment of the Spirit flowed from David's pen as he faced some very difficult challenges but trusted in God. David focused on the Lord as He waited for Him to comfort, deliver, forgive, and provide for him.

And the Holy Spirit of God still speaks to our hearts through what David discovered. The key, of course, was that he sat and listened to the Lord. We would be wise to do the same. In *Mere Christianity*, C. S. Lewis wrote:

> The real problem of the Christian life comes . . . the very moment you wake up each morning. All your wishes and hopes for the day rush at you like wild animals. And the first job each morning consists simply in shoving them all back; in listening to that other voice, taking that other point of view, letting that other larger, stronger, quieter life come flowing in.[2]

Friend, don't miss God. Slow down, listen to Him and discover the comfort, strength, and encouragement David enjoyed.

*Jesus, I am listening. Speak to me, my Savior. Amen.*

My hope is in Jesus because
He is worthy of my focus.

# THE ONE WHO HELPS YOU

*He who is the blessed and only Sovereign, the King of kings*
*and Lord of lords, who alone possesses immortality and*
*dwells in unapproachable light, whom no man has seen or*
*can see. To Him be honor and eternal dominion! Amen.*

1 TIMOTHY 6:15–16

Are there times in your life when you're overwhelmed and every-thing assailing you just seems to be too much? All of us have experienced such a season at one point or another. Thankfully, there is a remedy. Whenever these times arise in your life, focus on the majestic deity of Christ, which can be a brook of spiritual refreshment for your hurting soul.

In today's marvelous verses you see who Jesus really is—the immortal King of all creation. Christ, who formed and rules over all things—oceans, continents, stars, and galaxies—is the One who helps you endure and triumph.

Therefore, today, instead of measuring your troubles against your limitations, think of them in terms of God's unfathomable power. Can He deal with it all? Does He have the resources to pull you through? Of course He can and does! You are weak, but He is strong—and His strength becomes yours as you trust Him.

*Jesus, thank You for helping and defending me. Fill*
*me with understanding of who You truly are. Amen.*

My hope is in Jesus because He is the
omnipotent One who unfailingly helps me.

# HE WILL TEACH YOU

*"They will not teach again, each man his neighbor and each man his brother, saying, 'Know the LORD,' for they will all know Me."*

JEREMIAH 31:34

Do you ever feel as if the victorious Christian life is a mystery—as if something about it is eluding you? Certainly, being a believer can become confusing, especially as "experts" tout their unique plans for enjoying the abundant life. They unwittingly communicate that if you could just learn certain secret principles of spirituality, then you could finally take hold of all the blessings Jesus has given you.

Scripture, however, tells a much different story—as you can see from today's verse. The Word of God is the full revelation of the Lord's character and ways, and through it God Himself teaches you to know Him. This was at the core of Paul's teaching concerning the vibrant Christian life: "Christ in you, the hope of glory" (Colossians 1:27). Living the rich new life Jesus has provided for you is not a mystery but a reality for you to welcome. As a loving Father, God Himself leads you and teaches you how to embrace it.

So take joy in this truth: Jesus is all you need. Listen to Him, obey Him, depend on Him in every detail, and you will certainly experience the abundant life He created you for.

*Jesus, thank You for teaching me how to*
*experience the abundant Christian life. Amen.*

My hope is in Jesus because He
teaches me all I need to know.

# EXPANDING YOUR CAPACITY

*Do you not know that you are a temple of
God and that the Spirit of God dwells in you?*

1 CORINTHIANS 3:16

How does God—the omnipotent, omniscient, omnipresent Lord of creation—reside in such limited bodies as ours? How does He function in our finite human temples?

We know that the Lord lives in us through His indwelling Holy Spirit. But this does not mean we receive a partial or small-scale portion of Him. As the third Person of the Trinity, the Holy Spirit is just as much deity as the Father and the Son. And He is infinitely adequate to meet all of our needs.

No, God isn't limited, but our ability to give ourselves over to Him is. In fact, Romans 1:17 teaches, "The righteousness of God is revealed from faith to faith." Which is why we must continually allow Him to grow our capacity to experience Him by taking the steps of faith He leads us to.

So as you confront challenges that stretch the boundaries of your trust in Him, understand that He's allowed them in your life so He can reveal Himself to you in greater measure. Trust Him. He wants you to experience His fullness.

*Jesus, thank You for revealing Yourself to me in
increasing measure as I grow in my faith. Amen.*

My hope is in Jesus because He
grows my ability to experience Him.

# IDENTIFIED

*If we have become united with Him in the likeness of His death,*
*certainly we shall also be in the likeness of His resurrection.*

ROMANS 6:5

In the first five chapters of Romans, Paul taught us that through Christ's sacrifice on the cross, we have been declared righteous once and for all. We are securely saved forever, and there's nothing more we need to do to achieve our salvation.

But then in Romans 6, Paul introduced a new concept that we must embrace by faith and apply if we desire to experience the victorious Christian life. It is the principle of *identification,* and it is the first step to becoming more than a conqueror through Jesus (Romans 8:37). *Identification* means that we have been recognized as His—we take on His death, burial, and resurrection in our own lives.

In fact, Paul used the act of baptism as an example: we are submerged in Jesus and saturated with His character and likeness—like when fabric is immersed in dye and irreversibly takes on a new color.

Are you so identified with Jesus? Can others look at you and unmistakably see Him? Yes, this means suffering as He did, but it also means experiencing the glorious resurrection life that your soul longs for. And that is certainly worthwhile.

*Jesus, I want to bear Your image in all things so I can*
*fully experience Your resurrection life. Amen.*

My hope is in Jesus because
He conforms me to His image.

# ATTITUDES OF MINISTRY

*Be sober in all things, endure hardship, do the*
*work of an evangelist, fulfill your ministry.*

2 TIMOTHY 4:5

As you serve God and minister to others today, keep these attitudes in mind:

*Fearlessness*: as Paul told Timothy, "God has not given us a spirit of timidity, but of power and love and discipline" (2 Timothy 1:7). Why? Because the wisdom and power of God are with you as you serve Him. There's no reason to fear. *Faithfulness*: be devoted in your relationship to Jesus—not relying only on others' insights into His Word, but on what He teaches you through prayer and Bible study. *Fruitfulness*: your ministry should be productive—both you and those you are serving should be growing spiritually. *Fervency*: your love and devotion to the Lord should be the heartbeat of your ministry. Your desire to serve Christ should be "boiling hot," which is the Greek word picture of the word *fervent*. Because, as I often say, your intimacy with God determines the impact of your life.

When you're *fearless*, others will follow; when you're *faithful*, you'll persevere; when you're *fruitful*, you'll be encouraged; and when you're *fervent*, you will do the eternal work your spirit longs to accomplish. So serve Him well today.

*Jesus, I want to glorify You! Help me to be fearless,*
*faithful, fruitful, and fervent as I serve You. Amen.*

> My hope is in Jesus because
> He gives me purpose.

# OCTOBER

We do not lose heart, but though our outer man is decaying, yet our inner man is being renewed day by day. For momentary, light affliction is producing for us an eternal weight of glory far beyond all comparison, while we look not at the things which are seen, but at the things which are not seen; for the things which are seen are temporal, but the things which are not seen are eternal.

2 CORINTHIANS 4:16–18

# CONFESSION

*If we say that we have fellowship with Him and yet walk
in the darkness, we lie and do not practice the truth.*

1 JOHN 1:6

When Jesus died on the cross, He paid the debt for all the sins of the world. That means He died for the sins you committed *yesterday*—all your past transgressions. Likewise, He died for the sins you committed *today*—wherever you violate His Word, you are pardoned through Christ's sacrifice. It also means He died for the sins you'll commit *tomorrow*—regardless of what mistakes you make in the future, Jesus still accepts you.

In other words, your sin after salvation does not affect your *eternal standing* before God. Rather, what sin does is *disrupt your communion with Him*. You cannot walk with the Lord and continue in ungodly ways—those are two divergent paths. So if you want to be close to your Savior, it's imperative that you choose to walk in *His* direction.

With this in mind, the act of confession takes on a very important role. The Greek word for *confess* means "to agree." You acknowledge that God is right about your ungodly behavior so you can get on His path. So do it! Confess what displeases Him so you can know Him and serve Him better.

*Jesus, reveal all I need to confess so
I can walk with You always. Amen.*

My hope is in Jesus because
He corrects my course.

# STOP TRYING; START TRUSTING

*Having begun by the Spirit, are you
now being perfected by the flesh?*

GALATIANS 3:3

Have you ever heard that old Puritan motto, "If at first you don't succeed, try again"? Many believers not only know it, but they apply it to the Christian life. If they fail to conquer certain habits, they buckle down and try again.

Perhaps this is the way you've been living the Christian life. But maybe you've also learned that determination alone is not enough to overcome the stronghold of sin. You just keep hitting brick walls. The good news is that admitting you can't do it on your own is the first step toward a truly abundant life. You must come to the end of your own efforts, acknowledging that you can do nothing apart from Christ (John 15:5).

The only way to overcome sin is to allow Jesus to set you free from it. This means you do it *His way*—not yours. Yes, endurance is key. But you persevere in listening to Him, doing as He says, and allowing Him to transform your mind (Romans 12:2).

So stop trying and start trusting. He will lead you to a consistently satisfying Christian walk and set you free from all that holds you hostage.

*Jesus, my own efforts don't work, so I will
trust You to set me free from sin. Amen.*

> My hope is in Jesus because
> He leads me to freedom.

# PROVING US TRUE

*Even if I have to die with You, I will not deny You!*

MARK 14:31

If you had done an assessment of Jesus' disciples before His arrest and crucifixion, no doubt you would have found Peter to be impressively faithful. As you see in today's verse, Peter was consistent in voicing his trust in Jesus.

But when Christ was arrested and began the journey to the cross, Peter failed Him by denying his Lord. Peter may not have realized it, but he was accustomed to relying on his own strength, wisdom, and talents. And when confronted with the reality of Calvary, Peter's confidence crumbled—exposing the point of weakness in his faith.

Thankfully, Jesus did not give up on Peter. In fact, He continued to work on His disciple until Peter truly valued and trusted Christ above His own life. Jesus proved Peter's confession true, "Even if I have to die with You, I will not deny You!"

But understand, this is His goal with you as well. You will face challenges that force you to stop relying on your own resources so you can embrace all that Jesus longs to impart to you. So when you fail in your strength, don't despair. Jesus is exposing the weaknesses in your faith and teaching you to truly rely on Him.

*Jesus, thank You for proving my faith in You true. Amen.*

My hope is in Jesus because He
develops genuine faith in me.

# FORGIVE FOR GOOD

*You meant evil against me, but God meant it for good*
*in order to . . . preserve many people alive.*

GENESIS 50:20

When a person hurts us deeply, forgiveness can be difficult because of the intensity of the pain we feel. Only when our focus shifts from our suffering to God's sovereign work can we genuinely forgive.

We see this in the story of Joseph. As you may recall, his brothers sold him into slavery. When Joseph ascended to an exalted position of leadership in Egypt, those same brothers became afraid he would take revenge. Trembling, they asked Joseph's forgiveness. Thankfully, his response demonstrated his confidence in God's guidance and provision in the face of injustice.

But what's important for you to see in this example is that even the deliberate wounds of others cannot foil God's purposes for your life. He can integrate even the worst pain of betrayal into the rich fabric of His plan for you. And when you freely forgive, you liberate yourself to experience His love, grace, and mercy.

So in all your hurts, focus your attention on God's sufficiency. He can and will use what you've experienced for good if you allow Him to forgive others through you as He has forgiven you.

*Jesus, I will forgive. Thank You for working*
*through everything for good. Amen.*

> My hope is in Jesus because
> nothing can thwart His plans for me.

# RIGHTLY RELATED

*The one who loves God should love his brother also.*

1 JOHN 4:21

God has arranged the Christian life so that our relationship with Him is inseparably linked with our relationships to others. This is evident in the command He gives us in Matthew 5:23–24, "If you are presenting your offering at the altar, and there remember that your brother has something against you, . . . first be reconciled to your brother, and then come and present your offering." In other words, don't mistreat others and then expect Him to accept your spiritual offerings—honor Him in a practical way first.

Our earthly relationships ultimately reflect *how we would treat God Himself* (1 John 4:20). Remember, Jesus said, "To the extent that you [served] one of these brothers of Mine . . . you did it to Me" (Matthew 25:40). He places other people in our lives for His purposes, and if we reject them, we are ultimately rejecting Him.

Of course, we should never condone sinful behavior. But our focus should be on how *we* behave toward others and how *we* live out our faith in God in practical ways. We cannot shut ourselves in the prayer closet and then treat others—who are made in His image—badly. We must be loving to everyone as if we are relating to Jesus Himself.

*Jesus, it is often difficult to love others. Please fill me with Your love so I can honor You. Amen.*

My hope is in Jesus because
He teaches me to love.

# HE IS SUPREME

*By Him all things were created, both in the heavens
and on earth, visible and invisible, whether thrones
or dominions or rulers or authorities—all things
have been created through Him and for Him.*

COLOSSIANS 1:16

In Colossians 1, as Paul described Jesus' power and deity, he continually focused on Christ's superiority and supremacy. Why did he do so? Because he was reminding us of who it is we are living for and serving—who is the actual Ruler of all.

As believers we may reduce this down to where Jesus should fit into our priorities: we give time and resources to Christ first, family second, church third, job fourth, and so on. But Paul was telling us that Jesus is preeminently above and beyond everything in all creation *in authority.* That "He is the image of the invisible God" (v. 15) and has "first place in everything" (v. 18). Yes, Jesus is to be first in our work, homes, finances, relationships, and the rest. But Jesus doesn't merely fit in line with those other priorities—He must *rule over them.* And His will should come before our own.

So today consider: Is Christ the undisputed Lord over all of your life, reigning supreme? Is He leading or are you?

*Jesus, I want You to have the right place in my life—for
You to rule. To You be all honor and glory. Amen.*

My hope is in Jesus because
He rules over all.

# FORGIVE YOURSELF

*I am . . . not fit to be called an apostle, because I persecuted the
church of God. But . . . His grace toward me did not prove vain.*

1 CORINTHIANS 15:9–10

There is an old saying that instructs, "Be easy on others and hard
on yourself." To a point, it is a wise guideline. However, when it
comes to forgiveness, it can be disastrously misapplied, especially
when we are the ones at fault. An inability to forgive ourselves can
lead to deep discouragement, guilt, and hopelessness.

If anyone had a reason to judge himself harshly, it was the
apostle Paul. What if Paul had allowed his past as a persecutor of
the church to haunt him after his dramatic conversion to Christ?
Could he possibly have shared the good news of salvation so boldly,
passionately, and persistently? And David—what if he had dwelt on
his sin with Bathsheba, deeming himself unworthy of ever again
serving God? Could he have continued leading Israel with such
faith and conviction?

In each case, their refusal to forgive themselves would have had
disastrous consequences. The same is true for you. So don't be so
hard on yourself when it comes to forgiveness. Repent and accept
that Jesus not only welcomes you back gladly but restores you fully.

*Jesus, I repent of my sins. Thank You for forgiving
me, and help me to forgive myself. Amen.*

My hope is in Jesus because
He restores me fully.

# FIND FORGIVENESS

*Draw near to God and He will draw near to you.*

JAMES 4:8

Picture a son and a father in a heated argument. Upset, the son walks away angry and hurt. Days later, he still refuses to talk to his father—partly out of pride, but also out of fear he won't be accepted. Have you ever experienced a similar pain of separation—where you not only wish to be proven right but also long to be accepted back into a loving relationship?

When you receive Jesus as your Savior, one of the greatest privileges you are given is unhindered fellowship with God. Sadly, when you sin, your intimacy with the Father is broken. Like the angry son in the illustration, you want to be right—you want your own way. On the other hand, the shame of sinning against God may fill you with fear that He won't accept you. This naturally creates a separation between you and Him.

The answer to your conflicted feelings is *confession*—agreeing with the Father that He is right—because that is how your fellowship with Him is restored. When you live with unconfessed sin, your pride and shame separate you from the One your heart longs for, and that's painful. But God always wants you back. So go to Him and let Him heal your soul.

*Jesus, I agree with You—thank You for forgiving my sin. Amen.*

> My hope is in Jesus because
> He willingly forgives my sin.

# FINDING CONTENTMENT

*Godliness with contentment is great gain.*

1 TIMOTHY 6:6 NKJV

You may be a believer, but are you content in your Christian life? Have you discovered:

*That God has already provided all you need for a fulfilled life?* The Lord is the Giver of all good things, so contentment in the Christian life comes from realizing that He will always supply all of your essential needs.

*That the meaning and purpose you long for comes from Christ, not external circumstances?* You may feel happy when things are going right. But what happens when your situation turns sour? True contentment is based on knowing that no matter how things appear, God is in control, and He will carry out His plans for you.

*That life on earth is not as good as it gets—there is more for you in eternity?* In your present situation, joys may be mingled with sorrows, but one day pain and tears will be eliminated. The best is unquestionably yet to come!

So today, decide to be content with the assurances that God will provide for you, will carry out His wonderful plans for you, and is providing an everlasting home for you in heaven. Because certainly, a godly life with a joyful demeanor is great gain indeed.

*Jesus, thank You for providing all I need to be content. Amen.*

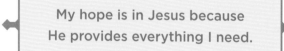

My hope is in Jesus because
He provides everything I need.

# FASTING FOR SPIRITUAL NOURISHMENT

*"When you fast, anoint your head and wash your face . . . and your Father who sees what is done in secret will reward you."*

MATTHEW 6:17–18

There are two common misconceptions when it comes to fasting. One is that our abstinence from food somehow impresses God and wins His favor. But Jesus condemned the Jews of His day because they weren't actually honoring the Lord—they were promoting themselves (Matthew 6:16). Likewise, if we fast to earn or prove our own holiness, we will be disappointed.

The other mistake believers make is to think that fasting is only an Old Testament practice. But we see throughout the New Testament (Matthew 4:2; Acts 13:2–3) that this is because fasting is meant to heighten our sensitivity to God's presence. In so doing, it is a valuable aid in worshipping the Lord and hearing His voice.

Fasting helps us concentrate on Christ and seek His will. By denying ourselves, we are demonstrating that we want His ways and desire His answers. We want to know Him more intimately, follow Him more obediently, and "not live on bread alone, but on every word that proceeds out of the mouth of God" (Matthew 4:4).

*Jesus, help me to hear and know You better. Amen.*

My hope is in Jesus because He satisfies my spiritual hunger.

# BURDENED

*When I heard these words, I sat down and wept and . . .*
*was fasting and praying before the God of heaven.*

NEHEMIAH 1:4

Nehemiah is a tremendous example of how God uses prayer burdens to unleash His power in others' lives. Nehemiah received a report from Jerusalem that its citizens were distressed, and its walls were in ruins. Hearing this made him weep and seek God's wisdom.

Likewise, when the Lord burdens your heart with His concerns, you may be surprised at how deeply it touches you. He may bring to your mind an individual, a group of people, or a situation that you connect with deeply on a spiritual level. Such burdens will force you into a new sense of dependence upon God because you know that only He can provide a solution.

Nehemiah wept, prayed, and fasted for the Lord's intervention for the people of Jerusalem, and three months passed before Nehemiah could do anything about it. Like Nehemiah, at times we must persevere in interceding for the burdens God places on our hearts.

So do you have a burden for someone in your life? Are you willing to pay the price for what God has placed on your heart? Friend, persevere. And like Nehemiah, you will see the Lord's glorious provision.

*Jesus, for this burden You've placed*
*on my heart—make a way! Amen.*

My hope is in Jesus because He answers
the burdens He places on my heart.

# HANDLING OPPOSITION

*David continued to succeed in everything he
did, for the LORD was with him.*

1 SAMUEL 18:14 NLT

After God gave David a great victory, something unexpected happened. King Saul turned against the young warrior. David's popularity unleashed a deadly strain of jealousy in Saul. Saul's envy was, of course, unfounded. Although David had been anointed as the next king and had popular support, he never did anything to undermine Saul. David simply lived such an exemplary and godly life that the nation was drawn to him. And Saul hated it.

Perhaps you find yourself in a similar situation. God gives you a victory, and all of a sudden opposition rises up against you from an unexpected place. Do not think it strange or become discouraged. Instead, take David's quiet example to heart. Do not defend your rights or become resentful; rather, behave wisely in all your ways. Maintain your confidence in God, fulfill your responsibilities, and respect those in authority—even if they are the ones attacking you.

Why? Because then the underlying theme of David's life will become yours as well: "The LORD was with Him." God will fight for you just as He did for David (Isaiah 54:17).

*Jesus, thank You for defending me. Help me to trust
You, to fulfill my responsibilities, and to respect those
in authority so that You will be glorified. Amen.*

My hope is in Jesus because He is with me.

# BATTLE IN PRAYER

*"Keep watching and praying that you may not enter into temptation; the spirit is willing, but the flesh is weak."*

MATTHEW 26:41

Do you realize that prayer can be a battleground where the fight of faith is carried out? Do you recognize that your adversary, the devil, is on the rampage, seeking to wreak havoc in your life? This is why prayerless believers are often in danger of living defeated Christian lives—because they are easy prey for the enemy. It is only by maintaining a strong, intimate relationship with God that we are able to overcome his assaults.

So consider: Is there a sin that has a stranglehold on you? Have you fallen in a certain area so many times that you have almost written off the victorious Christian life?

If your answer to any of the above is "yes," then realize your enemy has a foothold in your life. But do not despair—you can have freedom from it! Engage the battle in prayer! By the authority of Jesus' name, the power of His shed blood, and the leadership of the Holy Spirit, go with confidence to the throne of grace. Pray and listen to your God. He will certainly give you the victory that was already won for you by Christ at Calvary.

*Jesus, make me a prayer warrior and give me victory over the enemy's strongholds. Amen.*

My hope is in Jesus because He leads me to triumph over the enemy.

# THE COMFORT OF HIS PRESENCE

*"The Comforter . . . will . . . bring all things to your
remembrance, whatsoever I have said unto you."*
JOHN 14:26 KJV

Loneliness strikes almost everyone at one point or another. We can be popular and still miserably lonesome—feeling as if no one truly loves or understands us. The danger during such times is that we'll seek comfort in things or people that God never meant for us to be around—or that we'll turn so far inward that we sink deeper into despair.

But understand that God has given us His Holy Spirit to answer that profound need in our innermost parts. The Spirit is the Lord's permanent presence in our lives—our guarantee of His intimate friendship and ever-present help. No matter what our trials, the Helper is available to strengthen, encourage, and enable us.

You are never left without hope. So if you're feeling alone today, realize that He understands the pain you feel over crushed dreams and the disappointments you are facing because of others' broken promises. But the Holy Spirit doesn't stop there—He also heals your wounds and binds up your broken heart. So look to the friendship, help, and comfort of God's Holy Spirit. He is your best Friend—the One who will never leave you or forsake you.

*Jesus, thank You for always being with
me through Your Holy Spirit. Amen.*

My hope is in Jesus because His
constant presence comforts me.

# TO HOPE OR NOT?

*"Do not fear, for I am with you . . . I am your God.
I will strengthen you, surely I will help you, surely I
will uphold you with My righteous right hand."*

ISAIAH 41:10

Have you ever thought to yourself, *This is hopeless*? We all encounter seemingly impossible trials. But when we do, we must always make a decision: will we believe God's Word, or will we deny the truth of Scripture? The Bible testifies repeatedly that no matter how desperate your situation may appear, you can always count on the limitless resources of your Mighty God for your deliverance. Either you believe it or you don't.

You are not hopeless, "because greater is He who is in you than he who is in the world" (1 John 4:4). Is there anyone or anything that can overcome the One who created the heavens and the earth? Of course not! And you are promised His wisdom, strength, love, and counsel every step of the way. He knows the end from the beginning and works to accomplish His good and perfect will in and through you. He will lead you triumphantly to the finish line.

So today, decide to believe His Word above your own senses or understanding. Your Savior is the God of all hope, and He is yours forever.

*Jesus, I believe You above all else. I will trust You. Amen.*

> My hope is in Jesus because He is
> always with me in every situation.

# HUMBLE YOURSELF

*Humble yourselves under the mighty hand of God,*
*that He may exalt you at the proper time.*
1 PETER 5:6

There are pitfalls in life that we can avoid if we take precautionary steps. For example, we may be able to sidestep financial debt if we'll commit to living within our means. Likewise, it's possible to avoid certain obesity-linked illnesses if we're careful with our diet and exercise.

The same is true spiritually. Proverbs 16:18 reveals, "Pride goes before destruction." When we're conceited—or self-important—we're headed toward spiritual disaster. But we can circumvent the pitfalls of pride if we'll humble ourselves before God.

What that means is that we actively consider how dependent we are upon the Lord—we recognize how lowly we are in comparison to His sovereignty and magnificence. We may be smart, but how wise is God? We may be important, but how significant are we when standing before the King of kings?

In other words, we have worth and value, but as His handiwork, let us give our Creator the respect and honor He is due and humble ourselves before Him. Certainly that will keep us from pride—from becoming a god in our own eyes.

*Jesus, I humble myself before You—the King of kings. You are*
*sovereign, above all, and worthy of my devotion. Amen.*

> My hope is in Jesus because He is
> worthy of my respect and devotion.

# FRUSTRATIONS

*The creation was subjected to frustration, not by its own choice,*
*but by the will of the one who subjected it, in hope that the*
*creation itself will be liberated from its bondage to decay and*
*brought into the freedom and glory of the children of God.*

ROMANS 8:20–21 NIV

What frustrates you? Whether it's an area of life that just won't work for you, an aggravating relationship, or whatever else it might be, we're all forced to deal with irritations—areas where we just can't have our way. However, to deal with them successfully, we must realize that they've been given to help our spiritual growth.

The things that irritate you reveal what's really in you. So each time you're confronted with a circumstance that tries your patience, you have a choice to either lay down your personal rights or fight for them. In other words, you can either deny yourself and yield to the lordship of Christ or continue to battle in your own strength. Your choice will either advance your spiritual growth or neutralize it.

Instead of continuing in frustration and defeat, accept those irritations as the Lord's agents that scrape away the layers of pride and selfishness in you and reveal the liberated child of God you were created to be.

*Jesus, I choose to submit to You and grow spiritually. Amen.*

My hope is in Jesus because
He liberates and matures me.

# DYNAMIC DOCTRINE

*"Why do you call Me, 'Lord, Lord,' and do not do what I say?"*
LUKE 6:46

As you know, sound doctrine and a proper view of Scripture are crucial if we desire to have a correct understanding of who Jesus is as our Savior. Because of this, we must always hold on to our convictions and be careful never to abandon them.

However, where we often fall short is not in what we *believe* but in how we *act*. Our theology will never be complete until we live it out dynamically. There must be a fusion of our doctrine with who we are.

This means you may say you believe Jesus is truly God, but until you put Him first in every facet of your existence—until you really act as though He is Lord and obey His commands in practical ways—you will just be paying Him lip service.

So consider: Does Jesus have the final word as you make decisions, spend money, or plan for the future? When you interact with others, do you love them as He would? Is there anything that is more important to you than He is?

As your Sovereign Lord, Jesus demands total obedience and absolute surrender. So live it out—make Him first. And don't just talk about good doctrine—be a living example of it.

*Jesus, may my life be a dynamic example
that demonstrates You are truly God. Amen.*

My hope is in Jesus because He is truly God.

# RESTRAINING PASSIONS

*God's will is for you to be holy, so stay away from all sexual sin.*
1 THESSALONIANS 4:3 NLT

Beginning as a tiny rivulet in northern Minnesota, flowing through the heartland, and ending in the Gulf of Mexico, the Mississippi is America's mightiest river. Its swift currents could easily flood massive areas of land and cause terrible destruction if it were not for the system of earthen and cement banks that restrict its thundering flow.

Like the great Mississippi, we have a river running through us that can cause destruction if not properly restrained. Although sex is a gift God has given us for both procreation and pleasure, it has been provided for us to enjoy within the bounds of marriage. If allowed to flourish outside this commitment through adultery, fornication, pornography, or other sexual sins, there are always consequences. It may not seem like such a big deal to begin with, but like the Mississippi, the results of permitting our passions to flow without the restraints of God's commands will eventually allow them to gain destructive strength that we'll be powerless to harness.

First Corinthians 6:18 (NLT) is clear: "Sexual immorality is a sin against your own body." Don't hurt yourself. Instead, learn from God, obey Him, and trust Him to restrain the river of passion within you.

*Jesus, help me overcome the lure of lust so I can honor You. Amen.*

My hope is in Jesus because He protects me through His commands.

# OVERCOMING WEARINESS

*Let us not lose heart in doing good, for in due
time we will reap if we do not grow weary.*

GALATIANS 6:9

Have you ever felt spiritually weary—as if your capacity to experience Jesus' provision has been drained? This kind of fatigue hits everyone. In the pursuit to serve Christ, we can reach an overload point. If severe enough, our spiritual fatigue can paralyze us.

So how do you take hold of God's strength to endure? *First, you must repent.* "Lay aside every encumbrance and the sin which so easily entangles" (Hebrews 12:1). Why? Because unconfessed sin will wear you out. Get rid of it. *Next, cast your burdens on the Lord* (Psalm 55:22). Obey Him by refusing to carry anything He has not given you to bear. *Third, believe "that He is a rewarder of those who seek Him"* (Hebrews 11:6). God promises that your toil will be recompensed—so have faith that harvesttime will come. *Fourth, "do not worry about tomorrow"* (Matthew 6:34). Trust God one day at a time. This race can only be run step-by-step.

In other words, draw near to God—repent, obey, believe, and trust Him. For then you will be able to draw from His unlimited power supply and endure the journey.

*Jesus, help me to draw near Your supernatural strength. Amen.*

> My hope is in Jesus because He
> provides all I need for the journey.

# LEARN WHO YOU ARE

*As he thinks within himself, so he is.*

PROVERBS 23:7

Our usual defense against sin may be to recommit ourselves to personal disciplines and holiness. We may believe that through raw determination we can stem the tide of impure thinking or behavior. But if you've been a believer for a while, you know that the battle against temptation is not only unrelenting but can also be terribly discouraging. Thankfully, God has provided a defense for us—and it's a radical departure from how we usually fight (2 Corinthians 10:4–5).

How do we confront the onslaught of immorality we experience every day? *We must understand our new identity in Christ.*

Consider this example: You are putting together a model airplane. The box cover portrays a small plane, but you realize that the tools included are a jackhammer and a bulldozer. There's no way for you to build that delicate plane with the industrial tools you have. This is exactly what happens when you try to behave like Jesus in your earthly strength and with human tactics.

Thankfully, you are a new creation—different from your former self, spiritually alive, and eternal. And you have all you need for victory. So take hold of the tools you need to be *like* Christ by understanding your new identity *in* Christ.

*Jesus, teach me who I am in You so I can be like You. Amen.*

My hope is in Jesus because
He makes me brand-new.

# AN ETERNAL VIEW

*We look not at the things which are seen, but at the things*
*which are not seen; for the things which are seen are*
*temporal, but the things which are not seen are eternal.*

2 CORINTHIANS 4:18

Driving through a dense fog can be disorienting. Limited visibility requires a firm grip on the steering wheel and your focused attention on the road ahead. Such conditions can make a trip emotionally and physically draining.

Of course, the same can seem true about the Christian life this side of heaven—it may appear unsure and confusing, like that drive in the fog (1 Corinthians 13:12). We don't see clearly. This fallen world and our limited spiritual visibility can blur the reality of our eternal destination and can make our daily walk difficult.

But understand that even though you may not *see* what God is accomplishing, you can know for certain that *His plan is wonderful.* You are being conformed to the image of Christ, and the Lord is achieving eternal things through you. So center your attention on the fact that though you do not see, *God does*, and what He's accomplishing in you is glorious. Taking hold of that truth will help keep you on track and energized for the challenges you face.

*Jesus, I trust Your vision even when mine fails.*
*Thank You for leading me perfectly. Amen.*

> My hope is in Jesus because
> He clearly sees all that is ahead.

# BLESSED BY BROKENNESS

*"If you return, then I will restore you . . . ; and if you extract the*
*precious from the worthless, you will become My spokesman."*
JEREMIAH 15:19

Something unique happens when people undergo trials. They are broken in spirit—they come to a place where they're confronted with their own inadequacy, sin, and self-will. Then, in total desperation, stripped of all their devices and contingency plans, they look to God and recognize their complete dependence upon Him.

Have you come to such a place? Then realize that a person who has been broken has a greater potential to serve God with superior authority, fruitfulness, and productivity than even the most talented person who has never experienced that level of humble dependence upon Him. This is because the by-products of brokenness are spiritual growth, sensitivity, and godly character.

So today, take heart in the fact that the God who calls you by name is in complete control of your circumstances, and He has your best interests at heart—even in the places where you feel broken. He is fitting you for His service. Therefore, even if you cannot see His loving hand guiding you or evidence of spiritual growth, let the trial you're facing have its perfect work in your life.

*Jesus, I trust You to grow me spiritually. Thank*
*You for training me for Your purposes. Amen.*

My hope is in Jesus because
He knows how to build me up.

# CLOSED OFF

*He who separates himself seeks his own desire,*
*he quarrels against all sound wisdom.*

PROVERBS 18:1

Are you tempted to build an impenetrable wall around your life? Do you keep other people out so you can maintain the impression that you have your act together—that you're strong and unaffected by the things that disturb others?

Realize that in building this wall, you put yourself in opposition to God's intended work through you. You actually position yourself for adversity. This is because you are operating by the world's system, which views others as adversarial.

But in God's kingdom, we are called to "pursue the things which make for peace and the building up of one another" (Romans 14:19). In other words, we "rejoice with those who rejoice, and weep with those who weep" (Romans 12:15). You need encouragement from others so sin will not get a foothold in your life (Hebrews 3:13). Likewise, when you've passed through difficulties, you have comfort and wisdom to share with others (2 Corinthians 1:3–4).

So don't close yourself off. Allow God's people to edify you in your time of need so that you can be a light to them as well.

*Jesus, there are areas of my life that are difficult*
*to share. Reveal who I can trust. Amen.*

My hope is in Jesus because He
gives me a loving support system.

# FACING PERSECUTION

*Persecuted, but not forsaken; struck down, but not destroyed.*

2 CORINTHIANS 4:9

If you are truly living for the Lord, you can expect to encounter persecution—spiritual battle is a normal part of the Christian life (Ephesians 6:10–20). This is not adversity that arises due to any disobedience on your part; rather, it actually occurs because of your faithfulness to God (1 Peter 4:12–13). That may seem unfair to you, and you might be tempted to give in to fear or despair. But always remember that God is in control, and if He's allowed this hardship in your life, He most likely has a bigger plan in mind.

For example, when persecution broke out against believers in Jerusalem, they scattered throughout the Roman Empire—and so did the gospel. The good news spread like wildfire as a by-product of it.

So as you face harassment, don't try to defend yourself or figure your own way out; instead, trust God wholeheartedly. Keep your focus on the Lord—who has not left you or forsaken you, but is working through you for His greater purposes. And stand firm in His strength, knowing that the battle is His to fight. Because if you're where God has called you to stand, you can expect to be victorious, no matter what the outcome is.

*Jesus, thank You for fighting this battle for me. I will trust You regardless of the mistreatment I face. Amen.*

My hope is in Jesus because
He is always victorious.

# CLOSED DOORS

*"He who is holy, who is true, who has the key of David, who opens and no one will shut, and who shuts and no one opens."*
REVELATION 3:7

God has the power to open any closed door—no circumstance is too difficult for Him to overcome. Yet He may decide to let things that seem important to us remain blocked. Why does the Lord allow doors to stay shut?

*Protection*: perhaps He is keeping you from making a mistake. *Redirection*: He could be sending you on a more important path— with better opportunities, deeper satisfaction, or an opportunity to glorify His name. *Testing*: when God says no, your faith will be tested, and you'll discover what you really believe about Him. *Perseverance*: through shut doors, you have an opportunity to develop endurance—an indispensable quality for believers. *Timing*: God may simply be working out the correct timing for His will to be accomplished fully. *Disobedience:* God will discipline you so you can truly enjoy the blessings He gives you.

When your way is blocked, stop fretting. Instead, look to God and trust He will open the door when the time is right.

*Jesus, thank You for opening the right doors*
*and closing the wrong ones. Amen.*

> **My hope is in Jesus because He opens and closes doors for my good.**

# GOOD PURPOSES

*The Lord will not reject forever, for if He causes grief, then He*
*will have compassion according to His abundant lovingkindness.*
*For He does not afflict willingly or grieve the sons of men.*

LAMENTATIONS 3:31–33

How do you handle the disappointments? Do you immediately question God's love for you, or do you seek to comprehend what He is teaching you? Realize that your response will—in part—determine how long and intense the difficulty becomes.

If you turn away from Him and attempt to escape the pain, you will only make it harder on yourself. Therefore, accept God's purpose for allowing your suffering and act in a manner that honors Him. He may be purifying your faith—removing anything that you rely on as security or worship above Him. Likewise, the Lord may be removing a sinful stronghold, developing your character, or preparing you to minister to others. Some of the most impactful believers in history have walked through the valley of adversity. They understood both the struggles and triumphs of faith, which is what made them such a blessing to others.

Whatever the cause, know for certain that whatever God is accomplishing through your trial is *good*. Therefore, seek Him, keep trusting, and learn the lesson.

*Jesus, help me to learn from every trial, knowing You*
*have a purpose for everything I go through. Amen.*

My hope is in Jesus because
His purpose toward me is good.

# FORGIVE AS JESUS DOES

*"Lord, how often shall my brother sin against me and I forgive him? Up to seven times?" Jesus said to him, "I do not say to you, up to seven times, but up to seventy times seven."*

MATTHEW 18:21–22

In Peter's conversation with Jesus above, he asked what we often do: "Are there limits to what I can and should forgive?" This is because it's much more difficult to forgive some offenses than others. Some have consequences that are far greater and much more painful.

But what you are always to remember is the mercy Jesus offers you. He forgives *all* your sins—yesterday, today, and forever. And as you're called to emulate His example, the only right way to respond to others' offenses is to extend the same grace.

Two qualities mark such Christlike forgiveness. *First, it is unconditional—you cannot earn it.* Remember, there are no strings attached to the pardon Jesus offers you—all you have to do is receive it. The same must be true for you. Forgive freely.

*Second, His forgiveness is unlimited—He never turns you away.* Likewise, as a believer, always be a place of refuge for others. That doesn't mean condoning sinful behavior. Rather, it means you always demonstrate the loving-kindness that Jesus has shown you.

*Jesus, thank You for forgiving me. Help me to extend the same loving-kindness and grace to others. Amen.*

> My hope is in Jesus because He is my example of forgiveness.

# FIGHTING ANXIETY

*[Cast] all your anxiety on Him, because He cares for you.*
1 PETER 5:7

Do you feel fearful today? Understanding how susceptible you may be to anxiety as the trials of faith assail you, God reveals four biblical principles that can help dispel your apprehensions:

*First, you are of great value to God.* "Look at the birds of the air . . . your heavenly Father feeds them. Are you not worth much more than they?" (Matthew 6:26). The Lord sees your potential and wants to work through you. He has a stake in helping you.

*Second, you are not only useful to the Father; He also loves you unconditionally.* He affirms, "I have loved you with an everlasting love" (Jeremiah 31:3). Your Savior cares about you profoundly!

*Third, He is fully aware of your needs—even those you don't know exist—and He will supply them.* God knows what you're facing today. And you are assured: "He who did not spare His own Son . . . how will He not also with Him freely give us all things?" (Romans 8:32).

*Fourth, God is greater than whatever you face.* Your sovereign God is in total control, so stop fearing and let go. Cast your cares upon Him, for He is certainly able to care for all that concerns you!

*Jesus, thank You for Your purpose, love, provision, and protection! I will not fear—I will trust in You! Amen.*

> My hope is in Jesus because
> I can always count on Him.

# DEFEATING THE DECEIVER

*He will use every kind of evil deception to*
*fool those on their way to destruction.*

2 THESSALONIANS 2:10 NLT

Our archenemy, Satan, is described as the "father of lies" (John 8:44), and his chief weapon in his war against mankind is deception. We can see this in nations throughout the world where cultures are in moral upheaval—violent, addicted to illicit substances, sensually driven, and with little respect for human life. This comes in a modern, "enlightened" age, when global educational, scientific, political, and business communities are continually turning away from the Lord—setting up walls of separation between God and society. In this, we see the deceiver hard at work. His strategy is to blind people to the need for salvation so they won't turn to Christ.

This is why it's more important than ever that we remain prayerful, we're aware of his tactics, and we continue to build our lives on God's unchanging principles. We must also be salt and light wherever we go, understanding that the pain, bondage, and separation caused by sin remains deep in the souls of all those who reject the Savior. We must preach the truth and represent Christ well so that others can be freed from his grip and saved (2 Timothy 2:24–26).

*Jesus, help me to preach the truth and represent*
*You well so that others can be saved. Amen.*

My hope is in Jesus because
He is the only hope.

# WARFARE

*Our struggle is . . . against the powers, . . . against the*
*spiritual forces of wickedness in the heavenly places.*
EPHESIANS 6:12

In today's verse, the apostle Paul described the spiritual battle in which all Christians are engaged. He used words like "powers" and "spiritual forces" to indicate the supernatural nature of the conflict. Whether we realize it or not, we're in the fight of our lives.

Yes, we know Jesus is ultimately victorious. But in the daily frustrations and discouragements, we must realize that Satan's agents are actively making war with us—attempting to undermine our faith in God and our impact on the world. We tend to focus our anger on other people, situations, and even ourselves—on things that are seen. But this struggle against spiritual forces is real, and we must understand its unseen source in order to engage it successfully.

First Peter 5:8–9 admonishes, "Be of sober spirit, be on the alert. Your adversary, the devil, prowls around like a roaring lion, seeking someone to devour. But resist him, firm in your faith." In other words, be aware of the battle and fight it spiritually. Win it with unshakable trust in God and adherence to His Word. Because only in this way will you be truly victorious.

*Jesus, empower me to be victorious in the*
*spiritual warfare that assails me. Amen.*

My hope is in Jesus because He
overcomes the enemy of my soul.

# November

As for me, I will hope continually, and will praise You yet more and more. My mouth shall tell of Your righteousness and of Your salvation all day long.

PSALM 71:14–15

# PRIMARY MOTIVATOR

*"If I am lifted up from the earth I will draw all people to Myself."*
JOHN 12:32 HCSB

What is the motivating goal of your life? Do you realize that God has an objective for you as well? That, of course, is to exalt Jesus through you.

Now that you are spiritually alive through salvation, the Holy Spirit is working within you, drawing you into oneness with Christ and conforming you to His image. This is so much more than patterning your life after Jesus' moral and ethical teachings or attempting to emulate His character. Rather, unity with Christ has to come from within—it can only occur as you submit to His indwelling Spirit and allow Him to live His resurrection life in and through you. Much more than a mere imitation or follower of Jesus, you are becoming His visible representative in the world.

So consider: Do you obey the promptings of His Spirit? Can others see Christ through you? Do you care for others with His love, speak with His wisdom, and work in His strength? Your life can be a powerful testimony for Him. So agree with God, allow Him to conform you to Christ's image, and let that be the most important goal you pursue.

*Jesus, help me be conformed to Your image and exalt You so that others will know You as Savior. Amen.*

My hope is in Jesus because He speaks to others through my testimony.

# REDEEMING INJUSTICE

*The LORD caused all that he did to prosper.*

GENESIS 39:3

Do you ever feel as if your life has turned into an unfair worst-case scenario? Joseph probably did. He was sold by his brothers to Midianite traders, who in turn peddled him to Potiphar, the chief bodyguard of the Egyptian Pharaoh. Then Potiphar's wife falsely accused Joseph of sexual misconduct. He was subsequently jailed.

Thankfully, he was able to assist a cupbearer to the king while in prison, and it looked as if he would finally get a break when the cupbearer returned to service. But then the cupbearer forgot him.

In all, Joseph spent approximately thirteen years in slavery or imprisonment—all through no fault of his own. Yet Joseph remained free of an unforgiving spirit. How did he do so? He focused on the task before him and not his circumstances. He honored God and served with such skill that he was put in charge at every turn—eventually even ruling as second only to Pharaoh.

It's possible that you are facing a similar situation. You're in a terrible place because of the mistakes and sins of others. But don't lose heart. God knows exactly where you are, and victory is still possible. So like Joseph, keep obeying Him and trust that He *will* keep His promises to you.

*Jesus, thank You for being with me in this mess. I trust You. Amen.*

> My hope is in Jesus because
> He can redeem my situation.

# GOD WORKS IT OUT

*God causes all things to work together for good to those who*
*love God, to those who are called according to His purpose.*

ROMANS 8:28

Yesterday we saw how Joseph was able to keep his heart free from an unforgiving spirit in circumstances that cried out for revenge.

But understand, his triumph wasn't just because he didn't focus on his brothers' cruelty or Potiphar's wife unjustly accusing him. Rather, Joseph was able to concentrate on the task before him because he was confident that God Himself was behind every circumstance. We know this because of his testimony in Genesis 50:20: "You meant evil against me, but God meant it for good in order to . . . preserve many people alive." Behind every evil act by others was the Lord's wisdom and sovereign hand. He was divinely working through their actions to position Joseph for His greater purposes. And that same mighty God is at work in your life.

No matter who has hurt or undermined you, your heavenly Father is still orchestrating His good and gracious plan for you—often even working through the injustices to train you and get you where you need to be. So thank God that no matter what happens, He will use it to achieve His wonderful purposes in your life.

*Jesus, thank You that my situation is not a defeat,*
*but Your means for triumph. Amen.*

> My hope is in Jesus because He
> uses everything for my good.

# Getting God's Wisdom

*He who gets wisdom loves his own soul.*

PROVERBS 19:8

Do you ever receive an abundance of information but have no idea how to manage it all? Certainly there's a distinct difference between information and wisdom. Mere knowledge of the facts won't necessarily lead you to a good decision. You can have an abundance of data and still make terrible choices.

Rather, what you need is something that will connect the dots for you—facts you may not even realize are missing. And this is exactly what God offers you. This is why Proverbs 9:10 promises, "The fear of the LORD is the beginning of wisdom." Being both omniscient (all-knowing) and omnipresent (with everything in His presence), there is no detail, interaction, or relationship that escapes His notice. So when He gives you His perspective on an issue, you can be certain He is steering you in the right direction.

Best of all, you're promised, "If any of you lacks wisdom, let him ask of God, who gives to all generously and without reproach, and it will be given to him" (James 1:5). In other words, He loves to help you. So go to Him today for anything that confuses you and trust Him to lead you in the wisest course.

*Jesus, I trust Your wisdom. Show me the way I should go. Amen.*

> **My hope is in Jesus because He is wise and willing to direct me.**

# DYING FOR CONTROL

*"Unless a grain of wheat falls into the earth and dies,
it remains alone; but if it dies, it bears much fruit."*
JOHN 12:24

Does your life ever feel completely out of control? Like a car hydroplaning down a slick highway—the more you put on the brakes, the worse your slide.

Certainly it's human to want to be in charge of our lives—to steer our course with our own wisdom. This is why when God works to break us of this need for control through our circumstances, it's so difficult. He takes us out of the driver's seat and forces us to be passengers on the journey. And He keeps the pressure on until we confess we just cannot manage anymore. We have given it our best, and it wasn't enough—so we're ready to let go.

As you see from today's verse, this is exactly where your gracious Savior wants you. He wants you to die to your sense of control so that He can live through you.

You cannot accomplish in the flesh what only He can do through His resurrection power. But for Him to live through you, you have to give up. So stop fretting. Release control of the wheel and let Him drive.

*Jesus, giving You control is so difficult! But
I will have faith in Your leadership. Amen.*

My hope is in Jesus because the
resurrection life He gives is so much better!

# A Harvest That Lasts

*"I chose you . . . that you might go
and bear fruit—fruit that will last."*
JOHN 15:16 NIV

You plant a seed of corn beneath the rich earth. Within weeks, the stalk is out and reaching skyward. In a few more weeks, ears of corn begin to form. Before long, they are ready to harvest. You reap a dozen or so ears—each with hundreds of kernels. Amazingly, from that one single grain has come an untold bounty.

The problem is, that seed has to die before it can become fruitful. As we discussed yesterday, Jesus said, "Unless a grain of wheat falls into the earth and dies, it remains alone; but if it dies, it bears much fruit" (John 12:24). God allows you to experience brokenness so you can die to self, because it's self that limits the eternal influence you have with others. As you relinquish your need for control, you are able to experience the transforming life of Christ.

Think about it: it was a broken Peter who shepherded multitudes and a persecuted Paul who wrote the inspiring epistles that still encourage our hearts. That resurrection life that Jesus lives through you is what attracts others to Him and ushers in true power and eternal fruitfulness. But you have to let go and trust Him.

*Jesus, help me to let go of control and trust
Your wise and sovereign hand. Amen.*

> My hope is in Jesus because the
> life He gives me is worthwhile.

# THE RELIABILITY OF SCRIPTURE

*All Scripture is inspired by God and profitable for teaching,*
*for reproof, for correction, for training in righteousness.*

2 TIMOTHY 3:16

Do you realize that there's no other document on earth that is as reliable as the Bible? History testifies to the dependability of Scripture with more than five thousand Greek manuscripts of the New Testament. There is also overwhelming confirmation of the Old Testament's reliability because of the 1947 discovery of the Dead Sea Scrolls.

Sir Frederic Kenyon, former director of the British Museum, affirmed, "The Christian can take the whole Bible in his hand and say without hesitation that he holds in it the true Word of God."[3]

Archaeology and eyewitness attestations by extra-biblical writers all verify the trustworthiness of the Bible. But the most compelling reason we can unquestionably trust it is because *it is the revelation of God, which He Himself confirms through fulfilled prophecy.*

Yes, Scripture was written over a time span of fifteen hundred years by forty Spirit-inspired authors. But through it all is the consistent, unchanging, supernatural voice of our mighty God, helping us to know Him intimately and speaking the truth that sets us free. We can trust His Word because He Himself is trustworthy.

*Jesus, thank You for speaking to me so*
*powerfully through Your Word. Amen.*

> My hope is in Jesus because He has
> revealed Himself to me through Scripture.

# Resurrection Transformation

*"I am the vine, you are the branches; he who abides in Me and I in him, he bears much fruit, for apart from Me you can do nothing."*
John 15:5

Do you long for a deeper walk with God? Do you know what it means to work hard and be faithful—but fail to experience His resurrection power? Missionary John McCarthy explained the key to taking hold of it:

> Abiding, not striving not struggling; looking off unto Him; trusting Him for present power; trusting Him to subdue all inward corruption; resting in the love of an almighty Savior, in the conscious joy of a *complete* salvation, a salvation "from all sin" (this is *His* Word); willing that His will should truly be supreme. . . . Christ literally *all* seems to me now the power, the *only* power for service; the only ground for unchanging joy. May He lead us into the realization of his unfathomable fullness. (emphasis added)[4]

It's the concept Jesus spoke of in John 15:5. How does a natural branch bear fruit? As long as that branch is attached to the vine, it is given everything needed to produce. The same is true for you. So stop struggling. Attach yourself to Jesus and let His resurrection power flow.

*Jesus, I abide, I trust, and I praise You. Amen.*

My hope is in Jesus because
He transforms me.

# QUALIFIED

*God has chosen the weak things of the
world to shame the things which are strong.*

1 CORINTHIANS 1:27

A frequent assumption believers make is that they're not qualified to serve God because He only works through men and women endowed with extraordinary talents. But throughout history, the Lord has worked through seemingly insignificant individuals for truly miraculous purposes. The prophet Amos was a sheepherder. Most of the disciples were uneducated fishermen. William Carey, the great missionary, started as a cobbler.

God wants people who will glorify Him rather than themselves. Therefore, indispensable qualities for being useful to Him are humility and an understanding of one's own inadequacy. He is looking for people who want to honor Him and boldly trust *Him* as their Source rather than themselves. When that happens, the most common of people become heroes of the faith.

So if you've decided God cannot use you because you don't have the right connections, looks, money, training, past, or intellect, please reconsider. He can work through you to accomplish His wonderful purposes right where you are. All you have to do is trade your weaknesses for His strength by obeying Him. So place your willing, childlike faith in Christ and rejoice in all He does through you.

*Jesus, may You be glorified through my life. Amen.*

> My hope is in Jesus because
> He qualifies me for His service.

# SANCTIFICATION

*If we live by the Spirit, let us also walk by the Spirit.*

GALATIANS 5:25

Does the overcoming, joyous Christian life elude you? Perhaps you've embraced who you are in Jesus—loved, accepted, and saved forever—but something still isn't right.

As you can see in today's verse, Galatians 5:25, if you recognize that you have eternal life through faith in God, then you must also live it by faith in the wisdom and power of the Spirit. The same faith that saves you is what's necessary for the Holy Spirit to *sanctify* you—or set you apart to God.

You see, the Spirit is continuously revealing areas of your life—your body, mind, will, and emotions—that still need to be yielded to Him. That's the discomfort you feel in your relationship with Him. But when you choose His ways over your own, He imparts everything you need to grow, serve Him, and glorify Him—including His peace.

That feeling of being "off" in your relationship with God is actually Him completing what He has begun in you. He saves you fully (Hebrews 7:25)—not just eternally, but sanctifying every aspect of your life and character to set you free from your bondage to sin. So accept how He is working in you by obeying Him and depending on His Spirit to direct you.

*Jesus, I submit myself to Your sanctifying work. Amen.*

My hope is in Jesus because
He saves me completely.

# RESISTING THE ENEMY

*They have defeated him by the blood of
the Lamb and by their testimony.*

REVELATION 12:11 NLT

Perhaps you're feeling spiritually attacked today, and you wonder if the enemy has defeated you. There are two common mistakes we make when it comes to dealing with the adversary. The first is we *overestimate* his abilities. Yes, he is powerful and crafty—but not omnipotent, omniscient, or omnipresent. In other words, he is no match for God. Satan can never go beyond the Lord's sovereign boundaries.

The second issue is we *underestimate* his destructive potential. The prophet Ezekiel described him as one "full of wisdom and perfect in beauty" (Ezekiel 28:12). Make no mistake: Satan is an accomplished murderer, thief, and liar who has deceived and destroyed countless millions. So it's always dangerous and destructive to think we can fight him in our own power or on his territory. In other words, you cannot battle him through escapist sins—by eating your feelings, ingesting illicit substances, or engaging in other fleshly behavior. Only the Word and the Spirit of God can defeat him.

By being careful not to understate or overstate the enemy's abilities, we are better able to resist his assaults. He is a potent foe, but we are always victorious through Christ.

*Jesus, thank You for defending me from the
enemy and leading me to triumph. Amen.*

My hope is in Jesus because
He is always victorious!

# ONE OR THE OTHER

*Submit therefore to God. Resist the*
*devil and he will flee from you.*

JAMES 4:7

Resisting the devil implies spiritual combat—and indeed, it is. However, the tactics we employ to overcome him may seem almost paradoxical. The most powerful means of resisting the devil, James said, is to "submit to God." Why? Because it is God alone who has defeated Satan at the cross—and as believers we share in Jesus' triumph.

But also remember the enemy's main purpose, which is to subvert God's power and appropriate it for himself. All authority belongs rightly to the Lord, so when we fail to obey Him, we unwittingly advance the adversary's goals. That's right—anything we do apart from God's will actually serves the enemy. You submit either to one or the other. What a scary thought!

That is why it is so incredibly important to obey God, knowing that greater is He who is in us than the enemy (1 John 4:4). He deserves your devotion, and if you want victory and freedom, you must depend on Him. So however Satan is tempting you today, submit to God by relying on His mighty Spirit and Word. You will find astonishing victory and power over your most stubborn sins.

*Jesus, I submit to You! To You belongs all*
*authority, honor, and devotion! Amen.*

My hope is in Jesus because He
is worthy of my obedience.

# FROM THE HEART

*Watch over your heart with all diligence,*
*for from it flow the springs of life.*
PROVERBS 4:23

All of us have things we treasure—whether it's special possessions, relationships, activities, or experiences. And what we most value is usually what's closest to our hearts and influences our decisions.

The struggle within us exists, however, because of the conflict between our fallen nature and God's priorities for us. Our human hearts incline toward wickedness, but once we accept Jesus as Savior, His Holy Spirit continually admonishes us to honor Christ. This is why today's verse, Proverbs 4:23, exhorts us to employ all diligence in guarding our hearts—we have a choice about what we treasure and what drives us, whether for good or for evil. But how can we be certain we're doing a good job?

Thankfully, God knows exactly what's in us. And so, if we want to keep a clean heart before Him, we must continually take it to Him for examination. Like David, we too should pray, "Search me, O God, and know my heart. . . . See if there be any hurtful way in me, and lead me in the everlasting way" (Psalm 139:23–24). And if He targets something for removal, we must trust that He is eliminating what is stopping His life from flowing through us.

*Search me, Jesus, and remove anything that*
*impedes Your work in my heart. Amen.*

My hope is in Jesus because
He renews my heart.

# RESPECT HIS COMMANDS

*By this the children of God and the children
of the devil are obvious: anyone who does
not practice righteousness is not of God.*

1 JOHN 3:10

There is a tremendous difference between asking a question to gain more information and doing so to avoid surrendering to what God says. But this is what we often do. We go back to His throne of grace repeatedly, demanding more information or voicing our distrust in His purposes in order to sidestep the need to obey.

But understand, when the Lord communicates with you—it is *God* speaking. You may not understand or agree with what He is asking of you, but His authority and wisdom trump yours, and He deserves your complete respect.

So consider: When God calls, are you responding to Him immediately with the complete and loving obedience that should characterize His disciple? Are you demonstrating reverence for Him? No one is perfect. But the clearest evidence of your maturity in the Christian life is demonstrated through your willingness to do exactly as He says in faith. So stop arguing and submit to the One who leads you with perfect wisdom.

*Jesus, forgive me for questioning.
Help me to step out in obedience. Amen.*

My hope is in Jesus because He is
worthy of my complete respect.

# REPRESENT HIM

*If a brother or sister is without clothing and in need of*
*daily food, and one of you says to them, "Go in peace,*
*be warmed and be filled," and yet you do not give them*
*what is necessary for their body, what use is that?*
JAMES 2:15–16

You pass by people every day who are crying out to be touched by the love and power of Jesus Christ. Certainly, the needs of others are all around you. Do you notice? Do you see their pain and hear God calling you to be His answer to them? Perhaps someone has come to mind even as you've been reading this.

As a child of God, you are the visible and physical representation of Jesus on this earth. Christ is touching, saving, and healing lives through you—you are His mouth, hands, and feet. And you have so much to offer those in need through the power and wisdom of the Holy Spirit, who indwells you. As 2 Corinthians 5:20 explains, "We are ambassadors for Christ, as though God were making an appeal through us."

So what kind of impression are you making on His behalf? Do others see Him through you? Friend, don't ignore the needs around you. Allow Christ to touch others by the way you care for them.

*Jesus, reveal the needs You want me to meet*
*and glorify Yourself through me. Amen.*

My hope is in Jesus because He
works through me to reach the world.

# STAY FREE

*It was for freedom that Christ set us free; therefore keep standing firm and do not be subject again to a yoke of slavery.*

GALATIANS 5:1

A slave has little freedom to accomplish anything in accordance with his own desires. You can imagine the elation a person experiences when released from his confinement. His world takes on new meaning and possibilities—he can do things he'd only dreamt about before. But he is still responsible to live within the confines of the law of his nation. So even though he's free, in a sense, he is still under some restriction.

Likewise, the apostle Paul explained that we were once in bondage to the sin nature within us. Now, through Christ, we've been set free—our wrongdoing can no longer affect our eternal standing. Yet Paul admonished us to be careful not to feed the fires of fleshly desire, which can bring us back into enslavement. He explained, "All things are lawful for me, but all things are not helpful. . . . I will not be brought under the power of any" (1 Corinthians 6:12 NKJV).

When you try to meet your needs in your own way instead of how God has provided for you to fulfill them, you're confining yourself to a miserable existence that's far less than what He has for you. Don't do it. Focus on Jesus, who always leads you to freedom.

*Jesus, thank You for setting me free—and keeping me free. Amen.*

> My hope is in Jesus because
> He sets me free.

# His Good Will

*"If you keep My commandments, you will abide in My love."*
JOHN 15:10

Have you ever considered what motivates your commitment to Jesus? Is it because you *know* He loves you, and you are grateful? Or is it because you are afraid of *losing* His acceptance? Some may think today's verse suggests that you can lose His love when you fail to submit to Him and inherently doubt His motives. But actually, it means He works His loving will through you when you choose to trust His direction.

God's will is *always* good. So when you're not sure you want to obey Him, consider this question: would you rather obey God and experience His blessing, or disobey Him and spend the rest of your life wondering what He would have done if you had obeyed?

The truth is, there are many good people who find themselves looking back to a time when they stood on the threshold of a decision and, because of fear, lack of faith, stubbornness, or weakness, chose to serve self instead of God. They are forever left to wonder what He would have done if only they'd submitted to Him—would those deep desires have been met?

Don't allow that to happen to you. Obey His commands, abide in His love, and discover all He can do through your life.

*Jesus, I am grateful for Your love and will obey Your good will. Amen.*

> My hope is in Jesus because
> He has great plans for me.

# RESOLVE THE ISSUE

*There is no soundness in my flesh because of Your indignation;*
*there is no health in my bones because of my sin.*
PSALM 38:3

Is there an unresolved issue that keeps surfacing whenever you go before God? Is there something He has called you to surrender? Some ingrained sin that you deny He cares about—but which He brings up whenever you pray?

It may indeed be difficult to let go because of the pleasure, security, or comfort it seems to give you. But it's not really helping you. Instead, it is hindering you from being truly healed and enjoying life at its best. Let go of it! Purge it! Yes, it may be painful to take this step. But you are assured that God's power, wisdom, and sustaining comfort will set you free and heal your wounds.

Don't allow your unresolved issues to stand in the way of the amazing plan Christ has for your life. Weigh their value in the light of the life you could have and what the Lord could accomplish through you in eternity. Undoubtedly you will see how worthless these strongholds are—and how wonderful God's unlimited resources of love, strength, wisdom, and mercy are. Certainly He is worthy of your all.

*Jesus, I want to surrender, but it is difficult.*
*Show me what to do. Amen.*

My hope is in Jesus because
He frees me from bondage to sin.

# AN ANCHOR IN THE STORM

*Ask in faith without any doubting, for the one who doubts
is like the surf of the sea, driven and tossed by the wind.*

JAMES 1:6

Are there times when you struggle to maintain your level of faith in God? Do you find yourself trusting Him deeply one minute, then questioning and doubting Him just a little while later? It is indeed unsettling. So what can you do to strengthen your faith so that the storms of life don't overcome you?

Practice these three keys: *One, act in obedience*, not on how you feel or what you see. When you know God's direction on a matter, follow through by exercising your will. Choose to act in line with the truth He has revealed to you. *Two, focus your attention on God.* If your attention is on your circumstances, you will constantly battle defeat. So fix your eyes on your omnipotent Creator, who will never fail you. *Three, set your mind on Scripture.* The Lord is faithful to fulfill the promises He has given you. You can rely on His Word because it is always proven true.

Your God can be trusted—even more than what you can see or hear. So don't waver in your faith. Hold on to Him as the unshakable anchor for your soul.

*Jesus, help me to act in obedience, focus on You, and
embrace Your Word so my faith can stay strong. Amen.*

My hope is in Jesus because
He is trustworthy.

# ENDURE

*If when you do what is right and suffer for it you*
*patiently endure it, this finds favor with God.*

1 PETER 2:20

When God calls you to trust Him, there will inevitably be times when your faith is stretched to the limit and all of your dreams seem destroyed. Everything in you may say, "Give up." But don't! When you give up, you're saying that the Lord cannot be trusted to be faithful, and you abandon His help—relying instead on your own limited strength and understanding. You'll end up paying a terrible price: you'll damage your self-esteem, miss the blessing God has for you, and limit His ability to work through you.

But trust that God wants to do something very special in your life that requires your faith, strength, and perseverance to be exercised to the breaking point so that you'll learn to rely on Him rather than yourself.

Far too many believers give up right before they see victory. Don't be one of them. Stop looking at your circumstances—which, yes, may look terrible. But you're not seeing the full picture that God has in His sights. Instead, get back up, express your faith in His provision, and endure. Commit yourself to pressing on, claim the promises He has given, and cling to His faithfulness.

*Jesus, I want to see Your victory in this*
*situation. Help me to endure. Amen.*

My hope is in Jesus because
He is growing me.

# MOVING MOUNTAINS

*"If you have faith the size of a mustard seed, you will
say to this mountain, 'Move from here to there,' and it
will move; and nothing will be impossible to you."*

MATTHEW 17:20

The disciples tried to cast a demon out of a suffering boy but could
not. When they asked Jesus why they'd failed, He replied that it was
because their faith was too small, and that kind of demon could
only be removed by prayer and fasting. Then He taught the principle that you read above.

We often think of mountains as obstacles in our lives that
nothing can budge. In the case of the suffering boy, the enemy
had erected a stronghold in his life. But the disciples did not truly
believe that the Lord was stronger than that demonic force.

How about you—do you believe God is able to move any
mountain in your life? When you have a problem, do you talk to
your friends or turn to other sources for solutions, while not trusting God's wisdom? If you do, no doubt the result is that mountain
remains. But if you have even the smallest faith—the kind that
clings to God and does exactly as He says—He will knock down
those strongholds in ways that will astound you.

*Jesus, thank You for removing the mountains and leading
me to liberty. Help me to obey all You say. Amen.*

My hope is in Jesus because
He frees me from strongholds.

# SHIELDED WITH FAITH

*Take up the shield of faith, with which you can*
*extinguish all the flaming arrows of the evil one.*
EPHESIANS 6:16 NIV

Deliverance from the enemy's onslaughts requires the right kind of armor. So Paul admonished us to take up the shield of faith. Like the rectangular shields that soldiers used in his day, it is large enough to hide behind and can protect every part of the body.

It guards: *Your head*—your thoughts are vitally important in the battle to conquer self and sin. Faith can halt Satan from discouraging or tempting you. *Your heart*, which is the core of your being and the seat of your affections. Faith makes certain that the driving motivation of your life is influenced by God and not your adversary. *Your hands*—or the works you do. Faith ensures that what you're accomplishing is building the kingdom of God rather than that of the enemy. *Your feet*—with faith, nothing can dissuade your progress on the path God has for you.

Faith is central to the Christian life because it represents your trust and determination to do as the Lord says. From head to toe, it gives you victory over the enemy and the courage to do God's will. So no matter what happens, take it up and keep marching with confidence in Christ.

*Jesus, I believe You! Increase my faith and lead me to victory. Amen.*

> My hope is in Jesus because
> He protects me from the enemy.

# ENEMY TACTICS

*Has God said, "You shall not eat from any tree of the garden"?*

GENESIS 3:1

How often has Satan repeated the tactic he used on Eve in the garden of Eden? Note the progression of his attack against the command of God.

*First, the enemy presents the question*—with a subtext that implies that what the Lord has asked is unreasonable. Whenever you begin to question the logic or veracity of God's commands, let it be a warning sign to you. You are being tempted. You are doubting whether you should obey.

*Second, the enemy tells an outright lie*—"You surely will not die! . . . Your eyes will be opened, and you will be like God" (Genesis 3:4–5). In other words, Satan says the Lord isn't just misleading you; He's keeping you from something good—some pleasure, desire, or power you'd enjoy. But know for certain that God only ever wants the best for you and works for your benefit.

So be alert to the enemy's strategy and fight him as Jesus did in Luke 4:1–13—with the Word of God. The adversary is not unbeatable. He has already been eternally defeated at the cross. And armed with the indwelling Holy Spirit and the truth of Scripture, you never have to give in to his devastating lies.

*Jesus, I trust You fully. Help me to obey You wholeheartedly. Amen.*

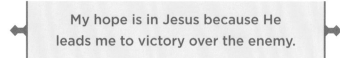

My hope is in Jesus because He
leads me to victory over the enemy.

# COMING STORMS

*Prepare your minds for action, keep sober in spirit,*
*fix your hope completely on the grace to be brought*
*to you at the revelation of Jesus Christ.*

1 PETER 1:13

In the Christian life, it's important for us to be on the watch for the storms that will arise. The trials will come. But what can you do when you recognize a tempest is headed your way?

*First, remove any hindrances.* Make sure you're right with God and get rid of anything that interferes with your relationship with Him. If you can't hear the Lord clearly, then you're not going to be able to obey Him. *Second, keep balanced in your judgment.* Don't panic or look for temporary solutions. Stay in Scripture and trust God to give you discernment about what to do. *Third, recognize that your hope is in Christ.* Rest in Him and remember that God has a divine purpose for allowing this storm. *Finally, make being more like Jesus your goal.* No matter what happens, set your heart to act like Him.

You *can* be prepared for the storms of life, and how you respond can make a tremendous difference. So don't just survive the tempest. Make it your goal to triumph in it.

*Jesus, help me prepare for the storms so*
*You will be glorified in them. Amen.*

My hope is in Jesus because
He is my shelter in the storm.

# FROM BROKENNESS TO STRENGTH

*Whoever serves is to do so as one who is serving
by the strength which God supplies.*

1 PETER 4:11

After Peter denied Jesus three times, it seemed as if his usefulness to Christ was destroyed forever. But in John 21:15, Jesus restored Peter by instructing, "Do you love Me . . . ? . . . Tend My lambs." He entrusted Peter with the important task of shepherding God's people—leading, teaching, and guarding them.

As Jesus revealed the new assignment, Peter must have thought back to Christ's words before the betrayal: "Behold, Satan has demanded permission to sift you like wheat; but I have prayed for you, that your faith may not fail; and you, when once you have turned again, strengthen your brothers" (Luke 22:31–32).

Like Peter, you may have failed God in some area. But Jesus has prayed for you, and He is close to you when you're at your lowest (Psalm 34:18). But also like Peter, when you realize your weakness, He is able to work through you more powerfully in the lives of others. You just have to return to Him in faith.

Knowing the depth of brokenness but also the sustaining power of God, you have a lot to offer others. So tend the lambs by leading other broken souls to the Shepherd who loves them.

*Jesus, thank You for restoring me and
making me useful for Your kingdom. Amen.*

My hope is in Jesus because
He gives me His strength.

# THE POWER OF WORSHIP

*"True worshipers will worship the Father in spirit and truth;*
*for such people the Father seeks to be His worshipers."*
JOHN 4:23

The late Christian pastor A. W. Tozer commented on what appeared to be the conspicuous absence of a vital spiritual ingredient. Despite the fervent and accurate exposition of Scripture, Tozer said that worship was "the missing jewel of the evangelical church." Though we may call our Sunday meetings "worship services," are we truly engaging in heartfelt praise and thanksgiving? Are the majesty and glory of God truly the focus of our gatherings?

The most noble and lofty act that you can engage in as a believer is to ponder the greatness and awesomeness of God and then proclaim His splendor both privately and publicly. Above your service, commitment, good deeds—even above leading others to Him—God both commands and delights in your hearty, sincere, and humble adoration. He must be first and foremost to you because when He is on the throne of your heart, all else—the service, evangelism, and godly character—will flow naturally.

So consider: is worship "the missing jewel" in your life? If so, make Jesus the resplendent centerpiece of your devotion today.

*Jesus, I thank and praise You! You are my*
*God and I rejoice in You! Amen.*

My hope is in Jesus because He is
awesome and deserves all my praise.

# WORSHIP HIM

*Praise the LORD! . . . Praise Him for His mighty deeds;*
*praise Him according to His excellent greatness.*

PSALM 150:1–2

Worship is not just an exhilarating exercise we engage in on Sundays; it is a concentrated focus on Yahweh God Himself. In Psalm 150:1–2, David's praise of the Lord reaches its crescendo, and in so doing reveals that worship should be our lifestyle—we should exalt Him wherever we are.

God's mighty acts should always invoke profound gratitude in our innermost beings. The Lord created the heavens and the earth; made man in His image; sent His Son, Jesus, as our sin-bearer; and raised Christ from the dead. He saved us from eternal death, gave us His nature through His indwelling Spirit, speaks to us through His Word, and guides us unerringly through the difficulties of life.

But not only do we praise God for His mighty deeds; still more, our adulation should focus on the excellency of His being. He is just, holy, faithful, merciful, longsuffering, truthful, trustworthy, gracious, omnipotent, omnipresent, omniscient, sovereign, eternal, and transcendent. Indeed, there is no one greater than Him. And He is so kind and compassionate that He loves us. Wow, what a God! Certainly He is worthy of all our adoration.

*Jesus, I worship You with all that I am! Praise You, Lord! Amen.*

My hope is in Jesus because of His mighty deeds and His excellent greatness.

# WORTHY

*Bless the LORD, O my soul, and all that
is within me, bless His holy name.*

PSALM 103:1

There are two compelling reasons we should worship the Lord. First, we worship God because *He is worthy*. The old English word for worship was *weorthscipe*, which means "worth-ship." The focus is on the One being exalted. So when we worship God, we are attributing to Him the eternal, magnificent worth that exclusively and eternally belongs to Him. As Psalm 29:2 instructs: "Ascribe to the LORD the glory due to His name."

Second, we are created to worship God because *we will become like what we worship*. If we worship money, we'll become greedy. If we worship things, we'll become materialistic. But if we worship God, we will become like Him, conformed to His image. We are "beholding as in a mirror the glory of the Lord . . . transformed into the same image from glory to glory" (2 Corinthians 3:18).

This is why you were created to adore God through your words and actions—because not only is He rightfully due such praise, but you have the fantastic privilege of reflecting His image. So praise your Creator, Redeemer, and King and bear His likeness with joy.

*Jesus, I adore You! To You belong all glory,
honor, power, and praise! Amen.*

> My hope is in Jesus because He is
> worthy of my worship and focus.

# COME HUMBLY IN WORSHIP

*My soul will make its boast in the LORD; the*
*humble will hear it and rejoice.*

PSALM 34:2

If worship is so central to the Christian life, why do so few of us genuinely magnify Him? Why are our prayers petitions instead of praises; complaining instead of singing?

One reason is because of our innate self-focus and pride. We are the center of our universe—inherently consumed with our own needs and desires. But the prerequisite for worshipping God is humility—the acknowledgment that He is greater than we are.

Another hindrance to worship is unconfessed sin, which plagues us with guilt and numbs our sensitivity to the Father. Perhaps we're unforgiving toward others, engaged in sinful behaviors, or unwilling to obey His call. Regardless of what it is, however, sin is essentially rebellion against God—and He will continually confront and condemn our resistance to Him. And since He will persistently demand our willing submission, we will run from worshipping Him.

If you truly desire to worship God, but have been prevented by pride or rebelliousness, understand that the choice is yours. You can turn this around because He *will* forgive you. So come submissively to Him today, confess your sin, and worship Him with all your heart.

*Jesus, I want to worship You! Thank You*
*for helping me return to You. Amen.*

My hope is in Jesus because
He always welcomes me back.

# JESUS IS LORD

*If you confess with your mouth Jesus as Lord, and believe in your heart that God raised Him from the dead, you will be saved.*

ROMANS 10:9

Romans 10:9 is a verse that's often used to lead the lost to Christ. However, as those who already believe in Jesus, it's an important confession for our lives as well. After all, "Jesus is Lord" should be something we are proclaiming with our lives every minute.

Understand, by our words we reveal the condition of our hearts (Matthew 12:34). So if we are saying, "I hate my life," or, "I hate this situation," are we proclaiming Jesus as Lord? No. Rather, the heart that acknowledges Jesus as Lord says, "Not my will but Yours be done." And, "I don't like this situation, but I know God has allowed it to teach me something through it."

Likewise, believing God raised Jesus from the dead—trusting that His resurrection power is working on your behalf—is powerful and transformative. You can act with faith in Him because you know nothing can thwart His plans.

So live "Jesus is Lord" with everything in you until it's flowing out of you and experience His resurrection power. And always trust that "whoever believes in Him will not be disappointed" (Romans 10:11).

*Jesus, please help me proclaim that You are Lord with every area of my life. Amen.*

My hope is in Jesus because He is my victorious, resurrected Lord!

# DECEMBER

"My soul exalts the Lord, and my spirit has rejoiced in God my Savior. . . . For the Mighty One has done great things for me; and holy is His name."

LUKE 1:46–47, 49

# The God You Can Know

*Seek the LORD while He may be found.*

ISAIAH 55:6

I have traveled to many countries in the world, and I have found three questions that people consistently have on their hearts, regardless of who they are or where they are from: *Who is the one true God? What is He like? Can I have a personal relationship with Him?*

The tragedy is that there are people who go to Christian churches every Sunday but are still unsure of who He is. Sometimes they doubt Him in an overt way—they can't tell you what He's like. Sometimes people will say they know Him well, but will live in a manner that tells a very different story.

Of course, you may already have a well-grounded idea about what the Lord is like. Or perhaps, like many people, you have some doubts or misconceptions about His character and what He expects of you.

The good news is that *you can know God.* In Jeremiah 29:13, He promises, "You will seek Me and find Me when you search for Me with all your heart." What is the key to doing so? Taking Scripture seriously. You don't have to make guesses about God because He has revealed Himself through His Word. And He guarantees He will make Himself known to you as you seek Him.

*Jesus, I want to know You. Show Yourself to me. Amen.*

> My hope is in Jesus because
> He reveals Himself to me.

# LORD UNLIMITED

*The God who made the world and all things in it, since He is Lord of heaven and earth, does not dwell in temples made with hands.*

ACTS 17:24

The God you serve is the Creator of all things. He isn't like lifeless idols that have no voice or power. Rather, He existed before the world began, and He has the unlimited power and unfathomable wisdom to coordinate every detail of this universe.

Although the Greeks and Romans Paul addressed served deities that were supposed to have dominion over certain areas or particular facets of life, the one true God has never been so limited. He is everywhere at all times and has concurrent dominion over all locations and aspects of life. He is the Ruler of all that exists—it all submits to His will and marches to His orders.

This, of course, is the difference between the one true God and a deity you've created in your mind—the Lord is absolutely unlimited and beyond you, while anything you can imagine is constrained to your imagination and acts in a predictable manner.

So if you are waiting on God today, don't be frustrated if He's not acting as you think He should. You can absolutely trust His character, but don't expect to track how He is working in the unseen.

*Jesus, I praise You! I am so grateful
You are completely unlimited! Amen.*

My hope is in Jesus because
He is King over all.

# Why We Obey

*Human hands can't serve his needs—for he has
no needs. He himself gives life and breath to
everything, and he satisfies every need.*

Acts 17:25 nlt

Consider a reason we sometimes do things for God: we long to win Him over. We yearn to keep Him on our side. We do so as if anything we can give Him satisfies something within Him. And yet whatever we can offer Him is like giving a piece of lint to a trillionaire—it is as nothing because He owns and rules all things. Rather, He has given us our very lives and everything we need.

So often we get this mixed up. We're so busy trying to make God into our image—ascribing our needs and standards to Him—that we become blinded to the grandeur of who He really is.

But our God is *already* in control of all things, so He isn't looking for more possessions or authority. Rather, He gives us commandments for our good because He loves us, not because He wants to oppress us. He is revealing whether we truly respect Him as God or if we still have bondage to the world in us.

So that's actually why we should serve Him—because He deserves it and knows what is best for us. To love Him out of gratefulness because He first loved us.

*Jesus, I will obey You out of love and respect. Amen.*

My hope is in Jesus because
He is so good to me.

# PURPOSEFUL

*He made from one man every nation of mankind to live on all the*
*face of the earth, having determined their appointed times and*
*the boundaries of their habitation, that they would seek God.*

ACTS 17:26–27

With the one true God, we can follow humanity back to the one
unique, identifiable man from whom every other person on earth
proceeds: *Adam*. God formed Adam from the dust, breathed life
into him, and gave him purpose. Isn't it astounding that we have
an account of his life even though he existed before there was an
alphabet to record it? Why is this possible? Because Adam's story is
not only significant *for us* to understand where we came from, but
it is also important *to God* because He cared about him so deeply.

But understand that the Lord created *you* with the same forethought and love that He did Adam. You are not an accident—you
are a special creation (Psalm 139:13–14). And your circumstances
are not based on a random set of events—they are purposeful and
what you require to realize your profound need for Jesus.

God actively creates conditions in your life so that you will seek
Him. And if He can do all of that, He can certainly reveal Himself
to you and lead you successfully.

*Jesus, I seek You. Thank You for always*
*leading me with wisdom and love. Amen.*

My hope is in Jesus because
He formed me with love.

# RESPECT YOUR MAKER

*For in Him we live and move and exist . . .*
*"For we also are His children."*
ACTS 17:28

Today understand: you are God's child—He is not your creation. He is your Maker; you are not His inventor. In other words, when you approach the Lord, you should do so as a humble learner rather than as one who already knows it all and should tell Him what to do.

If you've raised a teenager, you understand the dynamic. Once children enter into their teens, they feel the inherent need to express their autonomy. Naturally, you understand your child's potential, but you also know the limitations and areas where he or she still does not have sufficient experience to handle the temptations of life. So you do your best to teach your child well.

The same is true for your relationship with God. No matter how old or experienced you are, you do not have His all-encompassing, eternal point of view. There is a level of understanding that He has about this life and the life to come that you have no idea about. So with every challenge, obstacle, pain, heartbreak, trial, joy, and success, He is inviting you to trust Him and learn.

Therefore, as you face challenges, don't act like a headstrong teenager. Rather, have faith that your heavenly Father is leading you wisely in the right direction.

*Jesus, I respect You. Teach me—I want to learn. Amen.*

My hope is in Jesus because He is my Creator.

# RUNNING THE RACE

*Let us run with endurance the race that is set before us.*
HEBREWS 12:1

When Hebrews 12:1 admonishes you to run the race of life with endurance, the implication is that you are going to face times of hardships and suffering. But do not be dismayed. You can face each season with steadfast determination to complete the race.

God understands that it is difficult and that there will be times you stumble and falter. Running with endurance means that even when you fall, you get up and keep going. Likewise, you are diligently watching for entanglements—the sins that can impede your progress. How do you do so? "By keeping [your] eyes on Jesus, the champion who initiates and perfects our faith" (v. 2 NLT).

Jesus not only ensures that you never run alone, but He is always one step ahead to show you the most effective route, which is clear of sin and shame. He picks you up when you fall, gives you wisdom for the journey, and encourages you every step of the way.

So are you struggling in the race of life today? Has that time of difficulties come? Are there obstacles and entanglements on the course? Fix your eyes on Jesus so that you can live to the fullest and finish well.

*Jesus, thank You for leading, encouraging,*
*and protecting me in this race. Amen.*

My hope is in Jesus because
He is the Champion of my faith.

# INWARD VALUE

*"God sees not as man sees, for man looks at the outward appearance, but the LORD looks at the heart."*

1 SAMUEL 16:7

Man's way of looking at the world is not the same as the Lord's. Sadly, we have a habit of forgetting that important fact.

When Samuel went to anoint the next king of Israel, seven of Jesse's sons passed before him, but none were chosen. The boy God wanted was out tending the sheep because when no one else was watching, that boy, David, was honoring Him from the heart.

This is a very important principle for every believer. If you've ever felt rejected by others because you did not measure up in their eyes, you may have been tempted to work on your appearance or social skills to gain their acceptance. But at such times it's crucial to remember how the Savior sees you.

You aren't "less than" anyone—you were created by, were saved by, and belong to Christ. That means you have immeasurable worth. But what He values about you most is how deeply you love and obey Him from the heart. That's what God honors and blesses.

So don't be disheartened by how the world may see you. Look to God for the true measure of your worth. And trust that He will favor you in His time.

*Jesus, thank You for giving me worth*
*and making me worthy. Amen.*

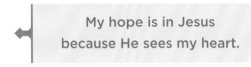

My hope is in Jesus
because He sees my heart.

# DISCOURAGED

*My flesh and my heart may fail, but God is the*
*strength of my heart and my portion forever.*
—PSALM 73:26

Have you ever opened your Bible and felt a sense of dread as you gazed on its pages? There can be many reasons for this, of course, but often it's due to unreconciled confusion over circumstances.

Asaph, who wrote Psalm 73, certainly struggled with difficult feelings over injustice. He watched the wicked prosper and receive the things he longed for as he continued to struggle. So he cried out, "Surely in vain I have kept my heart pure. . . . All day long I have been afflicted, and every morning brings new punishments" (Psalm 73:13–14 NIV).

Perhaps you've felt the same way. You look back over your years of faithfully serving God and see no benefit.

But notice: Asaph kept seeking God, and the Lord revealed what was really going on. The wicked were on a downward slide, while He was supporting Asaph in the unseen.

The same is true for you. Your Father has important, eternal things to show you about your situation. So don't reject Him because of feelings of injustice. When a dark cloud seems to settle over your soul, run to the light of His presence.

*Jesus, I need You. This situation seems so unfair.*
*But I know You have good plans for me. Amen.*

My hope is in Jesus because He
strengthens me even when I face injustice.

# THE PEACEFUL CENTER

*The steadfast of mind You will keep in perfect
peace, because he trusts in You.*

ISAIAH 26:3

Many people go to great lengths to achieve peace and satisfaction. But the truth is that—as a believer—you don't have to struggle to gain either. God has a plan for your life that will bring you both contentment and an abiding sense of tranquility. In fact, such fulfillment is the *result* of walking in the center of His will.

Take Nehemiah, for example. The Lord gave Nehemiah a desire to pray for Jerusalem. Of course, long before Nehemiah interceded on her behalf, God was already implementing His plan to rebuild Jerusalem's walls. But Nehemiah submitted to His direction—he joined God's plan in prayer and eventually by leading the people in the building effort. All the while, Nehemiah felt the assurance of being in the center of the Lord's will. This is why he could write, "The good hand of my God was on me" (Nehemiah 2:8).

Likewise, God often reveals His plans to you through the burdens He puts on your heart. So obey His promptings as He leads you on the path of His will. There, empowered by His strength and led with His wisdom, you'll feel the abiding sense of peace and satisfaction Nehemiah felt as well.

*Jesus, thank You for giving me contentment as You lead me. Amen.*

My hope is in Jesus because
He gives me peace as I obey.

# OBEDIENCE THROUGH SUFFERING

*Even though Jesus was God's Son, he learned*
*obedience from the things he suffered.*
HEBREWS 5:8 NLT

Take comfort in this thought today: even though Jesus is God in the flesh, *it took an act of His will to obey when pain and affliction were involved.* This is because anyone can submit to another's authority when there are rewards promised. But when the immediate effect of our obedience is hardship, the decision is not so easy.

The adversity you are facing today will help you decide whether you really believe in the Lord's wisdom and provision or not. We see Jesus make this decision at Gethsemane, when He said, "Father, if You are willing, remove this cup from Me; yet not My will, but Yours be done" (Luke 22:42). But understand, the process of growing your faith *is supposed to be challenging.* This is because when you have to choose the difficult path—when you must make painful decisions or you simply cannot imagine how the Lord could work things out for your good—it cements your commitment to Him. Obeying God in the tough decisions readies you for both His assignments and His great blessings.

Thankfully, you have a Savior who understands your pain and fears completely, and He's committed to leading you faithfully. So obey no matter the cost and trust Him.

*Jesus, help me to obey regardless of the cost. Amen.*

> My hope is in Jesus because
> He cements my faith.

# YOUR HEAVENLY FATHER

*See how great a love the Father has bestowed on*
*us, that we would be called children of God.*

1 JOHN 3:1

Our understanding of the Lord is directly affected by how we relate to our earthly dads. This is because our first awareness of authority, love, provision, and security comes from our parents. It's only natural that how we perceive them would influence how we view all of our relationships, including the one we have with the Lord.

But regardless of whether you had a godly father, one who was abusive, or one who was absent, understand that God wants to have a loving relationship with you—and has gone to great lengths to provide it (Romans 8:31–33). He always has time for you (Hebrews 4:16), will never fail or forsake you (Hebrews 13:5), and unfailingly accepts you (Romans 15:7).

Also, you may feel inadequate or unprepared to have an open and loving relationship with the Father because of your past, but remember—the One who saves you teaches you how to relate to Him. He will instruct you in how to walk with Him step-by-step.

So today, consider what negative traits you may be attributing to God because of earthly relationships. Then commit yourself to discovering the truth about Him.

*Lord, teach me who You are as my Father beyond*
*my perceptions and past experiences. Amen.*

My hope is in Jesus because
He never fails me.

# IMMOVABLE

*"The floods came, and the winds blew and slammed against that house; and yet it did not fall, for it had been founded on the rock."*

MATTHEW 7:25

How do you face the trials and difficulties that assail your life? Do you wish you could dull the pain in some way? The world offers many ways to do so—through illicit substances, entertainment, food, and a vast variety of activities. However, all those responses only allow you to escape the pain momentarily. And sadly, all they really do is undermine your life. Like the house built on sand, if you rely on them, you're destined for a fall.

Jesus was clear: the only viable foundation for your life is an absolute faith in Him and obedience to His Word.

So anchor your life upon the immovable Rock—Jesus Christ. He is the foundation that cannot be moved and that nothing can overcome. And when you choose to be established in Him, you won't be thrown into chaos when difficulties arise. You may have moments of discouragement and fear, but ultimately, the One who resides within you is the same One who said to the wind and waves, "Peace, be still!" (Mark 4:39 NKJV). And He's always available to speak tranquility to your soul if you'll seek Him.

*Jesus, thank You for giving me stability and speaking peace to my soul. Amen.*

My hope is in Jesus because
He is my immovable foundation.

# HE WILL ANSWER

*I have called upon You, for You will answer me, O God.*
PSALM 17:6

There may come a time in your life when it seems as if God is not answering your prayers. At that point, the natural response is to become discouraged and question His faithfulness. But don't. Understand that when the Lord doesn't respond in a way you expect, it's likely that you are on the verge of a dramatic discovery that may deepen, broaden, and strengthen your life in Christ.

So when you find yourself in this place of uncertainty, observe the following cautions: First, don't confuse *unanswered* prayer with *unheard* prayer. As His child, you are always heard by God. Second, if it seems as if He isn't responding, be careful about who or what you're listening to because it may be impeding what you hear. Third, God will often answer you with "no," "yes," or "wait"—and sometimes "wait" is the hardest answer to receive. So be prepared to accept what He says. Fourth, be honest with yourself. You must be humble and transparent if you want the Lord to work in your life.

Finally, understand that God knows best. Your heavenly Father knows all things—including *when* to answer you. So trust that not only will His response be wise, but His timing for it will be as well.

*Jesus, thank You for answering me with Your*
*perfect power, wisdom, and timing. Amen.*

My hope is in Jesus because
He always listens to me.

# PROTECTION FROM DECEPTION

*Be a good servant of Christ Jesus, constantly nourished
on the words of the faith and of the sound doctrine.*

1 TIMOTHY 4:6

Your Christian beliefs are your protection. Your convictions form
the mental grid through which you determine the validity and usefulness of what you hear. Of course, a filter with large holes isn't
very successful at keeping out unwanted material. The same is true
of your mental filter—it must be tightly woven with scriptural truth
in order to prevent you from being misled.

Remember how the adversary first infiltrated our relationship
with God? The enemy fooled Adam and Eve by disguising his lies
with partial truth—distorting the Lord's character and commands
(Genesis 3:1–7). Sadly, the first couple fell because of his falsehoods,
and it has affected humanity ever since. The enemy will try to
deceive you in this way too. Therefore, the more you understand
about the Lord's ways and plan, the more quickly you will recognize the enemy's lies, no matter how they are camouflaged.

So what is the best safeguard against the enemy's deception?
The unassailable truth—the infallible Word of God. Therefore, satu-
rate your mind with Scripture and allow the Lord to surface any
areas where the enemy's lies have already taken hold.

*Jesus, thank You for freeing me and
protecting me from the enemy's lies. Amen.*

My hope is in Jesus because
He leads me in truth.

# CONFORMED

*Those whom He foreknew, He also predestined to*
*become conformed to the image of His Son.*

ROMANS 8:29

Throughout your Christian life, God will work to conform you to the image of His Son. Have you ever stopped to think about what this *conformity* really means?

When you receive Jesus, He takes residence in your heart. However, there are many things in your life that actually work against His image in you. Therefore, as you grow in your relationship with Him, He continually refines your life so that you'll better reflect His image, character, and likeness.

This process is much like the art of sculpting. When he set out to produce his famous statue of David, Michelangelo chose a discarded piece of stone. Later, when he was asked how he had managed to carve the masterpiece from the slab of white marble, the artist replied that he did not carve David; rather, he saw David in that piece of stone and, with the tools he had, simply let him out.

That's what God is doing in your life—He works through adversity to "let Jesus out." So consider: what is God chipping away at in your life? Ask Him to reveal those things and request the strength to surrender your rough edges.

*Jesus, please reveal what hinders Your likeness from shining*
*through me and give me the strength to surrender it. Amen.*

My hope is in Jesus because
He sees Himself in me.

# THE LORD IS GOD

*The* LORD, *He is God.*

—1 KINGS 18:39

If ever there was a man who faced outlandish odds, it was Elijah. He stood as the sole prophet of the Lord God before 850 prophets of false deities (1 Kings 18:19).

The premise of the contest was simple: Elijah and the 850 false prophets would prepare a sacrifice. Then, as Elijah suggested, "You call on the name of your god, and I will call on the name of the LORD, and the God who answers by fire, He is God" (v. 24). The false prophets went to work. Although they shouted, danced, and prayed, there was only silence.

Then Elijah stepped up. He not only prepared the sacrifice, he also soaked the entire altar with water several times. Then he prayed. And the Lord God answered. Fire fell from heaven, consuming the entire sacrifice, altar, and every drop of water. Clearly, the true God had made Himself known—and even the 850 false prophets were forced to acknowledge it.

Are you facing overwhelming odds like Elijah? Remember, you serve the same God who delivered him—the One who still does miracles. Do not fear, but trust in His power. Certainly, He will make Himself known in a manner no one will be able to deny.

*Jesus, thank You for helping me regardless*
*of how overwhelming the odds. Amen.*

My hope is in Jesus
because He is the Lord.

# YOUR FAITHFUL FRIEND

*There is a friend who sticks closer than a brother.*

PROVERBS 18:24

When times are good, friends are aplenty. However, during difficult times, you may find that your friends become scarce. Perhaps they don't know how to console you. Or it could be that they are frightened by the circumstances you're experiencing. Whatever the case, they're gone when you need them most.

But understand that God is not like that. He is the best friend you'll ever have, and He reassures you of His presence by promising, "I will never desert you, nor will I ever forsake you" (Hebrews 13:5). By His nature, He is a comforter, standing by you and encouraging you through whatever dark valley you may traverse.

In fact, Jesus told you to *expect* storms: "In the world you have tribulation," He said. Then He added these words of encouragement: "but take courage; I have overcome the world" (John 16:33). In other words, yes, you'll have trouble, but the way to victory in it is to stay close to Him.

Likewise, be assured that the Lord never wastes your pain and suffering—He allows it for a reason. So if you're facing a difficulty or crisis, ask God to reveal His purpose for it; then give your worries to Him because certainly He cares for you (1 Peter 5:7).

*Jesus, thank You for being my best friend*
*and loving me through every difficulty. Amen.*

> My hope is in Jesus because
> He is always with me.

# OVERCOMING DISCOURAGEMENT

*We had the sentence of death within ourselves so that we would not trust in ourselves, but in God who raises the dead.*

2 CORINTHIANS 1:9

If you're feeling disheartened today, take heart. As you see in today's verse, even Paul faced feelings of intense discouragement. But Paul learned to live above his circumstances, and you can too.

*First, he focused on God rather than the problem.* As you deal with life's trials, center your attention on Jesus. He has the sovereign ability to handle whatever you're facing and can help you in miraculous ways. *Second, focus on the wisdom of God instead of the will of man.* Seeking the counsel of others is always a wise idea; however, be sure that what your friends tell you agrees with God's Word, which is your ultimate authority. Likewise, seek Him first on your own, because He always reveals Himself to those who seek Him. *Finally, focus on the positive results rather than the personal pain.* When trials come, ask the Lord to show you what He wants to accomplish through them and how you can join Him.

Paul lived above his circumstances because his focus was on Jesus and not on the trial. As a result, he gained the victory—and so can you. So don't be disheartened. Trust Him and triumph.

*Jesus, thank You for encouraging me.*
*May You be glorified in these trials. Amen.*

> My hope is in Jesus because
> He always leads me to triumph.

# A CRUCIFIED LIFE

*I have been crucified with Christ; and it is no*
*longer I who live, but Christ lives in me.*

GALATIANS 2:20

What keeps you from serving God? Is it fear of being misunderstood or even rejected? Are you afraid of what people may think about you?

Realize that your Savior, Jesus, was often unfairly attacked by enemies. But through it all, no one ever saw Jesus worrying about public opinion or the consequences in this life. Rather, Jesus was focused on the *eternal* mission. His desire was for people to know Him as Savior so they could be eternally reconciled to God. And because of it, He bears the name above all names (Philippians 2:9).

The same has been true of all Christ's disciples. Yes, many were not just misunderstood and rejected, but beaten, imprisoned, and even executed for their faith. Nothing stood in the way of their determination to do God's will. Why were they willing to make such sacrifices? Because they valued Christ above every other thing.

You must too. As missionary Jim Elliott so famously said, "He is no fool who gives what he cannot keep to gain that which he cannot lose." Never let the opinions of others become the focus of your life. Jesus always holds the key to your greatest and most lasting rewards.

*Jesus, help me to obey You faithfully with courage. Amen.*

My hope is in Jesus because
the life He gives is eternal.

# CEASE STRIVING

*"Cease striving and know that I am God."*

PSALM 46:10

Does your world sometimes feel as if it's been turned upside down? If so, how can you respond victoriously to the challenges you face each day?

The key is in today's verse: you must stop striving and take hold of the fact that God is in control. Of course, this may seem counterintuitive. If you stop, all the plates you have spinning will fall. But to "cease striving" does not mean you do nothing. What it means is that you stop fretting—trying to take care of it all with your limited wisdom. Instead, you actively watch, wait, and—most importantly—listen to the Lord.

In other words, to cease striving, you must trust God, be patient, submit your will to His, and focus on Jesus rather than circumstances. You do so by *getting alone with God continually*, waiting for Him to speak to your heart. Don't just talk; really listen. Likewise, *meditate on Scripture*, which helps you see your circumstances from the Lord's perspective. *And courageously say no to the things that pull you away from being still in God's presence.*

Can you be still and cease striving today? It is important that you do so. Because everything in your upside-down world can benefit from His guidance, and He has important things to tell you.

*Jesus, I'll let go and let You work. Show me what to do. Amen.*

> My hope is in Jesus because
> I can trust His leadership.

# CHOOSING HIM

*Come, let us worship and bow down, let us*
*kneel before the LORD our Maker.*
PSALM 95:6

When you choose to follow Jesus, some of your choices may be misunderstood. For example, taking time away from pressing matters to be still and to meditate on God's Word can seem indulgent—even irresponsible—to those who have different priorities.

Take Martha's reaction to Mary, for example. When Jesus visited their home, Mary chose to sit at His feet. But Luke 10:40 testifies: "Martha . . . came up to Him and said, 'Lord, do You not care that my sister has left me to do all the serving alone? Then tell her to help me.'" Because Martha was preoccupied with doing things *for* the Lord, she failed to see the importance of fellowshipping *with* the Lord. So Jesus answered, "Martha, you are worried and upset over all these details! There is only one thing worth being concerned about. Mary has discovered it" (vv. 41–42 NLT).

It's easy to become so preoccupied with life that your fellowship with God takes a backseat. Yet your relationship with Jesus is the most important one in your life. He gives you the spiritual sustenance to tackle the challenges with wisdom and grace. So don't fret over what others say. At the end of the day, when all else is forgotten, your relationship with Christ is what really counts.

*Jesus, I bow before You. Teach me, my Savior. Amen.*

My hope is in Jesus because He is my life.

# WITH YOU ALWAYS

*The LORD is the one who goes ahead of you; He will be with you.*
*He will not fail you or forsake you. Do not fear or be dismayed.*

DEUTERONOMY 31:8

When Moses prayed for God's guidance to Canaan, the Lord responded with these reassuring words: "My presence shall go with you" (Exodus 33:14). When Joshua was faced with the challenge of leading several million stubborn Israelites across the Jordan, God's encouraging command was: "Be strong and courageous! . . . For the LORD your God is with you wherever you go" (Joshua 1:9).

When the disciples were commanded to take the message of salvation to every nation, they were comforted when Jesus said, "Be sure of this: I am with you always, even to the end of the age" (Matthew 28:20 NLT).

And the good news is that through the indwelling Holy Spirit, you too have the comforting assurance of God's presence with you regardless of what you face. Absolutely nothing can ever sever you from Jesus. He is Immanuel—God with you (Matthew 1:23). His strength, wisdom, and love are yours forever.

As Paul exclaimed, "Nothing in all creation will ever be able to separate us from the love of God" (Romans 8:39 NLT). So let this truth encourage you today and go forward in faith.

*Jesus, I won't be afraid. for You are always*
*with me. Praise Your holy name! Amen.*

My hope is in Jesus because
He will never leave me.

# WAIT FOR MESSIAH

*May it be done to me according to your word.*

LUKE 1:38

As you prepare to celebrate Jesus' birth, there may be blessings that you've been requesting from God for a long time. But Christmas provides you with undeniable evidence that the Lord *always* fulfills His promises. Throughout history, every person to whom the Lord made promises faced circumstances that seemed absolutely impossible to overcome and many prolonged delays. Furthermore, the prophecies the Lord made about the Messiah seemed completely unattainable. But as the Christ, Jesus perfectly fulfills every detail that God has spoken through His prophets over the centuries.

In other words, the Lord has never failed any of those who trusted Him, and He will not let you down either. You can rest in the truth that God is faithful and able to accomplish all He has said He would do. Likewise, Jesus has been specially anointed to help you, guide you, and be with you in seasons of waiting.

So don't lose heart when you have to wait on God. Instead, remember the message of Christmas—and know for certain that the sovereign Lord of all creation, your heavenly Father, your Messiah and King, has heard your requests and will faithfully fulfill all of His promises to you in His perfect time.

*Jesus, I will wait for You, knowing You*
*always keep Your wonderful word. Amen.*

My hope is in Jesus because He
always keeps His promises faithfully.

# GOD WITH ME

*A virgin will be with child and bear a son, and
she will call His name Immanuel.*

ISAIAH 7:14

Approximately seven hundred years after the verse above was written, Jesus was born to Mary. His birth came at a time when spiritual darkness covered the land of Israel because the Jewish people had all but forsaken the ways of God (Matthew 4:16). The temple had become a marketplace, and people offered sacrifices more out of obligation than to worship and obey God.

Likewise, the interpretation of today's verse above carried a similar darkness. People believed the coming Messiah would bring a military revolution and eradication of Roman rule. However, as we know, Jesus came for a totally different purpose. He came to reestablish the intimacy with God humanity lost in the garden of Eden—to be "God with us" (Matthew 1:23).

The main message of Christmas is that God wants more for you than simply making your earthly life more bearable. He gives you His light, His life, and His freedom—He gives you Himself!

So today, stop seeking things from the Lord and enjoy the true Gift, the greatest Gift: Immanuel—God with you. Think about all that really means and praise Him for His grace.

*Jesus, You are the greatest Gift ever given!
Thank You for being so good to me. Amen.*

◆ **My hope is in Jesus because He is God with me.** ◆

# WHO IS THIS JESUS?

*"Who do you say that I am?"*
MATTHEW 16:15

Do you truly know who Jesus is? Is He more to you than a baby born in Bethlehem? More than just some religious leader in whom you're supposed to believe? Is He your life, your hope, your future?

We can go to church and sing songs about Jesus, but never actually honor Him. We can miss the joy and reverence of relating to Him personally and intimately. So I don't know of a better time to search our hearts than at Christmas.

We know the facts: Jesus was born to Mary and Joseph in Bethlehem and raised in the obscure village of Nazareth. We may even realize the impact of His life. His birth is the event that divides time into BC and AD. He didn't travel far from home, yet He has influenced the entire world. Satan couldn't tempt Him, death couldn't destroy Him, and the grave couldn't keep Him. He is the living God—and we can know Him because He sacrificially gives Himself to us (Philippians 2:5–11).

But do you really honor Him in the way He deserves? He's certainly worthy of all that you are. So this Christmas, really think about who He is and give Him the gift that truly represents what He means to you.

*Jesus, I want to truly honor You and*
*give my life as a gift to You. Amen.*

My hope is in Jesus
because He is God incarnate.

# RESURRECTION POWER

*I count all things to be loss in view of the surpassing*
*value of knowing Christ Jesus . . . that I may know*
*Him and the power of His resurrection.*

PHILIPPIANS 3:8, 10

Do you realize that adversity helps you experience Christ's resurrection power? Remember: there is no resurrection without a crucifixion. There must be an end to all of your self-reliance so that you can rely solely on God and His power can flow through you.

There's an illustration of this in the world of plumbing. When repairing a system, a plumber must wait until the pipes are completely dry before he can work on them. If there's even a drop of water left in the system, there's no point in trying to fix it because the heat from the soldering torch turns the water to steam—preventing the repairs from taking hold.

This is a striking picture of the Christian life. As long as there's even a drop of self-reliance in you, you will fight God from healing and working through you—from allowing His life to course through you. And so, through difficulties and challenges, the Lord cleans all that out so that you'll be an effective conduit for His resurrection power.

*Jesus, help me to become a conduit of*
*Your resurrection power. Amen.*

My hope is in Jesus because
He gives me resurrection power.

# FOCUS ON THE UNSEEN

*He endured, as seeing Him who is unseen.*

HEBREWS 11:27

Because we cannot see the future, our lives are full of unknowns. Some people respond to those unknowns with faith while many panic out of fear and frustration. So how can we be sure to react with courage and confidence?

In today's verse, we read about Moses and the confidence that carried him through many frightening unknowns. The Greek word for *endure* is defined as "the capacity to bear up under difficult circumstances." When we persevere, refusing to surrender our hope, we gain spiritual maturity.

So how did Moses endure? He did so by keeping his focus on "Him who is unseen"—on God. In other words, the key to perseverance in a world full of job insecurities, family instabilities, and unpredictable world events is to keep our eyes on the Lord.

Moses was not that different from you when it comes to fears, weaknesses, limitations, and faults. And daily he was challenged with persecution, the threat of death, and all sorts of trials. He simply chose to respond to his difficulties with hope, patience, and perseverance. You can too. So take his example—endure by keeping your focus on "Him who is unseen."

*Jesus, help me to focus on You regardless*
*of the trials or unknowns. Amen.*

My hope is in Jesus because
He never fails me.

# THIS IS FROM HIM

*"Take courage; it is I, do not be afraid."*
MARK 6:50

The disciples frantically wrestled with oars and sails as the little fishing boat became engulfed by the sea's angry waves. How did they get into this mess? The answer: Jesus had sent them there.

What a sobering thought. At times God may lead us along ways that seem very dark and lonely—stretching our ability to trust Him. The stormy trials come so quickly and hit so profoundly that we're left reeling. Our hearts feel crushed under the pressure, and we find ourselves crying out in anguish.

But notice that Jesus went to the disciples *during* the storm. He didn't go to them while the skies were blue and the waves were calm. Rather, He went when it appeared that all hope was lost and disaster seemed unavoidable. Yet His first words gave them hope: "Take courage; it is I, do not be afraid."

So in your trial today, take His words to heart: "Take courage; it is I, do not be afraid." This storm is from Him—the Lord has chosen this for you. But He is with you. Therefore, do not despair. Your sovereign Savior has His eye on you, and He will certainly work all things together for your good when the time is right.

*Jesus, thank You for comforting and*
*leading me in the storms of life. Amen.*

My hope is in Jesus because He
works through every trial for my good.

# FROM ORDINARY TO GLORIOUS

*"I have made them for my glory."*

ISAIAH 43:7 NLT

The greatest platform God has ever used to bless the world and accomplish His purposes was an ordinary tree. After it was cut down, it could have been fashioned into anything—a chair, a table, even furnishings for the temple. But it wasn't. Instead, it was formed into a cross. Of course, trees can't share their thoughts, but if it could, that tree may have expressed some concerns. That is, it may have doubted the Lord's purpose until it saw His ultimate plan fulfilled—that He would provide for the salvation of the world upon its wooden frame.

But understand, God is fulfilling His purpose with you as well—and it's why you shouldn't second-guess how He's leading you. The way He will ultimately work through you has yet to be revealed. But if you'll obey Him step-by-step, you'll experience firsthand how He uses the ordinary to accomplish His divine and glorious purposes. So don't fight God; rather, have faith in Him. And like so many others who have trusted Him throughout history, you'll be able to say, "God, I didn't realize what You wanted to do, but I thank You that it was far better than I ever could have imagined."

*Jesus, I don't understand what You're doing,*
*but I trust You with every step. Amen.*

My hope is in Jesus because
He makes my life worthwhile.

# PREPARING FOR HEAVEN

*"I go to prepare a place for you . . . that where*
*I am, there you may be also."*

JOHN 14:2–3

As children of God, we are on a journey. One day, however, it will end, and we will be called to our eternal home. Thankfully, we can be hopeful about going to heaven because Jesus has gone there to prepare a place for us. The warning for us as we await that day, however, is that we cannot grow apathetic in our faith or become discouraged because of hardships we face. Instead, we must make the most of the opportunities God gives us, knowing He will reward our faithfulness in a manner that will impact what we experience in the world to come (Revelation 22:12).

So remain steadfast in your faith, knowing that no matter what the future holds, God's grace will be sufficient for you. And be aware of how He may be calling you to serve Him. You may not know when you'll see Jesus, but you can and should live in joyful expectancy of that day. Certainly, you'll find it was all worthwhile when He greets you with, "Well done, my good and faithful servant. . . . Let's celebrate together!" (Matthew 25:23 NLT).

*Jesus, thank You for providing such a bright*
*and wonderful future for me. Amen.*

My hope is in Jesus because He
is preparing my home in heaven.

# LIVE FOR HIM

*"Behold, I am coming quickly, and My reward is with Me,*
*to render to every man according to what he has done."*

REVELATION 22:12

Consider your life. If Jesus were to return, would He find you living for Him? Would He see that you're fulfilling the purposes for which you were created?

I hope so, because that's the path to life at its very best. Yes, it's a road that's challenged with adversity, obstacles, and opponents. Sometimes you don't know where you're going or what the next step will be. But you're promised: "Trust in the LORD with all your heart and do not lean on your own understanding. In all your ways acknowledge Him, and He will make your paths straight" (Proverbs 3:5–6). You can be absolutely certain that Jesus will always lead you in the way imbued with His wisdom, strength, and hope.

It doesn't matter what mistakes you've made or what challenges you face—the Lord can do wonders in your situation. So make Jesus your perfect hope. As you stand at the threshold of a new year, decide to live your life for Him. Because certainly, this is how you can ensure that your life is invested in the most effective manner possible and that the best is still to come.

*Jesus, may the coming year make me more*
*wholly devoted to You than ever before. Amen.*

> My hope is in Jesus because
> He is the only perfect hope!

# About the Author

Dr. Charles Stanley is the senior pastor of the First Baptist Church of Atlanta, where he has served for more than 40 years. He is a New York Times bestselling author who has written more than 60 books, including the bestselling devotional *Every Day in His Presence*. Dr. Stanley is the founder of In Touch Ministries. The *In Touch with Dr. Charles Stanley* program is transmitted throughout the world on more than 1,200 radio outlets and 130 television stations/networks, and in language projects in more than 50 languages. The award-winning *In Touch* devotional magazine is printed in four languages with more than 12 million copies each year. Dr. Stanley's goal is best represented by Acts 20:24: "Life is worth nothing unless I use it for doing the work assigned me by the Lord Jesus—the work of telling others the Good News about God's mighty kindness and love" (TLB). This is because, as he says, "It is the Word of God and the work of God that changes people's lives."

# Notes

1. Henry Blackaby and Claude King, *Experiencing God* (Nashville: Broadman and Holman, 2004), 45.
2. C. S. Lewis, *Mere Christianity* (Nashville: Thomas Nelson, 2001), 198.
3. Frederic George Kenyon, *Our Bible and the Ancient Manuscripts* (London: Eyre and Spottiswoode, 1897), 11.
4. Howard Taylor and Mrs. Howard Taylor, *Hudson Taylor and the China Inland Mission* (London: Morgan and Scott, 1918), 169.